Teaching the Struggling Reader

Barbara R. Schirmer

University of Detroit

Boston   New York   San Francisco
Mexico City   Montreal   Toronto   London   Madrid   Munich   Paris
Hong Kong   Singapore   Tokyo   Cape Town   Sydney

Executive Editor: Aurora Martínez Ramos
Editorial Assistant: Jacqueline Gillen
Vice President, Marketing and Sales Strategies: Emily Williams Knight
Vice President, Director of Marketing: Quinn Perkson
Marketing Manager: Danae April
Production Editor: Gregory Erb
Editorial Production Service: Denise Botelho
Composition Buyer: Linda Cox
Manufacturing Buyer: Megan Cochran
Electronic Composition: Denise Hoffman
Cover Designer: Linda Knowles

For Professional Development resources visit www.pearsonpd.com.

Between the time website information is gathered and then published, it is not unusual for some sites to have closed. Also, the transcription of URLs can result in typographical errors. The publisher would appreciate notification where these errors occur so that they may be corrected in subsequent editions.

Library of Congress Cataloging-in-Publication Data

Schirmer, Barbara R.
 Teaching the struggling reader / Barbara R. Schirmer.
    p. cm.
 Includes bibliographical references and index.
 ISBN 978-0-13-701744-7 (0-13-701744-8 : alk. paper)
 1. Reading—Remedial teaching. I. Title.
 LB1050.5.S327 2010
 372.43—dc22   2009011332

Printed in the United States of America

10 9 8 7 6 5 4 3 2 1   RRD-VA   13 12 11 10 09

www.pearsonhighered.com

ISBN-10: 0-13-701744-8
ISBN-13: 978-0-13-701744-7

To my mom,
whose love of reading is now being
passed along to her great-grandchildren.
She may never have baked gingerbread cookies,
but her rendition of *The Gingerbread Man*
lasted far longer in my memory
than any tasty morsel could have.

About the Author

Barbara R. Schirmer is a Professor of Education and Special Assistant to the President at the University of Detroit. Her research on the literacy development of deaf children and other struggling readers has been published in numerous journals including *Exceptional Children, Review of Educational Research, Journal of Literacy Research, Journal of Deaf Studies and Deaf Education, Communication Disorders Quarterly*, and *The Journal of Special Education*. She has authored three books, *What Is Special about Special Education: Examining the Role of Evidence Based Practice* (published by Pro-Ed in 2006), *Language and Literacy Development in Children Who Are Deaf*, and *Psychological, Social, and Educational Dimensions of Deafness*  (both published by Allyn and Bacon). She presents regularly at national conferences such as the International Reading Association, the National Reading Conference, the American Educational Research Association, Council for Exceptional Children, and the Society for the Scientific Study of Reading. She is currently on the editorial review boards for the *Journal for Literacy Research, Literacy Research and Instruction*, and *Reading Psychology*. Dr. Schirmer received her doctorate and baccalaureate in education from the University at Buffalo, State University of New York, and her master's in the education of deaf and hard of hearing students from the University of Pittsburgh.

Contents

CHAPTER 4

Before-Reading Strategies: Prereading and Planning   99

CHAPTER 5

During-Reading Strategies: Supporting Strategic Reading   129

CHAPTER 6

After-Reading Strategies: Synthesizing and Extending   147

CHAPTER 7

*Attitude and Motivation: From Reluctant
to Enthused Reader   169*

CHAPTER 8

Families: Partnering with Parents   181

Preface

In my first teaching position, I was assigned as the resource room teacher to provide extra reading instruction for the students in kindergarten through sixth grade. At that point in my career, I had baccalaureate and master's degrees but no actual teaching experience beyond student teaching in regular and special education classrooms. It was common for the school to have visitors and one day, the person leading the tour stopped outside my classroom and said, "In this room is our reading expert." I looked around to see who he was talking about when I realized it was me. In large measure, this book was born that day because I was confronted with the reality that I was an imposter. The students coming to my resource room were counting on me, yet my own knowledge and skills fell far short of reading expert. I needed this book then, so wrote it now for all the teachers like me who want to offer the best possible reading instruction to their struggling students.

This book is for preservice, novice, and experienced teachers who understand the individual components of a developmental reading program but have never been shown how to put these components together into a coherent and effective instructional program. I provide a unifying framework to guide teachers in developing a reading program that will enable struggling readers to become proficient readers by showing how phonemic awareness, word recognition, fluency, comprehension, and attitude and motivation can be addressed in reading instruction every day through lesson structures that target the reader's needs. Graphic representations of this framework are provided that teachers can individualize to match their personal teaching styles and beliefs. Case studies provide real-life examples of applying each of the instructional approaches and strategies.

Some distinguishing features of the book include the following:

1. Four real-life case studies of struggling readers

2. A chapter on assessment presented at the beginning and stress on the importance of doing assessments first to determine the reader's strengths and weaknesses

3. Step-by-step guidelines for planning instruction within a framework that enables teachers to select approaches that fit with their own beliefs about learning

4. An explanation of the important differences between models for teaching reading and instructional strategies

5. An emphasis on including struggling readers rather than isolating them

6. Descriptions of how to group readers by ability and need rather than by risk factors

7. Ways to empower teachers to develop a reading program for struggling readers by using strategies and techniques they already know and adding ones that match their teaching styles

8. An explanation of the crucial aspects of reading within a unified framework for students who are struggling

9. A road map for creating an instructional program for struggling readers by planning instruction around their needs, rather than the other way around.

Every book is a lot of some things and not much of others, even though the other things might be related to the topic. At some point, the author has to decide when enough has been said and point the reader in other directions for more information on related topics. To meet this need, I have identified additional readings at the end of each chapter.

This book focuses on setting up a developmental reading program for students who struggle with reading. Since some of the challenges for emergent readers are the same challenges for struggling readers, it may also be of use to teachers of emergent readers, although it is not specifically about emergent readers. The approach that I present can be effectively applied with English language learners or students with disabilities when they struggle with reading because it is based on the student's needs, which some authors call differentiated instruction, although the book is not specifically geared toward teachers of these students. By improving their students' reading abilities through the approach that I present, content area teachers may be more able to incorporate subject matter reading material, although the purpose of the book is not to explain how to teach content subjects to struggling readers. And, finally, I have selected methods that have been shown to be effective in teaching children to read, whether these are traditional in nature or technology-based, rather than focusing strictly on ideas for incorporating technology when teaching word recognition, fluency, and comprehension.

Much has been written about evidence-based practices in recent years. Some educators feel that there is more to evidence than only what a set of research studies have found. They argue that evidence lies in the teacher's own personal observations about what is effective with a particular child or group of students. In this book, I present models and strategies that researchers have found to be effective. My own argument is that these evidence-based practices offer the highest likelihood for success with struggling readers. That said, I urge all teachers to decide for themselves whether a particular approach makes sense for the students they are teaching by asking and re-asking themselves two questions: "Is this model or strategy targeted for the instructional needs of this student?" and "Is this student making satisfactory progress in becoming a reader?" And if the answer is no (based on assessment of the student's achievement of reading goals), try a new approach.

Acknowledgments

No book is the product of only one person's hard work, ideas, and fervor and this book is no exception. I would like to thank, first, Aurora Martínez Ramos, the Executive Editor of this book. Aurora consistently offered valuable advice and just the right amount of prodding. I would also like to thank the reviewers for their careful and constructive comments. They include Heidi Davey, Hoffman Estates High School; Kelly M. Denison, Southside School District; ; Paul Markham, University of Kansas; and Karen Ward, Centennial Middle School. It is always delightful to read positive feedback and difficult to absorb critical advice, yet it is truly the criticisms that lead to better writing. I wrote the book as if I were having a conversation with the reader. It is the reviewers who made the conversation a real dialogue.

I also want to extend my deep appreciation to the colleagues who have helped shape my thinking about literacy learning. They include Patrick Finn, University at Buffalo, State University of New York; Cheri Williams, University of Cincinnati; Phillip Ginnetti, Youngstown State University; Michael Kibby, University at Buffalo, State University of New York; Barbara Strassman, The College of New Jersey; and Sam Weintraub, University at Buffalo, State University of New York.

Most important, I want to thank my family: husband Jack, who is willing to sit through black-and-white classic movies with me when the writing bogs down; daughter Alison, who cheers me by saying things like, "What, only one article written and no grants today?"; son Todd, who can offer statistical assistance with one hand and mental health advice with the other; son-in-law Jeffrey and daughter-in-law Christine, who put up with the weird Schirmers and usually pretend we're as normal as everyone else; and grandchildren Molly, Anne, and Sam, whose play is work and work is play, a good lesson for all of us.

The Reading Process
The Task and the Reader

2 Assessment: Putting the Reader at the Center of the Reading Program

3 Framework for Developing a Reading Program for the Struggling Reader

1 The Reading Process: The Task and the Reader

4 Before-Reading Strategies: Prereading and Planning

This chapter will discuss the reading process, describe theoretical perspectives, such as constructivism and behaviorism, that are important in understanding how children become readers, and discuss issues that make reading a challenge for some students.

5 During-Reading Strategies: Supporting Strategic Reading

8 Families: Partnering with Parents

6 After-Reading Strategies: Synthesizing and Extending

7 Attitude and Motivation: From Reluctant to Enthused Reader

*M*s. Edberg is taking a professional development course online in reading. The students come from a variety of school settings and geographic areas and all have classroom experience. In the first session, the professor asked the class to describe their most memorable teacher and the lesson learned as a teacher from a teacher. They were asked to post their essay on the course online bulletin board. Ms. Edberg's essay is about her tenth-grade social studies teacher, Linda Fields.

When I graduated from junior high school, I managed a solid "C" final average with my "B" in English nicely balancing my "D" in Algebra. When I met with my new high school guidance counselor, she seemed surprised when I said I would be going to college. At my high school, courses were tracked as SS, S, M, and some other letter that I no longer remember. I also do not remember what these initials stood for though SS was clearly for Super Smart, S for Smart, and M for Mediocre. College bound students took all S and SS courses. When I told my guidance counselor that I wanted to take S courses, she was uneasy and urged me to reconsider. I must have stood firm, though at age 14, I wonder how I came to be so steadfast. She capitulated for English, Science (Biology), and Math (Geometry) but she was adamant that I take M Social Studies. I also took French but languages weren't tracked.

As it turned out, M Social Studies with Miss Linda Fields was serendipitous. Miss Fields (I can hardly think of her as Linda, though she asked me to call her that when I met her years later) seemed quite excited to have me in her class. No teacher had shown that level of enthusiasm about my presence for several years, probably one-third of my school life up to that point. I don't know if she was as enthused about the other students but frankly I believe she was not. It was obvious to me that the students in M Social Studies were a lot different from the students in my S classes. In M Social Studies, there were lots of absences, few raised hands, and regular incomplete homework submissions.

I remember the day when Miss Fields asked me what I was doing in M Social Studies. I'm sure I mumbled something like, "I didn't do very well last year." She had that look on her face that indicated she was wondering what the guidance department does. What she said was, "You need to take all S courses, Barbara. You're too smart for this course." That certainly gave me something to think about. Only my mother had expressed the same sentiment. My response was, "I really like this course, Miss Fields. I don't want to change." What I wanted to say was, "Oh my gosh, please don't make me leave the one place in this huge, unfriendly high school where I feel good." She must have sensed my panic and said she'd talk to my guidance counselor about taking S Social Studies next year.

I had many memorable teachers but Linda Fields tops the list of the positive memories. Today we have educational and medical jargon to describe the distractibility that I displayed in school. Starting in M Social Studies, I began to channel this distractibility positively and to block out stimuli in order to concentrate. So when I look for the lesson in this story, it is the power of one teacher to influence one child, particularly the one who is struggling.

Mrs. Hong, Mr. Ginnetti, Mr. Rumrill, and the other teachers taking the online course also wrote essays about their memorable teachers. The common element in their stories is that memorable teachers have enormous influence over the learning, self-confidence, attitude, and motivation of the students in their classes. In some stories, the influence was positive and in some, negative lessons were taught and learned. Whether positive or negative, each of these individuals reflecting on their memorable teacher recognized that they had integrated the experience into their own beliefs about teaching, beliefs that served to frame their orientation as a teacher.

Beliefs about the Reading Process

What happens when a student processes text to obtain meaning? As these four teachers in the online course learned, the answer depends on their philosophical and theoretical orientation.

One philosophical orientation is empiricism. Empiricists are interested in describing the environment through the gathering and measuring of data. When applied to the reading process and reading instruction, empiricists focus on the student's perception of sounds, understanding how sounds relate to letters and words, and recognition of print. The opposite of orientation is rationalism. Rationalists are interested in understanding the actions and reactions of the human mind. When applied to the reading process and reading instruction, rationalists focus on the meaning of text. If these orientations seem a lot like the theories of behaviorism and constructivism discussed in psychology and applied to the reading process, they are.

These are the two theories most often cited to support particular approaches to the teaching and learning of reading. According to behaviorists, learning is explained in terms of an individual's observable responses to environmental stimuli (Cooper, Heron, & Heward, 2007). According to constructivists, learning is explained in terms of an individual's assimilation of new experiences based on prior experience, knowledge, and belief (Fosnot, 2005).

How do behaviorists and constructivists answer the question about what happens when a student processes text to obtain meaning? As you can see in Table 1.1, their answers can be compared along the three critical roles involved in the teaching of reading: teacher, reader, and material.

For the behaviorist, the role of the teacher is to directly and systematically teach the component skills involved in the reading process, offer ample opportunity for student response, provide practice and review, and offer immediate and precise feedback. The role of the student is to respond actively to instruction. The role of the material is to provide opportunity for the student to apply and practice new skills and strategies.

For the constructivist, the role of the teacher is to create an instructional environment that provides meaningful and relevant activities for the student.

4

....

CHAPTER 1

The Reading
Process:
The Task and
the Reader

The role of the student is to interact with the environment and construct his or her own understanding, ideas, and solutions to problems. The role of the material is to provide opportunity for the student to explore, reflect, and discover.

How are these roles applied to teaching reading? For behaviorists, instruction focuses heavily on word recognition. The model of reading that aligns with behavioral theory is typically referred to as *bottom-up*. Bottom-up processing assumes that the act of reading begins with letter-sound information. For constructivists, instruction focuses heavily on comprehension. The model of reading that aligns with constructivist theory is typically referred to as *top-down*. Top-down processing assumes that the act of reading begins with the reader's prior knowledge, which enables the reader to predict the meaning of print.

A third philosophical orientation has emerged to explain the mutual influence of print and prior knowledge. This orientation has been termed

TABLE 1.1 Reading Beliefs According to Behaviorism, Constructivism, and Interactivism

Role of the:	Behaviorism	Constructivism	Interactivism
Teacher	• Directly and systematically teaches the component skills involved in the reading process • Offers ample opportunity for student response • Provides practice and review with appropriate feedback	• Creates an instructional environment that provides meaningful and relevant activities for the student	• Clearly, directly, and systematically teaches the component skills involved in the reading process • Provides significant opportunity to apply new skills within the context of reading materials
Reader	• Responds to the instructional stimuli	• Interacts with the environment and constructs his or her own understanding, conceptualizations, and solutions to problems	• Responds to the instructional stimuli • Constructs understanding within the context of interaction with written material
Material	• Provides opportunity for the student to apply and practice the new skills	• Provides opportunity for the student to explore, reflect, and discover	• Provides opportunity for the student to apply skills, develop understanding, and draw on prior knowledge

interactivism or the *interactive model* of the reading process. The interactive model assumes that reading begins with a prediction of meaning based on the decoding of graphic symbols (Stanovich, 2000). Unlike the bottom-up model, which assumes that the reading process flows from part to whole, and unlike the top-down model, which assumes that the reading process flows from whole to part, the interactive model assumes that the reading process flows back and forth between part and whole.

For the interactivist, the role of the teacher is to clearly, directly, and systematically teach the component skills involved in the reading process while providing significant opportunity to apply new skills with reading materials that enable students to draw on their prior knowledge. The role of the student is to respond actively to instruction and construct his or her own understanding of the written material. The role of the material is to provide opportunity for the student to apply skills and develop understanding.

Instructional approaches based on the interactive view of the reading process are called *balanced reading* or *balanced literacy* approaches. Balanced reading instruction involves the teaching of skills and support of students as they apply these skills to reading material. Pressley (2006) used the following analogy in describing balanced reading:

> Whole language is like Little League baseball if players only played games. Their playing of whole games would be substantially impaired by lack of skills. Just as bad, skills emphasis is like Little League baseball if it involved mostly infield, outfield, and batting practice. As good as players experiencing such an approach might be at picking up grounders, running down fly balls, and hitting consistently, they would not be baseball players. They would not know how the components interrelate as part of an entire game. Baseball, like all sports, involves both the development of skills and practice in applying those skills in whole games, played at a level appropriate to the developmental level of the players. (pp. 438–439)

As you reflect on your own beliefs about teaching, are you more closely aligned with the behaviorism, constructivism, or interactivism view? In their online discussion, the four teachers found themselves evenly split between constructivism and interactivism, though some of their classmates who are special education teachers were aligned with behaviorism.

Regardless of whether your beliefs about teaching and learning are more closely aligned with behaviorism, constructivism, or interactivism, you must address specific reading tasks in instruction. The emphasis placed on these tasks, and the strategies taught and used, will reflect your philosophical orientation. If you are an experienced teacher, the following descriptions will be a reminder about the tasks that are mastered by skilled readers and toiled over by struggling readers. If you are a novice teacher, you might want to review material on these reading tasks in your introductory reading texts such as Reutzel and Cooter (2009), Vacca et al. (2009), and Cooper and Kiger (2009).

6

CHAPTER 1

*The Reading
Process:
The Task and
the Reader*

Reading Tasks

Every reader is faced with three major tasks: identifying the words, reading text fluently, and understanding the meaning. As Figure 1.1 shows, word recognition and comprehension involve particular knowledge and skills, and fluency is the bridge between word recognition and comprehension.

Word Recognition

Word recognition involves the identification of words in print. The terms *word recognition* and *word identification* are typically used to mean the same thing. The term *decoding* is also often used interchangeably with word recognition, however, decoding is more likely to be used for the process involved in identifying a word not instantly recognized as a sight word. When decoding is used in this way, word recognition is used to refer to immediate word recognition. In this book, the term word *recognition* will be used to refer to the broad task of identifying words in print, whether those words are in the reader's sight vocabulary or whether those words are not immediately recognized and have to be figured out. Sight words will be referred to as simply *sight words* or *automatic word recognition*.

The goal of word recognition is to identify a word as being in the reader's vocabulary and therefore activate knowledge about the word's meaning. In other words, the reader understands the word when someone else speaks it and may even use it in conversation. The task in word recognition is to identify the printed version of the word. (If the student does not know the meaning of the word, the task is vocabulary development rather than only word recognition.) The more quickly and successfully the student can identify words in print, the more attention can be devoted to comprehension. The corollary is true also. The more attention the student must pay to word recognition, the less attention can be devoted to comprehension. Readers who struggle with word recognition are likely to have weak comprehension.

Phonemic Awareness

Phonemic awareness is the awareness of the phonemes in spoken words. Phonemes are the smallest meaningful sound units of speech. Thus, the word *book* has three phonemes (*b-oo-k*) though it has four letters. Phonemic awareness is considered to be particularly important in reading English because English is an alphabetic language. As in all alphabetic languages, the basic unit of writing reflects a correspondence (though not perfect match) between phonemes and graphemes, or sounds and letters. Thus, it is a great advantage if the reader is aware of the phonemes that make up spoken words and is able to map these sounds to English letters, letter combinations, syllables, and words.

The terms *phonemic awareness* and *phonological awareness* are often used interchangeably. However, many authors view phonemic awareness as the first of three components of phonological awareness. Phonemic awareness is strictly the awareness of the phonemes in words. The second component is syllabic awareness, which is the awareness of syllables. The word *book* has one syllable, and the word *bookstand* has two syllables. The third component is onset-rime awareness, which is the awareness of the two units within any syllable. The onset corresponds to the phonemes before the vowel and the

FIGURE 1.1   Reading Tasks

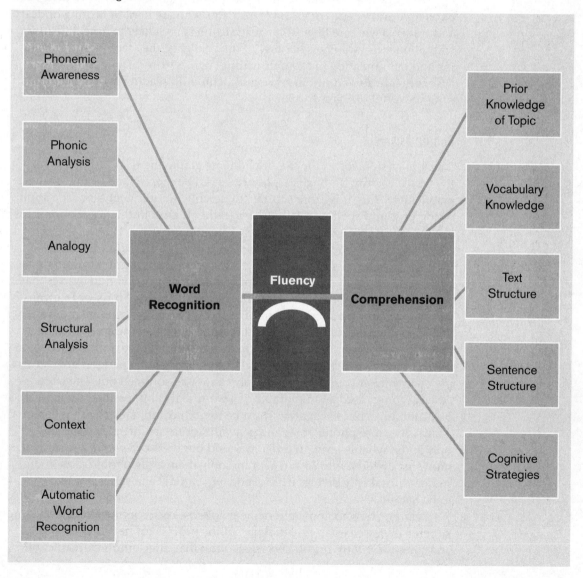

8
....

CHAPTER 1

*The Reading
Process:
The Task and
the Reader*

rime corresponds to the vowel sound and any phonemes following the vowel. In the word *book*, *b* is the onset and *ook* is the rime. (It is important to note that some syllables have a rime but no onset, as *at* and *and*.) In this book, the term *phonemic awareness* is used broadly to include the student's awareness of the sounds that make up words, the syllables that make up words, and the onset and rime within words.

From research in the 1960s by Elkonin (1963) through the findings of the National Reading Panel (2000), the importance of phonemic awareness in early reading instruction has been established. Further, evidence of the relationship between phonemic awareness and reading ability has been shown in numerous research studies (e.g., Allor, 2002).

We know that readers are more likely to struggle if they have deficits in phonemic awareness. For example, students who are hard of hearing or deaf and students who are English language learners are likely to have difficulties with phonemic awareness because of the challenge they face in discriminating and manipulating the sounds within English words. Deficits in phonemic awareness are also common among students with reading disabilities (Catts & Kamhi, 2005; Torgeson, 1996).

Phonic Analysis

Phonic analysis involves the use of phoneme-grapheme relationships to identify words in print. In English, phonemes can be represented by one or more graphemes. Thus, it is more accurate to describe phonic analysis as the application of sound-spelling relationships (rather than sound-letter relationships) to the identification of words in print.

Although phonic analysis is an important word recognition strategy, it is far from fail-safe. First, phonic analysis makes no contribution toward understanding a word's meaning. The assumption in using phonic analysis is that pronouncing the word correctly will trigger knowledge of the word's meaning. For students who have language learning difficulties, this assumption may not hold true for many words they encounter. For example, the reader may be able to sound out the word *fling*, but it won't help if the student doesn't know what *fling* means. Second, English spelling patterns are complex; some letter combinations simply cannot be sounded out. The word *women* is often used as an example of a word that is impossible to sound out. And third, phonic analysis must be used in combination with syllabic analysis because phonic rules and generalizations are directly applicable only at the syllable level. In order to sound out the word *belong*, the student must first divide it into *be* and *long* and only then apply phonic rules. If the student mistakenly divides it as *bel* and *ong*, phonic analysis is not likely to be helpful.

Learning how to apply phoneme-grapheme correspondences and spelling patterns is viewed as an essential part of the process for beginning readers and since the 1960s, researchers have found that direct phonics instruction has a positive effect on early reading development (Chall, 1967; National Reading Panel, 2000; Snow, Burns, & Griffin, 1998).

Given that no one-to-one correspondence between letters and sounds exists in English, the use of phonics must involve the learning of common letter-sound relationships and phonic generalizations while recognizing the necessity of flexibly applying and shifting sounds when encountering an unknown word. This flexibility is not often a characteristic of struggling readers.

Analogy

Analogy involves the use of cues that similar words offer. For example, to identify *same*, the reader might use the familiar word *name*. To use analogy, the reader must separate the onset from the rime and then use phonic analysis to work out the unknown letter-sound relationship. As you can see, analogy is dependent on phonic analysis, and phonic analysis is dependent on phonemic awareness.

Analogy is also dependent on sight word recognition. In order to be successful at analyzing a word by analogy, the reader needs to identify a familiar onset or rime pattern from recognizable words. For example, in order to identify the unknown word *same*, a word such as *name* must already be a sight word, or a word the student can recognize automatically.

Students who have difficulty with phonic analysis are also likely to have difficulty with analogy because analogy depends in part on knowledge of sound-letter relationships. On the other hand, they may be able to capitalize on their knowledge of sight words to use analogy as an effective word recognition strategy.

Structural Analysis

Structural analysis involves the use of morphemes to identify written words. Whereas phonemes are the smallest meaningful units of speech, morphemes are the smallest meaningful units of language. Linguists typically categorize morphemes as free and bound. Free morphemes, such as *light* or *walk*, can occur alone. Bound morphemes, such as the *ly* in *lightly* and the *ing* in *walking* must be attached to another morpheme. Compound words often contain two free morphemes, such as *flashlight* and *walkway*. Except for compound words, free morphemes are usually thought of as roots and bound morphemes as prefixes and suffixes.

Unlike phonic analysis, structural analysis does contribute toward understanding a word's meaning. Given that many prefixes and roots come from Greek and Latin words, knowledge of these can assist students in predicting a word's meaning. For example, *tele* means "far off" and *scope* means "instrument for observing." By putting them together, the word *telescope* could be deduced to mean "instrument for observing things that are far off." Many prefixes and suffixes in English carry grammatical meaning. Thus, *biannual* is

10
....

CHAPTER 1

*The Reading
Process:
The Task and
the Reader*

likely to mean "every two years" and *semiannual* to mean "every half a year," *player* would be a person who plays, *unmask* could be analyzed to mean "take off a mask," *helpless* would mean "without help," and *kittens* would involve more than one.

Structural analysis may be a more accessible word recognition strategy than phonic analysis or analogy for students who have difficulty using sound-letter relationships, such as students with hearing loss or those unfamiliar with the sounds of English because it is their second language.

Context

Context involves using the semantic and syntactic cues of known words in the text, usually within the same sentence. Semantic cues involve the meaning of these known words. For example, in the following sentence, it would not be difficult to identify the unknown word as *homework* even if the reader was unsuccessful using phonic analysis, analogy, or structural analysis.

My teacher assigns two hours of _____ every night.

Syntactic cues involve the structure of these known words in the sentence. As a language that relies heavily on word order, many markers in English signal particular grammatical categories. For example, if *teacher* was the unknown word in the previous sentence, the reader would know it was a noun because the pronoun *my*, just before the unknown word, would signal a noun. If *assigns* was the unknown word, the noun preceding it would signal a verb.

In combination, semantic and syntactic cues are more powerful than used singly. And in combination with the word recognition strategies of phonic analysis, analogy, and structural analysis, context is even more powerful. The use of semantic and syntactic context for word recognition is obviously a challenge for students who are not proficient in spoken English, such as students who are learning English as a second language, students who are deaf or hard of hearing, and students with language learning difficulties.

Automatic Word Recognition

Automatic word recognition, often referred to as *sight word recognition*, involves the ability of the reader to identify a word instantly. The ultimate goal of all word recognition strategies is automatic recognition. It is with quick and effortless word recognition that the reader can devote attention to comprehension.

A relatively small number of words make up the majority of words appearing in print, particularly the written material of young readers. For decades, various lists have been comprised of these high-frequency words. Recognizing these words automatically is crucial because they appear so often. Certain neurological disabilities predispose some students to have difficulty retaining sight words. It is unknown why others struggle with automatic word recognition.

Fluency

Fluency involves reading accurately, quickly, and with appropriate expression. It is based on successfully carrying out the task of word recognition. When readers are free from word recognition difficulties, they can concentrate fully on the task of comprehension. Fluency is viewed as a bridge between word recognition and comprehension (Welsch, 2007).

Though fluency is most often assessed and taught through strategies involving oral reading, it is manifested in silent reading, and the goal of teaching fluency is to develop fluent silent reading.

Comprehension

Reading comprehension involves understanding what the author has written. Some educators would argue that comprehension involves reconstructing the author's meaning because meaning resides in the text. Others would argue that comprehension involves constructing meaning because meaning is not fixed by the author but is generated through an interaction between the written material and the prior knowledge and experiences of the reader. In classrooms of teachers who believe in the first definition, the goal of instruction is to guide the reader toward correctly identifying the author's meaning. In classrooms of teachers who believe in the second definition, the goal of instruction is to encourage the reader to identify meaning that makes sense based on his or her personal knowledge and experience. In this second kind of classroom, different meanings might be generated by different students.

If you go back to the discussion of behaviorism, constructivism, and interactivism, you will see that teachers who believe that meaning resides solely in the text are more closely aligned with behaviorism, teachers who believe that meaning resides solely in the interaction between the reader's background knowledge and the author's words are more closely aligned with constructivism, and teachers who believe that there is a degree of fixed meaning that the author intended along with a degree of interpretation are more closely aligned with interactivism. Later in the text, you will see how your instructional questions and classroom discussions link to your belief about where meaning resides.

Comprehension is dependent on the knowledge and skills of the reader along several dimensions. One dimension is knowledge of topic, vocabulary, text structure, and sentence structure. Another dimension is the cognitive strategies used by the reader before, during, and after reading. These comprehension tasks are shown in Figure 1.1.

According to Kibby (1995a), a third aspect of comprehension is the situational context for reading, which includes the purposes for reading, the setting, and the instructional support. The student's motivation and interest are included in this third aspect because motivation and interest are intertwined with the purpose for reading (e.g., assignment versus self-selected material) and setting (e.g., school versus home). This third aspect of comprehension does not involve reading tasks per se and so will not be discussed in this chapter. Purpose, setting, and instructional support will be discussed in Chapters 4 through 6; motivation and interest will be discussed in Chapter 7.

Prior Knowledge of Topic

Prior knowledge of topic includes the reader's general world knowledge, particular information about the topic, and personal experiences with the topic. Evidence suggests that background knowledge directly influences reading comprehension (Anderson, Spiro, & Anderson, 1978; Pressley, 2006; Recht & Leslie, 1988), and indeed, activating and expanding background knowledge before reading is conventional wisdom to veteran teachers.

Students who struggle with reading may experience four problems in the task of applying prior knowledge during reading. The first involves possessing (or not possessing) the prior knowledge the author assumes. The second involves being aware (or not being aware) of having relevant background knowledge and tapping into it during reading. The third involves focusing on important (or unimportant) features of the text passage and drawing on background knowledge that is relevant (or not relevant) toward understanding the material. The fourth involves flexibly (or not flexibly) tapping into pockets of background knowledge as appropriate to shifting topics within the text.

In other words, the reader may not have the prerequisite prior knowledge. Or the reader may have appropriate prior knowledge but isn't aware of it and, therefore, doesn't apply it toward understanding the text. Or the reader may have appropriate prior knowledge but apply it to an unimportant part of the text or apply irrelevant prior knowledge, both of which lead to misunderstanding the text. Or the reader may have difficulty applying different areas of knowledge as the content shifts. Given these different problems, simply teaching background information may not be sufficient for struggling readers.

Vocabulary Knowledge

The relationship between *vocabulary knowledge* and reading comprehension is well established (Anderson & Freebody, 1981; Baumann, 2005). The more words readers recognize, the better the readers' comprehension will be. However, what is meant by a word being "new" or "known" to the reader depends on the definition of *vocabulary*.

Vocabulary *knowledge* can be characterized as receptive and expressive, oral and reading, and sight. The size of a person's receptive vocabulary is not usually the same as the size of that person's expressive vocabulary. Similarly, the size of a person's oral vocabulary is not necessarily the size of that person's reading vocabulary.

- Receptive vocabulary includes what the student understands when vocabulary is presented in text or in listening; expressive vocabulary includes what the student uses in writing or speaking to others.
- Oral vocabulary includes words the student recognizes when listening; reading vocabulary includes words the student understands when reading.
- Sight vocabulary includes words the student recognizes automatically when reading.

Vocabulary *learning* can be differentiated by levels of the student's current word knowledge. Like prior knowledge of topic, teaching vocabulary is not simply a matter of teaching a new word.

- Sight word learning involves learning to identify words in print that the student understands receptively and uses expressively in speech.
- Learning new meanings for known words involves learning multiple meanings.
- Clarifying and enriching the meanings of new words involves deepening knowledge of word concepts.
- Learning new labels for known concepts involves attaching a word to an idea, experience, or image.
- Learning words that represent new and difficult concepts involves developing a new concept and attaching a label simultaneously.
- Learning to use words expressively that are known receptively involves being able to use words productively in speech and writing.

As reading material becomes more difficult, the number of different words per passage increases dramatically. More important, the concepts attached to new vocabulary become significantly more complex. Thus, deficiencies in vocabulary knowledge become increasingly more problematic and more likely to contribute to the difficulties of the struggling reader as reading materials move from lower to higher levels. Content area teachers, particularly in middle and high school, face this issue when assigning text selections that have high vocabulary loads and written at the readability of the subject grade level, which is well above the struggling reader's own reading level.

Text Structure

The pattern of organization that characterizes typical narrative and expository text is referred to as *text structure*. The reader's mental organization of how typical text is structured is referred to as *text schema*. When the reader's text schema matches the text structure, comprehension is enhanced because the reader's expectations about the way the text should unfold are confirmed. The reason many readers stick with certain genres is because they are comfortable with a predictable structure. It is just easier to comprehend when the structure of material is familiar.

Most of the research on text structure has focused on narrative text, often referred to as *story structure*. Researchers have found that stories written for children characteristically include a setting, series of episodes, and resolution. In the setting, the central character is introduced, and location and time may be described. Within each episode is an initiating event that causes the central character to react and formulate a goal. The goal is generally intended to solve the problem presented by the initiating event. The central character then attempts an action designed to achieve the goal. For each attempt, there is either a successful or failed outcome or consequence. If there is more than one episode in the story, the consequence is the initiating event of the subsequent episode. The resolution or ending represents the final outcome.

Children who expect stories to have predictable structures demonstrate better comprehension of stories that adhere to predictable structures. More able readers demonstrate more highly developed story schema (Pappas & Brown, 1987; Rahman & Bisanz, 1986). We know that story schema develops as a result of much exposure to stories, such as reading and read-aloud by parents and teachers. Children may be slower in developing story schema when they have had fewer of these experiences. For example, children who have not had much experience with bedtime read-aloud may have weak story schema when encountering their first reading material in school.

Expository text typically follows the patterns of collection (such as lists of information), description (such as presenting a concept and describing its attributes or providing examples), cause-effect relationships, problem-solution relationships, and similarities-differences relationships. It is common for expository text to incorporate all five structures. Awareness of expository text structure increases with age, increases with reading ability, and improves comprehension and recall of text information (McGee, 1982; Ohlhausen & Roller, 1988).

If the struggling reader has a poorly developed schema for story structure and expository text structure because he or she simply has not done enough wide reading to internalize these text structures, the problem can become cyclical. The less reading the child does, the fewer exemplars of text structure are experienced. The fewer the exemplars, the less likely it is that the child will internalize the structures.

Sentence Structure

Just as the reader must recognize most written words quickly and effortlessly to devote ample attention to comprehension, so must the reader process *sentence structures* quickly and effortlessly. If the syntactic structures used by the author are familiar, then the reader will be able to turn attention to other comprehension skills such as applying background knowledge, using vocabulary knowledge, considering text structure, and activating cognitive strategies. However, if the syntactic structures are unfamiliar, the reader must devote considerable attention to deciphering the syntax before attending to the meaning of the material.

Some linguistic structures are clearly more difficult to comprehend than others. Because English relies heavily on word order to express meaning, the structure of simple active declarative sentences (*Elihu completed his homework*) provides straightforward cues to the meaning. Transformations of the structure complicate the reader's road to meaning as indicated by simple questions (*What did Elihu complete?*), negatives (*Elihu didn't complete his homework*), and passives (*Homework was completed by Elihu*). Complex structures make the task even more difficult (*Elihu wanted to complete his homework in time to watch his favorite television program*). The links, ties, order arrangements, and patterns that connect and integrate sentences to create a coherent text can add to syntactic complexity (*Before Elihu completed his homework, he had to take the trash to the curb. As soon as he went outside, his friend asked if he wanted to play.*). Figurative language provides further challenge (*Elihu completed his homework as fast as a slide into home plate*).

It is self-evident that students who are not proficient in English are likely to struggle with written sentence structures. Even early reading material is replete with complex structures that may be unfamiliar to children with language learning difficulties, children who are English language learners, and children with hearing loss.

Cognitive Strategies

As Figure 1.1 showed, most of the tasks associated with comprehension involve the reader's prior knowledge. The greater the match between the reader's prior knowledge of topic, vocabulary, text structure, and sentence structure and those used by the author, the better the reader's comprehension will be. It is important to realize that although these tasks are necessary, they are not sufficient for skilled reading. The reader must also be able to consciously carry out strategies that will enhance comprehension. *Cognitive strategies* involve the ways that readers consciously monitor their comprehension and adapt their strategies to improve comprehension. These cognitive strategies are employed before, during, and after reading.

Before reading, strategies can include setting goals, overviewing, activating prior knowledge of topic and vocabulary, and predicting.

During reading, strategies can include noting relationships between ideas in text, distinguishing important from less or unimportant information, inferring, interpreting, monitoring comprehension by being aware when understanding breaks down, recognizing problems in concentration and pacing, recognizing inconsistencies in text, recognizing discrepancies between predictions and new information, deciding to skim or read carefully, deciding to skip or reread, self-questioning, visualizing, paraphrasing, getting the gist or main idea, and engaging in higher level and critical thinking.

After reading, strategies can include summarizing, evaluating, integrating, and concluding.

Instruction in cognitive strategies improves comprehension (Pressley & Woloshyn, 1995; Rosenshine & Meister, 1997) and can have particular benefits for struggling readers who may not independently realize when and where they are having comprehension difficulties and what to do to resolve problems in understanding.

At-Risk Factors and Issues

The major reading tasks of word recognition, fluency, and comprehension are so challenging to some students that they struggle with reading and fall behind their in peers in achievement. For decades, researchers and teachers have tried to identify the factors and issues that appear to place some students at risk for reading difficulties. Two fundamental reasons underlie this search for at-risk factors and issues. The first reason is based on the belief that if something within the child is an at-risk factor, intervention could be aimed at fixing the problem. For example, if poor visual acuity is an at-risk factor, the problem could likely be corrected through medication, surgery, eyeglasses, or contacts. The second reason is based on the belief that if something within the child is an at-risk factor, intervention could be aimed at reducing the need to rely on the factor, strengthening a skill that could compensate for the factor, or strengthening the factor itself. For example, if poor visual acuity is an at-risk factor, and correcting the visual problem itself is not an option, the child could be taught to read with large print or Braille books. What researchers and teachers have found is that it is rarely as straightforward as addressing the issue of visual acuity.

As you consider these at-risk factors, it is important to recognize that the influence of these factors on reading performance will vary from student to student. We know that the presence of any one of these factors, let alone several, places the child at risk for reading difficulty. Alternatively, we know that their presence does not ensure that the child will have difficulty and that some students who struggle with reading do not exhibit any of these at-risk factors. Most important, we know that none of these factors predetermines reading failure.

Understanding the potential influence of these factors on reading performance will enable you to carry out two important activities. The first is to take these factors into consideration when you assess the student's reading abilities. The second is to adapt instruction appropriately.

Cognitive Factors

According to Reed (2007), *cognition* is defined as the acquisition and use of knowledge. With this definition in mind, the relationship between cognition and language development is interdependent. As an aspect of language, reading development is both dependent on cognitive ability and, in turn, contributes to cognitive development.

Intelligence is associated with reading ability. That is, the relationship between intelligence and reading ability is positive. However, lower intelligence does not cause reading disability just as higher intelligence does not cause reading ability. Students with lower intelligence are likely, however, to have more difficulty encoding, storing, and retrieving words in memory. They are also likely to have more restricted background knowledge to apply to new text topics, a smaller vocabulary, more difficulty with complex English sentence structures, and less ability to employ cognitive strategies in reading than students with average or high intelligence.

Linguistic Factors

Three linguistic factors are related to reading ability: learning disability, language disability, and second language learning.

Learning disabilities involve significant difficulties in acquiring, understanding, and using spoken and written language, reasoning, and mathematical abilities. According to the National Joint Committee on Learning Disabilities (1998), it is presumed that these difficulties are due to central nervous system dysfunction. Difficulty with reading is the most common feature of students with learning disabilities (Kavale & Forness, 2000). The reading problems of these students are characterized by poor phonological awareness, inadequate use of letter-sound relationships for identifying words, and weak performance in a task called rapid naming speed, which is the speed with which the reader can name visually presented letters, numbers, or pictures (Lovett, Steinbach, & Frijters, 2000; Torgesen & Wagner, 1998; Wolf, 1991). The term *dyslexia* is currently used to refer specifically to children and adults with exceptional difficulty in developing phonological awareness and who, thus, have great difficulty mapping letters to spoken words (Shaywitz et al., 2000).

Some students with learning disabilities have persistent difficulty in attending to tasks and are diagnosed as having attention deficit disorder. Others display high rates of purposeless or inappropriate movement along with difficulty in attending. These students are diagnosed as having attention deficit/hyperactivity disorder (ADHD). In order to be diagnosed with ADHD, the determination must be made by a physician who uses the diagnostic criteria found in the *Diagnostic and Statistical Manual of Mental Disorders* (American Psychiatric Association, 2000). Symptoms include inattention,

18
....

CHAPTER 1

*The Reading
Process:
The Task and
the Reader*

hyperactivity, and impulsivity. Not all students with learning disabilities have ADHD and not all students with ADHD have learning disabilities. Reading problems can stem from the reader's difficulty in giving close attention to reading material and sustaining attention through extended written passages. Reading disability and ADHD co-occur at a relatively high rate with approximately one-third of grade one children and over half of grade nine students having a dual diagnosis (Dykman & Ackerman, 1991; Shaywitz, Fletcher, & Shaywitz, 1995).

Language disability often accompanies learning disability. The proportion of students with learning disabilities who also experience language delays and difficulties may be as high as 80 percent (Wiig, 1994). Language disability may include any or all of the four components of language: syntactic, semantic, phonological, and pragmatic development.

Syntactic development involves learning how morphemes are combined into words and how words are combined into sentences. The child with delayed syntactic development will have difficulty comprehending sentence structures and using structural analysis, analogy, and context for word recognition.

Semantic development involves learning the meaning of words and the relationship of word meanings. The child with delayed semantic development will have difficulty learning new vocabulary and applying vocabulary knowledge when reading. Some students have specific difficulty with word finding. Snyder and Godley (1992) found word-finding difficulties to be characterized by pauses, fillers such as "um," circumlocutions, repetitions, use of nonspecific words, and phrases such as "you know."

Phonological development involves learning the sound patterns of language. The child with delayed phonological development will have difficulty with phonemic awareness and using phonic analysis for word recognition.

Pragmatic development involves learning how to use language for interacting with others. For example, learning the "rules" for opening, maintaining, and closing a conversation are part of pragmatic development. The child with delayed pragmatic development may have difficulty using cognitive strategies such as predicting, inferring, and interpreting.

Students for whom English is a second language, or English language learners (ELLs), may also experience difficulties in becoming readers. Research shows that it takes the average English language learner two years or less to use English easily in conversation but at least five years to be at grade level in English proficiency (Cummins, 2001). Given that reading material requires English proficiency rather than simple conversational proficiency, English language learners are likely to spend at least one-third of their school years with language abilities well below what is required for reading at grade level. As Cummins noted, "Every year native English-speaking students gain more sophisticated vocabulary and grammatical knowledge and increase their literacy skills. ELL students, therefore, must catch up with a moving target" (p. 120).

Social and Cultural Factors

Students from socially and culturally diverse backgrounds may experience difficulty in school because of incongruence of expectations and norms between the child's home culture and the school environment, which can result in a mismatch between the child's preferred learning and interactive style and the teacher's (Au, 2000; Barrera, 1995). *Culturally responsive teaching* involves instructional practices aimed at affirming the culture of students and reflecting the student's culture in the teaching process. According to Gollnick and Chinn (2009), culturally responsive teaching mitigates against learning problems because it involves high teacher expectations, reflects students' cultures in academic subjects, includes multiple perspectives on issues and events, involves positive and caring student-teacher interactions, and incorporates effective cross-cultural communication between students and teachers. As Cartledge and Kourea (2008) note, "Creating culturally responsive classrooms that include developing culturally competent teachers is a transformative process of the American educational system. . . . Assessments that are culturally fair should inform teachers about the quality and integrity of their instruction and should enable them to make changes for increasing student outcomes, a coveted end goal of education in America" (pp. 366–367).

Carnine and colleagues (Carnine, Silbert, Kame'enui, & Tarver, 2004; Carnine, Silbert, Kame'enui, Tarver, & Jungjohann, 2006) distinguish between students who struggle with reading because they have adequate general language ability but weaknesses in translating between oral language and printed language from students, largely from families of lower socioeconomic status, who struggle because they have inadequate oral language knowledge and literacy-related knowledge.

Emotional Factors

Attitude and *motivation* play an important role in reading success. It is rare to find a young child who is not enthused about reading but some children evolve into reluctant readers. The major reasons appear to involve frustration with a task at which they fail repeatedly, avoidance of poor reading performance in front of peers, desire to be perfect and inability to perform error-free, wish to protect their self-esteem, and learned helplessness or a sense that no matter what they do, it will not improve their performance. The student with a negative attitude toward reading is likely to avoid school-related and recreational reading. Attitude and motivation will be discussed in depth in Chapter 7.

Educational Factors

The research on effective reading instruction is extensive. Thus, it seems obvious to identify inappropriate reading instruction as a reason that some students struggle with reading. Strategies and materials that are appropriate

20
....

CHAPTER 1

*The Reading
Process:
The Task and
the Reader*

for one student may be inappropriate for another. No simple one-size-fits-all reading program works for every student. The student's educational program is an at-risk factor if the same strategies and materials are used regardless of the progress he or she makes. The teacher should be able to answer yes to the following questions:

- Have I assessed the student's abilities?
- Do my instructional strategies and materials make sense based on what I learned about the student's abilities and needs through my assessment?
- Am I differentiating instruction?
- Are my strategies ones that are evidence-based practices?
- Have these strategies been found to be successful with readers who have similar abilities and needs as my student?
- Am I willing to adapt or change my strategies if the student is not succeeding?

Physical Factors

Three physiological factors are related to reading ability: hearing, vision, and neurological factors.

Similar to intelligence, there is a direct relationship between *hearing loss* and reading ability. Degree of hearing loss is correlated with reading achievement level; the greater the hearing loss, the more likely it is that the child will have lower reading achievement. The average student who is deaf gains one third of a grade equivalent change each school year and the average reading level is fourth grade at high school graduation (Gallaudet Research Institute, 2003). The cause of low reading achievement appears to be related to oral language development. For children to learn language, they need a considerable amount of experience in conversation with adults. Through these interactions, children discern the underlying rules of the language used by adults. Children who are deaf and hard of hearing are exposed to inconsistent and incomplete language models because they do not hear English without some distortion. The amount of distortion depends on their degree of hearing loss, ability to benefit from amplification, and use of visual modalities, such as American Sign Language (Schirmer, 2000). Thus, students who are deaf and hard of hearing are likely to experience difficulty with phonemic awareness, phonic analysis for word recognition, and English sentence structures. They may also have less background knowledge than hearing students who benefit from the incidental information available through overhearing others talking, listening to the radio while driving in the car, and the myriad other daily opportunities to hear what is happening without looking.

Vision is not directly related to reading difficulties unless a visual problem is undiagnosed. The reading process of students with low vision is not qualitatively different from the reading process of students with normal vision (Bosman, Gompel, Vervloed, & von Bon, 2006). Students with blindness and low vision do not have a higher prevalence of reading problems than students with normal vision although they are likely to have less background knowledge than students with normal sight who gain this knowledge from the ongoing stream of visual information within everyday experiences. They also have difficulty connecting and organizing their experiences, understanding abstract concepts, and comprehending figurative language (Kingsley, 1997). Beyond visual acuity per se, *visual perception* and *visual discrimination* received a great deal of attention by researchers during the last quarter of the twentieth century. Ultimately, research showed no evidence that visual perception or discrimination problems cause reading disabilities or that visual training or visual tracking exercises improved reading ability (O'Shea & O'Shea, 1994).

Neurological factors related to reading ability include traumatic brain injury and neurological disorders. Traumatic brain injury is an acquired condition that is caused by an external physical force (unlike other neurological disabilities that are caused by disease or congenital malformation of the brain such as cerebral palsy and some causes of mental retardation). The student with traumatic brain injury displays impairment in cognition, language, memory, attention, reasoning, abstract thinking, judgment, problem solving, psychosocial behavior, physical functions, information processing, speech, and/or sensory, perceptual, and motor abilities (Heward, 2009). According to Hill (1999), students with traumatic brain injury may have difficulty concentrating, understanding oral and written language, and expressing themselves orally and in writing.

Neurological disorders can result from diseases and toxic substances during pregnancy, birth, and childhood. Other neurological issues have been proposed as causes of reading difficulties including preferred learning style, dominance of left- and right-brain hemispheric functioning, and the concept of multiple intelligences. None of these issues have been found to have a direct bearing on reading ability and instruction aimed at these domains has not been found to influence reading achievement (McCormick, 2007; Riccio & Hynd, 1996).

Recent research on brain function, particularly the use of magnetic resonance imaging technology, has shown that individual brain differences are present in many individuals with reading disabilities but it is unclear whether brain differences cause reading disabilities or are the result of years of poor reading (Catts & Kamhi, 2005). New technologies hold great promise for learning about the influence of brain structure and neural networks on learning to read.

22

CHAPTER 1

*The Reading
Process:
The Task and
the Reader*

Next Step

Two major assumptions were made in this chapter that will follow through each subsequent chapter. The first is that teachers are knowledgeable of the many components of the reading process and strategies common in teaching students to read through their introductory reading courses in preservice teacher education. The second assumption is that teachers do not have a unifying framework for putting the pieces together into a coherent reading program designed to enable struggling readers to become proficient readers.

This chapter provides the first of several graphic representations that you will use as a tool in putting together a reading program for any student in your classroom who is not succeeding. This chapter has also provided you with an overview of factors and issues that can place students at risk for struggling with reading.

The next chapter will present a process for assessing reading. Its placement after the chapter on the reading process and before the chapter on teaching lesson models and strategies is deliberate. You have to know which reading tasks to assess and you cannot decide on instruction until you have assessed the student's reading abilities, attitudes, and motivation. Thus, the next step in this book is assessment.

QUESTIONS FOR REFLECTION AND APPLICATION

1. What are your beliefs about the reading process and how do these beliefs influence how you interact with other teachers who hold the same or different beliefs?

2. If you were asked to prioritize reading tasks, how would you justify the ones you selected as most and least important?

3. Which at-risk factors present the greatest challenge in designing reading instruction?

4. What is the difference between being at-risk for reading difficulty and being a struggling reader?

SUGGESTED RESOURCES FOR ADDITIONAL READING

Finn, Patrick J. (2009). *Literacy with an Attitude: Educating Working-Class Children in Their Own Self-interest* (2nd ed.). Albany, NY: State University of New York.

Heward, William L. (2009). *Exceptional Children: An Introduction to Special Education* (9th ed.). Upper Saddle River, NJ: Allyn and Bacon/Merrill.

Klingner, Janette K., Hoover, John J., & Baca, Leonard M. (2009). *Why Do English Language Learners Struggle with Reading?: Distinguishing Language Acquisition from Learning Disabilities.* Thousand Oaks, CA: Corwin.

Obiakor, Festus E. (2001). *It Even Happens in "Good" Schools: Responding to Cultural Diversity in Today's Classrooms.* Thousand Oaks, CA: Corwin.

Taylor, Barbara M., & Ysseldyke, James E. (Eds.). (2007). *Effective Instruction for Struggling Readers, K–6.* New York: Teachers College.

Assessment

Putting the Reader at the Center of the Reading Program

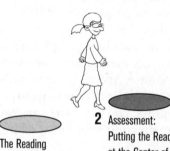

2 Assessment: Putting the Reader at the Center of the Reading Program

1 The Reading Process: The Task and the Reader

3 Framework for Developing a Reading Program for the Struggling Reader

4 Before-Reading Strategies: Prereading and Planning

This chapter will present a process for assessing reading using both formal and informal tools. This chapter is presented early in the text because assessment of the student's reading abilities, attitude, and motivation is the first step in developing a reading program for the struggling reader.

5 During-Reading Strategies: Supporting Strategic Reading

8 Families: Partnering with Parents

6 After-Reading Strategies: Synthesizing and Extending

7 Attitude and Motivation: From Reluctant to Enthused Reader

*R*eading assessment involves the process of gathering information about the student's reading knowledge and abilities and using this information to make judgments about instruction and intervention. In this view of reading assessment, the connection between assessment and instruction is direct. The connection is also iterative. Assessment information is used to plan instruction, and the student's performance during instruction provides assessment information for subsequent instruction.

24

....

CHAPTER 2

*Assessment:
Putting the Reader
at the Center
of the Reading
Program*

The topic of assessment typically appears in introductory literacy textbooks toward a later chapter because assessment is seen as a follow-up to instruction. These texts are typically structured to address, usually in this order, emergent and early literacy, word recognition, fluency, vocabulary development, and comprehension because these are viewed as the major elements of literacy instruction. This is certainly an appropriate structure for apprentice teachers who are studying how children learn to read. At the other end of textbook structures, texts designed to instruct teachers on carrying out an in-depth reading diagnosis for students who have fallen significantly behind their peers in reading typically incorporate assessment as part of each chapter on the topics of word recognition, fluency, vocabulary knowledge, and comprehension because the teacher's task is to identify the student's specific reading problems. This is assuredly an appropriate structure for apprentice, novice, and experienced teachers who are learning how to develop a program of remediation.

In this book, assessment is presented early in the text because for struggling readers, assessment is the essential first step in developing a reading program. You are aware of the components of the reading process because you have taken an introductory reading course. And whether or not you have taken or will take a reading diagnosis course to learn how to instruct students with severe and persistent reading difficulties, you will have struggling readers in your classroom. For these readers, assessment is your first teaching activity.

Sources of Assessment Information

....

There are seven major sources of assessment information: observations, recollections, tests, artifacts, diagnostic teaching, extant information, and professional judgments (Cohen & Spenciner, 2007; Hargis, 2004; Kibby, 1995a; Salvia, Ysseldyke, & Bolt, 2007; Taylor, 2006).

1. *Observations.* Observations involve watching the student during reading activities and noting behaviors, characteristics, and interactions. Observations can be informal or structured. In informal observations, you simply notice and notate behaviors that indicate the reader's acquisition and application of new knowledge and skills. In structured observations, you predetermine behaviors and activities to observe, as well as how to record the observations.

2. *Recollections.* In recollections, the teacher, parents, child, and others familiar with the child are asked to provide information from memory. Typically, this information is gathered from interviews or questionnaires. Formats for obtaining recollections include published versions that incorporate developmental milestones as well as teacher-created questions tailored to specific classrooms and students.

3. *Tests.* A test is simply a set of questions or tasks. The questions are predetermined and the results are scored in a consistent manner across all test takers on preset criteria and standardized scoring procedures.

In one type of standardized scoring procedure, normative standards are used. These are typically referred to as norm-referenced or standardized tests. The key characteristic of norm-referenced tests is that the student's performance is compared to the performance of a group of individuals considered to be peers. By understanding the match between the group on which the test was standardized and the student being tested, you can judge the relevance and value of the test results.

In a second type of standardized scoring procedure, absolute standards are used. These are typically referred to as criterion-referenced tests. The key characteristic of criterion-referenced tests is that the student's performance is compared to a predetermined level of mastery. By understanding the match between the level of mastery expected on the test and the student being tested, you can judge the appropriateness of the test and value of the results. Although norm-referenced tests are virtually always published tests, criterion-referenced tests may be published or developed by the teacher.

4. *Artifacts.* Artifacts are collections of items that reflect the reader's strengths, weaknesses, growth, and goals. Artifacts are a major component of portfolio assessment, which is a system for gathering student work over time to reflect changes in skills and knowledge.

5. *Diagnostic Teaching.* In diagnostic teaching, you conduct a mini-lesson for the purpose of identifying the strategies and skills used by readers, assessing how effectively they incorporate these strategies and skills, determining which ones they do not utilize, and ascertaining whether they can learn a new strategy or skill.

6. *Extant Information.* Information that has previously been gathered and is available to be reviewed is typically in the form of school records. For example, cumulative school records regularly include report cards, results of standardized tests, attendance records, Individualized Education Programs (IEPs) for students being served under the Individuals with Disabilities Education Act (IDEA), and reports from specialists such as speech-language pathologists and school psychologists. Extant information might also include the artifacts and anecdotal records kept by the student's previous teachers

7. *Professional Judgments.* All of the assessment information is interpreted by the teacher, who exerts professional judgment about its meaning and importance. The information gathered from observations, recollections, tests, artifacts, diagnostic teaching, and extant records is as valuable as the teacher is skilled. As Salvia, Ysseldyke, and Bolt (2007) observed, "Judgments represent both the best and worst of assessment data. Judgments made by conscientious, capable, and objective individuals can be invaluable aids in the assessment process. Inaccurate, biased, and subjective judgments can be misleading at best and harmful at worst" (p. 32).

CHAPTER 2

Assessment: Putting the Reader at the Center of the Reading Program

CHAPTER 2

Assessment:
Putting the Reader
at the Center
of the Reading
Program

The kinds of assessment conducted and the purposes for the assessment depend on the stakeholders who want the information. Stakeholders rely differently on the sources of assessment information.

Public policymakers, the general public, and the press want information related to groups of students to determine if publicly supported programs are effective. The impetus for the No Child Left Behind Act (reauthorization of the Elementary and Secondary Education Act), signed in 2002, was based on the perceived lack of success in raising achievement levels of our nation's youth, particularly those from low income backgrounds and those for whom English is a second language. These stakeholders are interested in assessment that indicates if schools are doing a good job, accountable to standards of performance, and meeting state and national goals. They are interested almost exclusively in norm-referenced test results.

Program administrators, such as school principals and superintendents, want information that helps them judge the effectiveness of the programs they direct within schools. These stakeholders are interested in assessment that indicates the quality of curriculum, materials, and instruction. They are predominantly interested in norm-referenced test results though increasingly have been interested in state-adopted tests that measure achievement of state curriculum standards by students at selected grade levels.

Parents and family members want information that helps them determine whether their child is making good progress within the current educational program. These stakeholders are interested in assessment that compares their child to the achievement of other children so that they can decide if the educational program is appropriate or whether their child needs a different program. These stakeholders are interested largely in tests, both norm-referenced and criterion-referenced, and the professional judgment exerted by the teacher in interpreting these test results.

Students want information about their own strengths and needs so that they can decide where to place their energies. They are interested in the match between the expectations of their teachers and their own abilities and interests. Students are interested in all sources of assessment information and rely most heavily on teacher judgment.

Teachers want information that enables them to plan instruction, monitor learning, and adapt instruction. They are interested in assessment that helps them make good instructional decisions. They are interested in all sources of assessment information. No Child Left Behind, state curriculum standards, and other accountability measures have placed norm-referenced tests and state-adopted criterion-referenced tests at the forefront of all assessments, though these tests provide little information on what adjustments in instruction would be helpful for a particular reader.

Five principles should guide teachers in reading assessment.

1. Assessment and Teaching Are Bound Together.
   - Assessment is grounded in what students are learning about reading.
   - Assessment is linked with reading activities.
   - Assessment enhances the teacher's ability to observe and understand learning.
   - Teaching goals are focused enough to be assessed.
2. Assessment Is a Continuous, Systematic, and Evolving Process.
   - Some types of assessment take place moment by moment and some on regularly scheduled bases.
   - Assessment changes over time as students demonstrate the ability to engage in new kinds of reading tasks.
3. Assessment Is Multidimensional.
   - Assessment techniques and instruments are varied.
   - Diverse contexts are used to gather information on the full spectrum of knowledge and skills possessed by the student.
4. Assessment Includes Formative and Summative Measures.
   - Formative assessment is ongoing during instruction.
   - Summative assessment is conducted before and after instruction.
5. Assessment Is a Shared Endeavor between Teacher and Student.
   - Assessment informs the teacher and student mutually so that they can make joint and individual decisions about what to do next.
   - Assessment is effective when the result is positive change in instruction and learning.

27

CHAPTER 2

*Assessment:
Putting the Reader
at the Center
of the Reading
Program*

Assessment Process

The subtitle of this chapter, "Putting the Reader at the Center of the Reading Program," is meant to emphasize the relationship between assessment and instruction. Unlike instruction that derives from reading programs or reading materials, instruction for struggling readers must derive from assessment of the student. As shown in Figure 2.1, when the reader is the centerpiece, the reading program is developed for the student and materials are selected for the student. Instead of choosing a reading program and set of materials for a group or class of students, which is a fairly typical approach for classroom teachers, the assessment provides a road map to the teacher for selecting a reading program and set of materials for the student.

If the reader is put at the center, does it mean that you have to develop individualized programs for each student? The answer is, absolutely not. As will be shown in the next chapters, individual assessment is compatible with a range of instructional lesson models and teaching strategies that involve individual, peer, small-group, and large-group instruction.

28

CHAPTER 2

*Assessment:
Putting the Reader
at the Center
of the Reading
Program*

FIGURE 2.1   Relationship between Assessment and Instruction

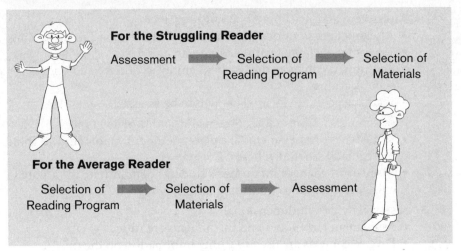

The first major assessment activity involves assessing the student's reading ability for the purpose of selecting a reading program and materials. The second major activity involves ongoing assessment for the purpose of modifying and adapting instruction. The third major activity involves assessing the reader's progress. The three may intertwine but the assessment techniques and instruments tend to vary between the three activities. The focus in this section on the assessment process is most specifically on assessing reading ability. The point in time of this assessment is generally when the student is new to the teacher, either at the beginning of the school year or if the student has transferred to the classroom. Assessing the reader's progress is also included in this section because the process for this summative assessment is essentially an abbreviated form of assessment at the outset of instruction. Ongoing assessment is included in a separate section later in the chapter.

Table 2.1 provides suggestions for assessment tests and techniques that can be used as a reference tool. This list is not exhaustive and not meant to be a protocol. The names of published tests were chosen as examples because they are widely used and are considered trustworthy measures. The popularity of tests is not always based on how reliable and valid they are, and certainly not always based on how appropriate they are for assessing your students. The information in Table 2.1 is intended to help you determine which tests are the right ones for assessing the students you teach. Further information on these tests and others that you might be interested in using, or may be mandated to use by your school district, are more thoroughly discussed in several current assessment texts listed at the end of this chapter.

Walpole and McKenna (2006) suggest that teachers put together a toolkit of assessments of phonemic awareness, the alphabetic principle, word recognition, oral reading fluency, reading comprehension, and reading motivation. Such a toolkit can be developed from the assessments in Table 2.1.

(text continues on page 43)

TABLE 2.1 Tests and Techniques

Skill/ Strategy	Name	Age/Grade Range	Description	Source
Phonemic Awareness	1. Stanford Diagnostic Reading Test-4th	Grade 1.5–12	Consists of six levels. Phonetic analysis is sampled at grade levels 1.5–4.5 through items assessing skill in associated letters and word segments with consonant and vowel sounds.	Criterion-referenced and norm-referenced test
	2. Gates-MacGinitie Reading Tests-4th	Emergent–Grade 12	Prereading subtest assesses phonological awareness, ability to attend to phonemic units in spoken English words, and letters and letter-sound correspondences. Beginning reading subtest assesses the student's ability to decode combinations of consonants and vowels that make up English words.	Norm-referenced test
	3. Woodcock-Johnson III Diagnostic Reading Battery	Age 5–adult	Incomplete word subtest assesses the student's ability to supply one or more missing phonemes. Sound blending subtest assesses the student's ability to synthesize syllables into words.	Norm-referenced test
	4. Yopp-Singer Phoneme Segmentation Test	Grade K–1	Consists of 22 words. The examiner says each word and asks the student to say each sound in the word, in order.	Criterion-referenced test
	5. Test of Phonological Awareness-2+	Grade K–1	In the kindergarten version, the student compares first sounds in words. In the first-grade version, the student compares last sounds in words.	Norm-referenced test
	6. Phonological Awareness Test-2	Grade K–4	Consists of six subtests assessing the student's ability to discriminate and produce rhymes; segment sentences, compound words, syllables, and phonemes; pronounce separately the beginning, ending, or medial sound in short words; delete a syllable or phoneme from a word and pronounce the word that remains; use colored blocks to show	Norm-referenced test

(continued)

TABLE 2.1   continued

Skill/ Strategy	Name	Age/Grade Range	Description	Source
Phonemic Awareness (continued)			the number and order of phonemes in words; and blend together separately presented syllables or phonemes to make words	
	7. Comprehensive Test of Phonological Processing	Grade K–12	For kindergarten to first grade, tasks involve sound comparison, segmentation, and phoneme blending. For second grade and beyond, tasks involve phoneme segmentation and blending. The test also includes measures of rapid naming ability and short-term memory for phonological information.	Norm-referenced test
	8. Developmental Reading Assessment-2	Grade K–3 and 4–8	Assessment is conducted with Benchmark Books to identify levels for independent reading and guided reading instruction.	Criterion-referenced test
Automatic Word Recognition	1. Teacher-made Informal Reading Inventory	Grade Pre-primer–9	Consists of brief narrative and/or expository passages at each grade level (25–50 words at preprimer-primer, 50–100 words at grades 1–2, 100–200 words at grades 3+). Two comparable passages are chosen for each grade level; 6–10 factual and inferential questions are written for each passage. The first passage is read orally and the teacher records any miscues such as substituting, adding, omitting, mispronouncing, repeating, or inverting words. The second passage is read silently. The teacher records reading behaviors such as effort, concentration, expression, and strategies for identifying unknown words. After each passage is read, the teacher asks the comprehension questions.	Criterion-referenced test

TABLE 2.1 continued

Skill/ Strategy	Name	Age/Grade Range	Description	Source
Automatic Word Recognition (continued)	2. Published Informal Reading Inventory (e.g., Analytical Reading Inventory-6th, Qualitative Reading Inventory-4, Standardized Reading Inventory-2nd)	Grade 1–9	Consists of a set of graded word lists and graded passages for each form. One form is read silently and one is read orally. Each form is followed by multiple-choice comprehension questions.	Criterion-referenced test
	3. Developmental Reading Assessment-2	Grade K–3 and 4–8	Assessment is conducted with Benchmark Books to identify levels for independent reading and guided reading instruction.	Criterion-referenced test
	4. Gray Oral Reading Test-4th	Ages 6–18	Consists of reading passages of progressive difficulty. After reading each passage orally, five comprehension questions are asked.	Norm-referenced test
	5. Gates-MacGinitie Reading Tests-4th	Emergent– Grade 12	Beginning reading subtest assesses the student's ability to identify common words in written text.	Norm-referenced test
	6. Woodcock Reading Mastery Tests-Revised	K–adult	Word identification subtest measures skill in pronouncing words in isolation.	Norm-referenced test
	7. Wide Range Achievement Test-4th	Ages 5–adult	Reading subtest includes assessment of words in isolation.	Norm-referenced test

(continued)

TABLE 2.1 continued

Skill/ Strategy	Name	Age/Grade Range	Description	Source
Automatic Word Recognition (continued)	8. High-frequency word lists (e.g., Dolch Basic Sight Word List, The New Instant Sight Word List, Ekwall list, Harris-Jacobson Core Lists)	K–adult	Each word is printed on a card and the student reads each aloud. For contextual tests, the words are placed into sentences or stories, grouped by level (preprimer, primer, grade 1, etc.). The student reads the sentences aloud.	Criterion-referenced test
	9. The Names Test	Grade 3–8	Consists of a list of first and last, single and multi-syllabic words.	Criterion-referenced test
	10. Mini-lesson (e.g., Directed Reading Thinking Activity, Reciprocal Teaching, Reading Workshop)	Grade K–12	Teacher develops a lesson implementing a reading model and strategies thought to be appropriate for the student, with reading material likely to be at the student's indepen-dent or instructional reading level. The lesson provides opportunity to observe the student's automatic word recog-nition abilities and assess the student's ability to learn new sight words.	Diagnostic reading lesson
Word Analysis	1. Teacher-made Informal Reading Inventory	Grade Preprimer–9	See #1 for Automatic Word Recognition.	Criterion-referenced test
	2. Published Informal Reading Inventory (e.g., Analytical Reading Inventory-5th, Qualitative Reading Inventory-4, Standardized Reading Inventory-2nd)	Grade 1–9	See #2 for Automatic Word Recognition.	Criterion-referenced test

TABLE 2.1 continued

Skill/ Strategy	Name	Age/Grade Range	Description	Source
Word Analysis (continued)	3. Developmental Reading Assessment-2	Grade K–3 and 4–8	See #3 for Automatic Word Recognition.	Criterion-referenced test
	4. Gray Oral Reading Test-3rd	Ages 7–18	See #4 for Automatic Word Recognition.	Norm-referenced test
	5. Gates-MacGinitie Reading Tests-4th	Emergent–Grade 12	Grades 1 and 2 subtests assess the student's ability to decode words.	Norm-referenced test
	6. Woodcock Reading Mastery Tests-Revised	K–adult	Word attack subtest assesses skill in using phonic and structural analysis to read nonsense words.	Norm-referenced test
	7. Woodcock Diagnostic Reading Battery	Age 4–adult	Word attack subtest measures phonic and structural analysis with non-words and unfamiliar words.	Norm-referenced test
	8. Running records and miscue analysis	Grade 1–12	Teacher asks the student to read a passage aloud. During reading, the teacher makes a check mark for each word the student reads correctly, notates when the student doesn't know a word, and writes the word used by the student when it is a substitution, repetition, omission, or incorrect pronunciation.	Criterion-referenced test
	9. Mini-lesson (e.g., Directed Reading Thinking Activity, Reciprocal Teaching, Reading Workshop)	Grade K–12	Teacher develops a lesson implementing a reading model and strategies thought to be appropriate for the student, with reading material likely to be at the student's independent or instructional reading level. The lesson provides opportunity to observe the student's ability to identify words through phonic analysis, analogy, and structural analysis and to learn and apply new word analysis skills.	Diagnostic reading lesson

(continued)

TABLE 2.1 continued

Skill/ Strategy	Name	Age/Grade Range	Description	Source
Using Context for Word Recognition	1. Gates-MacGinitie Reading Tests-4th	Emergent– Grade 12	Grade 1 test assesses context clues.	Norm-referenced test
	2. Mini-lesson (e.g., Directed Reading Thinking Activity, Reciprocal Teaching, Reading Workshop)	Grade K–12	Teacher develops a lesson implementing a reading model and strategies thought to be appropriate for the student, with reading material likely to be at the student's independent or instructional reading level. The lesson provides opportunity to observe the student's ability to use syntactic and semantic context for identifying words and to learn to use context for word recognition.	Diagnostic reading lesson
Fluency	1. Teacher-made Informal Reading Inventory	Grade Pre-primer–9	See #1 for Automatic Word Recognition.	Criterion-referenced test
	2. Published Informal Reading Inventory (e.g., Analytical Reading Inventory-5th, Qualitative Reading Inventory-4, Standardized Reading Inventory-2nd)	Grade 1–9	See #2 for Automatic Word Recognition.	Criterion-referenced test
	3. Developmental Reading Assessment-2	Grade K–3 and 4–8	See #3 for Automatic Word Recognition.	Criterion-referenced test
	4. Gray Oral Reading Test-3rd	Grade 1–12	See #4 for Automatic Word Recognition.	Norm-referenced test

TABLE 2.1 continued

Skill/ Strategy	Name	Age/Grade Range	Description	Source
Fluency (continued)	5. Dynamic Indicators of Basic Early Literacy (DIBELS)	Grade K–3	Subtests include oral reading fluency, initial sounds fluency, letter naming fluency, phonemic segmentation fluency, nonsense word fluency, and word use fluency. The oral reading fluency test includes a retell fluency test to assess comprehension. Each subtest takes no more than a few minutes to administer.	Criterion-referenced test
	6. Running records and miscue analysis	Grade 1–6	Teacher asks the student to read a passage aloud. During reading, the teacher makes a check mark for each word the student reads correctly, notates when the student doesn't know a word, and writes the word used by the student when it is a substitution, repetition, omission, or incorrect pronunciation.	Criterion-referenced test
	7. Fluency scale (e.g., Oral Reading Fluency Scale)	Grade 1–6	Teacher asks the student to read a 250–1000 word passage at the student's instructional level. The teacher observes three factors: phrasing, following the author's syntax, and expressiveness. At level 1, the student reads primarily word by word. At level 2, the student reads primarily in two-word phrase groups. At level 3, the student reads primarily in three- or four-word phrase groups, demonstrates mostly appropriate phrasing, attends to the author's syntax, and demonstrates little or no expressive interpretation. At level 4, the student reads primarily in meaningful phrase groups, attends to the author's syntax, and reads with expressive interpretation.	Criterion-referenced test

(continued)

TABLE 2.1 continued

Skill/ Strategy	Name	Age/Grade Range	Description	Source
Fluency (continued)	8. Reading rate	Grade 1–6	Teacher asks the student to read a passage at or slightly below grade level in difficulty. At the end of 60 seconds, the teacher asks the student to stop reading. The teacher counts the number of words that were read. The teacher repeats the procedure several times with different passages and calculates the average correct words per minute (cwpm). The teacher compares the student's oral reading rate to expected 53 cwpm for first, 89 cwpm for second, 107 cwpm for third, 123 wpm for fourth, 139 cwpm for fifth, and 150 cwpm for sixth grades.	Criterion-referenced test
Prior Knowledge of Topic	1. Mini-lesson (e.g., Directed Reading Thinking Activity, Reciprocal Teaching, Reading Workshop)	Grade K–12	Teacher develops a lesson implementing a reading model and strategies thought to be appropriate for the student, with reading material likely to be at the student's independent or instructional reading level. The lesson provides opportunity to observe the student's ability to activate background knowledge, learn new information about the text topic, and apply background knowledge during reading for comprehension.	Diagnostic reading lesson
Vocabulary Knowledge	1. Stanford Diagnostic Reading Test-4th	Grade 1.5–12	Consists of six levels. Vocabulary is assessed through listening vocabulary, skill in identifying synonyms, and classification of words into categories.	Criterion-referenced and norm-referenced test
	2. Gates-MacGinitie Reading Tests-4th	Emergent–Grade 12	Grades 1–12 subtests assess vocabulary through multiple-choice questions.	Norm-referenced test

TABLE 2.1 continued

Skill/ Strategy	Name	Age/Grade Range	Description	Source
Vocabulary Knowledge (continued)	3. Woodcock Reading Mastery Tests-Revised	K–adult	Word comprehension subtest assesses the student's ability to provide antonyms, synonyms, and analogies.	Norm-referenced test
	4. Woodcock Diagnostic Reading Battery	Age 4–adult	Reading and oral vocabulary subtests measure the student's skill in providing synonyms and antonyms.	Norm-referenced test
	5. Test of Reading Comprehension-3rd	Age 7–17	General, math, social studies, and science vocabulary subtests assess the student's ability to read three related words and select two of four response words that are related to the other three words.	Norm-referenced test
	6. Peabody Picture Vocabulary Test-4th	Age 1.5–adult	Consists of a list of vocabulary words and a series of plates with four pictures per plate. The examiner reads the word aloud and the student points to the most appropriate picture.	Norm-referenced test
	7. The Word Test 2: Elementary and Adolescent	Age 6–11 (El) and Age 12–17 (Ad)	Elementary level tests six vocabulary and semantic areas: associations, multiple definitions, semantic absurdities, antonyms, definitions, and synonyms. Adolescent level includes four tasks: brand names (explaining why a semantically descriptive name of a product or company is appropriate), synonyms, signs of the times (telling what a sign or message means and why it is important), and definitions.	Norm-referenced test
	8. Expressive and Receptive One-Word Picture Vocabulary Tests	Age 2–11	Consists of 100 stimulus pictures. The examiner presents each picture and asks the student to name it.	Norm-referenced test

(continued)

TABLE 2.1 continued

Skill/ Strategy	Name	Age/Grade Range	Description	Source
Vocabulary Knowledge (continued)	9. Cloze procedure	Grade Pre-primer–12	Consists of a brief passage (250–300 words) in which words are omitted (e.g., every 5th word), with first and last sentences left intact. In modified cloze, the student is given several word choices.	Criterion-referenced test
	10. Mini-lesson (e.g., Directed Reading Thinking Activity, Reciprocal Teaching, Reading Workshop)	Grade K–12	Teacher develops a lesson implementing a reading model and strategies thought to be appropriate for the student, with reading material likely to be at the student's independent or instructional reading level. The lesson provides opportunity to observe the student's vocabulary knowledge and ability to learn new vocabulary words.	Diagnostic reading lesson
Knowledge of Text Structure	1. Stanford Diagnostic Reading Test-4th	Grade 1.5–12	Consists of six levels. The comprehension subtest uses recreational, informational, and functional text. Four kinds of comprehension are assessed: initial understanding, interpretation, critical analysis, and reading strategies. Within the reading strategies segment, recognizing and using text skills structures and types of text are assessed.	Criterion-referenced and norm-referenced test
	2. Test of Reading Comprehension-3rd	Age 7–17	Sentence sequencing subtest assesses the student's ability to put five randomly ordered sentences into a meaningful story.	Norm-referenced test
	3. Storytelling, retelling, and story writing	Grade K–12	Teacher asks the student to write a story, retell a story previously read, or describe the story in a wordless picture book.	Criterion-referenced test

TABLE 2.1 continued

Skill/ Strategy	Name	Age/Grade Range	Description	Source
Knowledge of Text Structure (continued)	4. Mini-lesson (e.g., Directed Reading Thinking Activity, Reciprocal Teaching, Reading Workshop)	Grade K–12	Teacher develops a lesson implementing a reading model and strategies thought to be appropriate for the student, with reading material likely to be at the student's independent or instructional reading level. The lesson provides opportunity to observe the student's ability to retell the story, complete a story cloze, or answer questions aimed at eliciting knowledge of story components.	Diagnostic reading lesson
Knowledge of Sentence Structure	1. Test of Reading Comprehension-3rd	Ages 7–17	Syntactic similarities subtest assesses the student's ability to select two of five sentences that are the most closely related in meaning.	Norm-referenced test
	2. Test of Language Development-3rd	Primary and Intermediate	Primary subtests are picture and oral vocabulary, grammatic understanding and completion, sentence imitation, word articulation, and discrimination. Intermediate subtests are sentence combining, vocabulary, word ordering, generals, grammatic comprehension, and malapropisms.	Norm-referenced test
	3. Cloze procedure	Grade Preprimer–12	Consists of a brief passage (250–300 words) in which words are omitted (e.g., every fifth word), with first and last sentences left intact. In modified cloze, the student is given several word choices.	Criterion-referenced test
	4. Mini-lesson (e.g., Directed Reading Thinking Activity, Reciprocal Teaching, Reading Workshop)	Grade K–12	Teacher develops a lesson implementing a reading model and strategies thought to be appropriate for the student, with reading material likely to be at the student's independent or instructional reading level. The lesson provides an opportunity to observe the student's ability to understand the author's sentence structures and to learn syntactic structures.	Diagnostic reading lesson

(continued)

TABLE 2.1   continued

Skill/ Strategy	Name	Age/Grade Range	Description	Source
Cognitive Strategies	1. Stanford Diagnostic Reading Test-4th	Grade 1.5 –12	Consists of six levels. The scanning subtest measures skill in scanning for important information. The comprehension subtest uses recreational, informational, and functional text. Four kinds of comprehension are assessed: initial understanding, interpretation, critical analysis, and reading strategies. Also includes a reading strategies survey.	Criterion-referenced and norm-referenced test
	2. Gates-MacGinitie Reading Tests-4th	Emergent– Grade 12	Grade 1–12 tests assess comprehension through multiple-choice questions.	Norm-referenced test
	3. Woodcock Reading Mastery Tests-Revised	K–adult	Passage comprehension subtest assesses the student's ability to read silently a passage with a word missing and to choose from several choices the appropriate word.	Norm-referenced test
	4. Woodcock Diagnostic Reading Battery	Age 4–adult	Passage comprehension subtest measures the student's ability to point to pictures representing what has just been read and identify missing words in phrases or short passages. Listening comprehension subtest assesses the student's ability to listen to a passage and supply the last word.	Norm-referenced test
	5. Test of Reading Comprehension-3rd	Age 7–17	Paragraph reading subtest assesses comprehension by asking the student to read paragraphs and answer multiple-choice questions requiring the student to select a best title, recall details, and infer.	Norm-referenced test
	6. Meta-comprehension Strategy Index	Middle– upper elementary	Consists of 25 multiple-choice questions that assess the student's awareness of reading strategies the student uses before, during, and after reading a narrative passage. Strategies include	Criterion-referenced test

TABLE 2.1 continued

Skill/ Strategy	Name	Age/Grade Range	Description	Source
Cognitive Strategies (continued)			predicting and verifying, previewing, purpose setting, self-questioning, drawing from background knowledge, summarizing, and applying fix-up strategies.	
	7. Survey of Reading Strategies	Adolescent– Adult	Consists of 30 5-point Likert scale items that assess the type and frequency of reading strategies that adolescent and adult English as a second language students perceive they use while reading academic materials in English.	Interview/ Questionnaire
	8. Mini-lesson (e.g., Directed Reading Thinking Activity, Reciprocal Teaching, Reading Workshop)	Grade K–12	Teacher develops a lesson implementing a reading model and strategies thought to be appropriate for the student, with reading material likely to be at the student's independent or instructional reading level. The lesson provides an opportunity to observe the student's ability to monitor comprehension and adapt strategies to improve comprehension.	Diagnostic reading lesson
Attitude and Interests	1. Stanford Diagnostic Reading Test-4th	Grade 1.5–12	Includes a reading questionnaire to measure attitude toward reading and reading interests.	Interview/ Questionnaire
	2. Estes Attitude Scale	Grade 3–12	Students rank 20 statements to indicate attitudes on a 5-point scale (strongly agree to strongly disagree).	Interview/ Questionnaire
	3. Elementary Reading Attitude Survey	Grade 1–6	Uses the comic strip character Garfield the cat to solicit information about the student's attitude toward school-based and recreational forms of reading.	Interview/ Questionnaire
	4. Reader Self- Perception Scale	Intermediate	Consists of 35 statements that reflect how the student feels about him- or herself as a reader on a 5-point scale (strongly agree to strongly disagree).	Interview/ Questionnaire

(continued)

TABLE 2.1   continued

Skill/ Strategy	Name	Age/Grade Range	Description	Source
Attitude and Interests (continued)	5. Motivation to Read Profile	Grade 2–6	The reading survey consists of 20 items with a 4-point response scale designed to assess self-concept as a reader and value of reading. The conversational interview consists of questions designed to elicit general motivation and motivational factors related to reading narrative and informational texts.	Interview/ Questionnaire
	6. Teacher-made questions	Grade K–12	Consists of questions or statements designed to elicit the student's attitude and interests toward reading.	Interview/ Questionnaire
	7. Teacher observations	Grade K–12	Teacher observes the student during the school day to assess the student's attitude and interests.	Observations

Bibliography

Beaver, J., & Carter, M. (2003). *Developmental Reading Assessment Levels 4-8* (2nd ed.); (2006) *Developmental Reading Assessment Levels K-3* (2nd ed). Eagan, MN: Pearson Assessment.

Bowers, L., Huisingh, R., LoGiudice, C., & Orman, J. (2005). *The Word Test 2: Elementary*. East Moline, IL: LinguiSystems.

Brown, V., Hammill, D., & Wiederholt, J. L. (1995). *Test of Reading Comprehension* (3rd ed.). Austin, TX: Pro-Ed.

Gardner, M. F. (2000). *Expressive and Receptive One-Word Picture Vocabulary Tests*. Novato, CA: Academic Therapy.

Clay, M. M. (2000). *Running Records for Classroom Teachers*. Portsmouth, NH: Heinemann.

Cunningham, P. (1990). The Names Test: A quick assessment of decoding ability. *The Reading Teacher, 44,* 124–129.

Duffelmeyer, F. A., Kruse, A. E., Merkley, D. J., & Fyfe, S. A. (1994). Further validation and enhancement of the Names Test. *The Reading Teacher, 48,* 118–128.

Dunn, L. M., & Dunn, D. M. (2007). *Peabody Picture Vocabulary Test* (4th). Eagan, MN: Pearson Assessment.

Dynamic Indicators of Basic Early Literacy Skills (6th ed.). (2002). *DIBELS*. Retrieved July 10, 2008 from http://dibels.uoregon.edu.

Estes, T. H. (1971). A scale to measure attitudes toward reading. *Journal of Reading, 15,* 135–138. [Estes Attitude Scale]

Gambrell, L. B., Palmer, B. M., Codling, R. M., & Mazzoni, S. A. (1996). Assessing motivation to read. *The Reading Teacher, 49,* 518–533. [Motivation to Read Profile]

Henk, W. A., & Melnick, S. A. (1995). The Reader Self-Perception Scale (RSPS): A new tool for measuring how children feel about themselves as readers. *The Reading Teacher, 48,* 470–482.

Huisingh, R., Bowers, L., LoGiudice, C., & Orman, J. (2005). *The Word Test 2: Adolescent*. East Moline, IL: LinguiSystems.

Karlsen, B., & Garland, E. F. (1996). *Stanford Diagnostic Reading Test* (4th ed) San Antonio, TX: Harcourt Brace.

Leslie, L., & Caldwell, J. (2006). *Qualitative Reading Inventory-4*. Boston: Allyn and Bacon.

MacGinitie, W. H., & MacGinitie, R. K. (1998). *Gates-MacGinitie Reading Tests* (4th ed.). Itasca, IL: Riverside.

Mather, N., Sammons, J., & Schwartz, J. (2006). Adaptations of the Names Test: Easy-to-use phonics assessments. *The Reading Teacher, 60,* 114–122.

McKenna, M. C., & Kear, D. J. (1990). Measuring attitudes toward reading: A new tool for teachers. *The Reading Teacher, 43,* 626–639. [Elementary Reading Attitude Survey]

Mokhtari, K., & Sheorey, R. (2002). Measuring ESL students' awareness of reading strategies. *Journal of Developmental Education, 25*(3), 2–10.

Newcomer, P. L. (1999). *Standardized Reading Inventory* (2nd ed.). Austin, TX: Pro-Ed.

Pinnell, G. S., Pikulski, J. J., Wixson, K. K., Campbell, J. R., Gough, P. B., & Beatty, A. S. (1995). *Listening to children read aloud*. Washington, DC: U.S. Department of Education, National Center for Education Statistics. [Oral Reading Fluency Scale]

Pitcher, S. M., Albright, L. K., DeLaney, C. J., Walker, N. T., Seunarinesingh, S. M., Headley, K. N., Ridgeway, V. G., Peck, S., Hunt, R., & Dunston, P. J. (2007). Assessing adolescents' motivation to read. *Journal of Adolescent and Adult Literacy, 50,* 378–396. [Motivation to Read Profile]

Robertson, C., & Salter, W. (2007). *Phonological Awareness Test-2*. East Moline, IL: LinguiSystems.

Schmitt, M. C. (1990). A questionnaire to measure children's awareness of strategic reading performance. *The Reading Teacher, 43,* 454-461. [Metacomprehension Strategy Index]

Torgeson, J. K., & Bryant, B. R. (2004). *Test of Phonological Awareness-2+* (2nd ed.). Austin, TX: Pro-Ed.

Wagner, R. K., & Torgeson, J. K. (1999). *The Comprehensive Test of Phonological Processing*. Austin, TX: Pro-Ed.

Wiederholt, J. L., & Bryant, B. R. (2001). *Gray Oral Reading Test* (4th ed.). Austin, TX: Pro-Ed.

Wilkinson, G. S., & Robertson, G. J. (2006). *The Wide Range Achievement Test* (4th ed.). Lutz, FL: Psychological Assessment Resources.

Woodcock, R. (1987). *Woodcock Reading Mastery Tests* (rev.). Circle Pines, MN: American Guidance Service.

Woodcock, R. W., McGrew, K. S., & Mather, N. (2001). *Woodcock-Johnson III Tests of Achievement*. Itasca, IL: Riverside.

Woods, M. L., & Moe, A. J. (1999). *Analytic Reading Inventory* (6th ed.). Upper Saddle River, NJ: Merrill/Prentice Hall.

Yopp, H. K. (1995). A test for assessing phonemic awareness in young children. *The Reading Teacher, 49,* 20–29. [Yopp-Singer Phoneme Segmentation Test]

Note: Sight word lists can be found by using the key term "sight words" on a web browser.

Rather than administer a preset series of tests to each student, putting the reader at the center of the reading program also means selecting assessment instruments based on questions about a particular student's reading abilities. Kibby (1995a) described this as a decision-making process and noted that the "process is essentially a problem-solving process: it requires identifying needed information, obtaining that information, interpreting and evaluating it, and then determining what further information (if any) is needed. Without a conceptual framework or decision-making model, this process may become either haphazard and nondirected or standardized and inflexible" (p. 2).

Reutzel and Cooter (2009) suggest that when interpreting reading assessment data that you engage in if/then thinking, which is illustrated as the following: "*If* the student has this reading need, *then* I should teach the reading skill _____ using _____ teaching strategy" (p. 228).

In order to keep track of the information, you will need a system to record what you have found and what you still need to learn about the student's reading abilities and difficulties. Figure 2.2 provides one way to organize this information. The left side of the chart identifies the sources of information you have selected for each skill area. The right side of the chart summarizes what you know from the assessments just conducted and what you still need to learn.

Student Background

The first step is to obtain information about the student's background. The sources for this information include recollections, extant records, and artifacts.

- Developmental milestones, diagnosis of disability, and relevant medical history can indicate cognitive, physical, and linguistic issues that may affect learning.

- Language used at home can indicate if the student is learning English as a second language.

- The age at which the student began school or began receiving educational services (such as an early intervention program) can provide information on the student's previous educational experience.

- School report cards or progress reports can provide information on the student's accomplishments in relation to prior teachers' expectations.

- IEPs for students with disabilities offer detailed information regarding the student's educational needs, goals, and services as well as strategies for addressing these goals.

- Test results from previously administered achievement tests provide information regarding how well the student is achieving compared to peers. When combined with tests of intelligence, you can compare expected achievement to actual achievement. Tests of reading, oral language, and written language provide information about performance at

FIGURE 2.2 Assessment Process

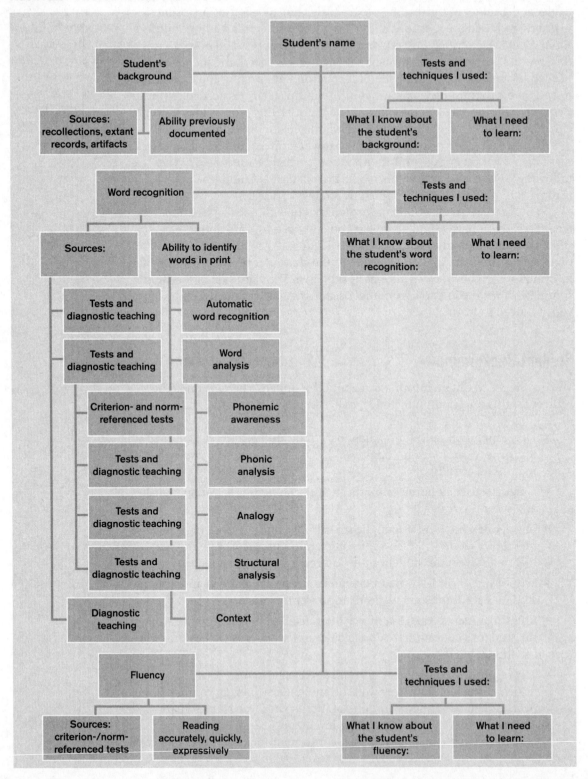

FIGURE 2.2 continued

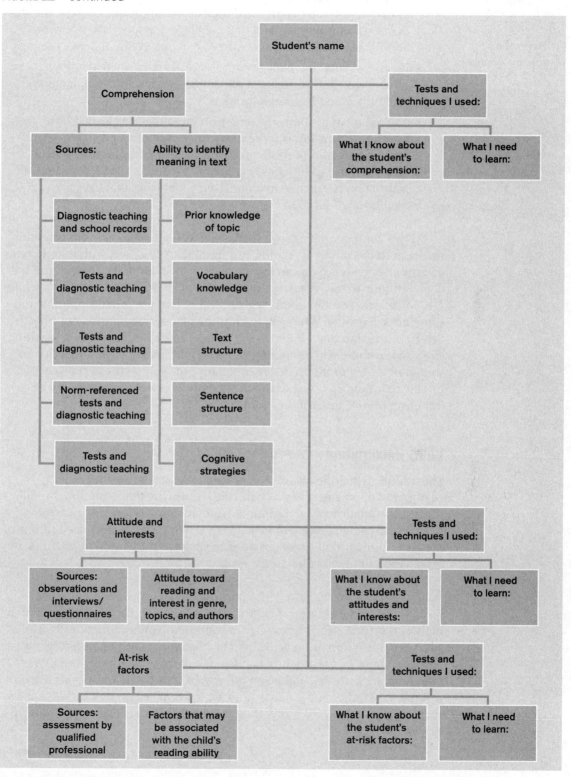

46

CHAPTER 2

Assessment:
Putting the Reader
at the Center
of the Reading
Program

the point in time in which these tests were administered and if all are available, you can determine if there is a relationship between the student's reading, writing, and oral language development. If tests were administered over time, you can see patterns in the student's progress.

- Reports of speech-language pathologists and school psychologists can offer diagnostic information regarding speech difficulties, language disabilities, and learning problems.
- The nature of previous reading instruction may be gleaned from progress reports but is more likely to be available in the form of artifacts gathered for portfolio assessment. Knowledge of the models, strategies, and techniques that previous teachers used for reading instruction is valuable in identifying approaches that have a likelihood of success.

When you examine the cumulative file, you are looking for information pertinent to the student's reading abilities. When you meet with the student's parents or caregivers, you can learn a great deal about home literacy, the student's attitude toward reading, and factors not evident in the student's school file. Sometimes you can obtain a great deal of background information and sometimes very little. What you learn is the first step in figuring out how to design instruction that builds on the reader's strengths and skills. Everything else you learn in the assessment process and ultimately in your instruction should be added to the student's cumulative file so that the next teacher will be able to follow up rather than to repeat unnecessary assessments or carry out unsupportive instruction.

Word Recognition

The second step in the assessment process is to determine the reader's strengths and weaknesses in recognizing words. The three component skills include automatic word recognition, word analysis (phonemic awareness, phonic analysis, analogy, and structural analysis), and context. Definitions of these component skills were provided in Chapter 1; this section provides an explanation of how to assess each skill.

Automatic Word Recognition.   The purpose of assessing automatic word recognition is to determine, first, the size of the student's current sight vocabulary and second, his or her ability to learn new words automatically. The source of this information is likely to be diagnostic teaching mini-lessons, criterion-referenced tests (such as informal reading inventories and lists of high-frequency words), and norm-referenced tests (such as the ones listed in Table 2.1). An example of a diagnostic teaching lesson that includes assessment of automatic word recognition is provided in the Diagnostic Teaching Lesson box.

(text continues on page 51)

47

CHAPTER 2

Assessment:
Putting the Reader
at the Center
of the Reading
Program

Diagnostic Teaching Lesson

Directed Reading Thinking Activity for
Stacey Says Good-bye by Patricia Reilly Giff

STEP 1: Concept Development

[Ms. Tankersley uses the ReQuest strategy, discussed in Chapter 4, to build Aimin's background knowledge of concepts in the story.]

Ms. Tankersley: Here's a new book that we'll begin reading today. [She points to the cover.]

Aimin: *Stacy Says Good-bye.*

Ms. Tankersley: Look at the picture on the cover. [The picture shows children with presents standing near the teacher at her desk.] Then read the first sentence. You can ask me anything you want to know about the story.

Aimin: "It was morning, almost time for school."

Ms. Tankersley: What would you like to ask me? [She pauses for a few seconds.] One question might be, what are the presents for?

Aimin: What are the presents for?

Ms. Tankersley: They're for the teacher. Do you have another question?

Aimin: Is it the teacher's birthday?

Ms. Tankersley: No. Read the second sentence and see if you have any other questions.

Aimin: "Stacy Arrow picked up her baby picture." What is the baby picture for?

Ms. Tankersley: All the children are bringing a baby picture to school. There's a contest for the best picture. What do you think will happen in the story?

Aimin: Maybe Stacy will win.

Ms. Tankersley: Maybe she will. Before we begin reading, I have a few new words to show you.

STEP 2: Sight Vocabulary

[Ms. Tankersley presents nine words (*bounce, toothpaste, mess, sloppy, stuff, picture, beautiful, envelope, spectacular*). Each word is written on a separate flash card. She discusses the meaning of each and points out letter-sound relationships, prefixes, suffixes, and compounds, as shown with the following two words.]

(continued)

48
....

CHAPTER 2

Assessment:
Putting the Reader
at the Center
of the Reading
Program

Ms. Tankersley: Bounce; o-u makes the sound /ou/.

Aimin: Bounce.

Ms. Tankersley: What does bounce mean?

Aimin: Jump, you know, up and down.

Ms. Tankersley: Right. A person can bounce. A ball can bounce. Here's another word. *Toothpaste.* It has two words. *Tooth. Paste.* What do you do with toothpaste?

Aimin: Brush my teeth.

Ms. Tankersley: Right.

[After teaching each word, Ms. Tankersley reviews them one at a time. She then mixes them up and flashes them quickly as Aimin says each word.]

STEP 3: Guided Reading

[Ms. Tankersley divides the chapter into one-page segments. For each page, she asks Aimin to predict what will happen and then to read the page silently. When he finishes a page, she asks him whether his prediction is correct and then one or two questions. When he answers a question, she asks him to read orally the sentence or more that helped him answer the question, as shown with the following for the second page of the story. This method allows Ms. Tankersley to pinpoint aspects of the passage that cause Aimin comprehension difficulty, determine if he is able to apply background knowledge, see if he remembers the new sight words she taught, and identify which word recognition strategies he uses to figure out unknown words.]

Ms. Tankersley: What do you think will happen?

Aimin: I think Stacy will be sloppy.

Ms. Tankersley: Let's see if you're right. Read this page silently.

[Aimin reads the page and then looks up at Ms. Tankersley.]

Aimin: She's sloppy.

Ms. Tankersley: Read me the part that made you think she's sloppy.

Aimin: "The bedroom was a mess."

Ms. Tankersley: How do you know that Stacy is sloppy?

Aimin: Sloppy and mess are the same.

Ms. Tankersley: You remembered from our words at the beginning. Wonderful. Is there any other place that shows you Stacy is sloppy?

Aimin: I don't know.

Ms. Tankersley: Let me show you. Here it says, "She liked a messy bedroom."

Aimin: Messy?

49

CHAPTER 2

Assessment:
Putting the Reader
at the Center
of the Reading
Program

Ms. Tankersley: Messy has the same root word as mess. You can say the bedroom was a mess or she had a messy bedroom. Tell me about Stacy's picture.

Aimin: She was a fat baby.

Ms. Tankersley: Read me the part that helps you know she was fat.

Aimin: "Her sister Emily picked up a picture. 'Boy, were you fat,' she said."

Ms. Tankersley: That's right. Great, Aimin. What do you think will happen next in the story?

Aimin: I don't know.

Ms. Tankersley: Which picture do you think she'll pick?

Aimin: She'll be a fat baby in the picture.

Ms. Tankersley: Okay. Let's see if you're right. Read the next page to yourself.

STEP 4: Discussion

[After reading all the segments, Ms. Tankersley asks several questions she had prepared. The first few questions were designed to elicit Aimin's ability to apply his understanding of story structure. The other questions were designed to assess his ability to think beyond the literal level.]

Ms. Tankersley: What was Stacy doing at the beginning of the story?

Aimin: Looking at pictures.

Ms. Tankersley: Yes. She and her sister, Emily, were looking at baby pictures. They were where?

Aimin: In their room.

Ms. Tankersley: Right. They were in their bedroom. Which picture did Emily choose?

Aimin: She looked beautiful.

Ms. Tankersley: Yes. She was in a pretty blue dress. How did Stacy feel?

Aimin: Happy. She was excited.

Ms. Tankersley: How did she bring the picture to school?

Aimin: She had it.

Ms. Tankersley: She had it in what?

Aimin: I don't know.

Ms. Tankersley: In an envelope. Do you remember what an envelope is? [She shows Aimin an envelope.]

Aimin: An envelope.

Ms. Tankersley: Yes, so the picture wouldn't get . . .?

Aimin: Messy.

Ms. Tankersley: Right. The word Stacy used was *wrinkled*. Folded and messy. Did Mrs. Zachary like the picture?

(continued)

50

CHAPTER 2

Assessment:
Putting the Reader
at the Center
of the Reading
Program

Aimin: Yes.

Ms. Tankersley: How do you know she liked it?

Aimin: Mrs. Zachary liked it.

Ms. Tankersley: She said, "spectacular."

Aimin: Spectacular.

Ms. Tankersley: How did the chapter end?

Aimin: She was waiting.

Ms. Tankersley: What was Stacy waiting for?

Aimin: To see all the pictures.

Ms. Tankersley: Anything else?

Aimin: Mrs. Zachary's news.

Ms. Tankersley: What do you think Mrs. Zachary's news will be?

Aimin: I don't know.

Ms. Tankersley: What's one idea?

Aimin: Maybe she has a baby picture.

Ms. Tankersley: Of herself?

Aimin: Maybe.

Ms. Tankersley: Tomorrow we'll find out more. What kind of person is Stacy?

Aimin: She's nice.

Ms. Tankersley: Does she seem like anyone you know?

Aimin: No.

Ms. Tankersley: I think she's like Corda because Corda is a nice person.

Aimin: I like Corda.

Ms. Tankersley: When we read more, maybe Stacy will seem like someone you know.

Aimin: Maybe like Corda.

Ms. Tankersley: Maybe there are things they have in common. And maybe there are things different about them. We'll think about it when we read more about Stacy.

[During the lesson, Ms. Tankersley noticed that Aimin remembered several of the new sight words and all of the definitions. Ms. Tankersley used the new sight word "toothpaste" and the previously known sight word "bedroom" as examples of compound words in a brief lesson when Aimin had difficulty reading the words "classroom" and "downstairs." Aimin seemed to understand the new words but given that these words did not appear again in the chapter, Ms. Tankersley could not be sure he would recognize them in print. Ms. Tankersley also noticed that Aimin was able to answer the questions that followed story structure and questions asking for story details but had difficulty with questions requiring him to analyze or synthesize text information and to make inferences.]

Word Analysis.   The purpose of assessing word analysis is to determine the reader's ability to identify words through phonic analysis, analogy, and structural analysis. Given the relationship between phonemic awareness and phonic analysis, if he or she shows difficulty with phonic analysis, then assessment of phonemic awareness is indicated.

51

CHAPTER 2

*Assessment:
Putting the Reader
at the Center
of the Reading
Program*

The major source of information for *phonemic awareness* is tests. The most commonly used criterion-referenced test is the Yopp-Singer Phoneme Segmentation Test, which takes relatively little time to administer. Several norm-referenced tests, such as the Phonological Awareness Test and Comprehensive Test of Phonological Processes in Reading, were designed specifically to assess phonemic awareness; several diagnostic reading tests, such as the Stanford and Gates-MacGinitie, include phonemic awareness subtests.

The source of information for the reader's current *word analysis* ability is tests, both criterion-referenced and norm-referenced. Informal reading inventories are considered criterion-referenced tests because reading levels are based not on how the student's performance compares to other students' but rather on criterion measures of numbers of running words read accurately and comprehension questions answered correctly.

Whether you use a published informal reading inventory or create one from classroom reading material, the premise and the procedure are the same. The student orally reads brief passages thought to be just below, at, and just above his or her reading level. When the student recognizes at least 98 percent of the words and answers correctly 90 percent of the comprehension questions, the material is at his or her independent level. (Some authors use a 95 percent target, but when the student has to stop and figure out 5 out of every 100 words, the material is not very accessible.) When the reader recognizes at least 90 percent of the words and answers correctly 75 percent of the comprehension questions, the material is at his or her instructional (or mediational) level. When word recognition and comprehension fall below these levels, the material is at the reader's frustration reading level. All such tests use a notation system similar to miscue analysis (Goodman, Watson, & Burke, 2006) and running records (Clay, 2000) in which substitutions, repetitions, omissions, and incorrect pronunciations are notated while the student is reading each passage aloud. Indeed, you can use any notation system, even one that you personally develop, as long as notations are made consistently.

When using oral reading for assessing word analysis, you are assuming that the reader's errors (or miscues) reflect his or her working hypothesis about how to use the word's structural elements and letter-sound relationships to discern the actual word. This is why some educators prefer to use the term *miscue* because it shows the reader's emerging understanding of how to figure out the identity of an unknown word.

Word analysis can also be assessed through norm-referenced tests (such as the Woodcock and Gates-MacGinitie listed in Table 2.1). In these tests, the reader is asked to read a set of actual and nonsense words and performance is compared against norms for peers at the same grade level.

52

CHAPTER 2

*Assessment:
Putting the Reader
at the Center
of the Reading
Program*

As important as it is for you to know the reader's current ability to use word analysis strategies, it is more important to know whether he or she can learn and apply new strategies. The source of this information is largely diagnostic teaching, such as the lesson in the Diagnostic Teaching Lesson box, though some information may be available from school records if previous teachers have included descriptions of the reader's learning of word analysis skills.

Context. The purpose of assessing the reader's ability to use context for word recognition is to determine whether he or she can use syntactic and semantic cues for identifying words. The source of information regarding context is principally diagnostic teaching, as shown in the diagnostic teaching lesson.

Fluency

The third step in the assessment process is to determine the reader's ability to read accurately, quickly, and with appropriate expression. The correlate to fluency is freedom from word recognition difficulties. Given its relationship to word recognition skills and its importance in comprehension, fluency represents an important step between assessing the reader's word recognition skills and assessing comprehension abilities.

The sources of information about the student's reading fluency are tests, particularly criterion-referenced tests. Informal reading inventories and the use of running records or miscue analysis with teacher-selected material are most popular. In conjunction with these tests, reading rate and fluency scales described in Table 2.1 can provide additional information.

To determine *reading rate*, you count the number of words the student can read in a 60-second period with material at or slightly below instructional reading level and compare this number to the following grade-level averages: 53 correct words per minute (cwpm) for first, 89 cwpm for second, 107 cwpm for third, 123 cwpm for fourth, 139 cwpm for fifth, and 150 cwpm for sixth grades (Hasbrouk & Tindal, 2006; Padak & Rasinski, 2008).

Fluency scales are based on three factors: phrasing, following the author's syntax, and expressiveness. By observing the student reading a 250- to 1000-word passage at his or her reading level, you can categorize the reader's fluency as falling along a continuum of reading primarily word by word to reading primarily in meaningful phrase groups, attending to the author's syntax, and reading with expressive interpretation.

Comprehension

The fourth step in the assessment process is to determine the reader's strengths and weaknesses in comprehension. Four of the component skills involve prior knowledge of topic, vocabulary, text structure, and sentence structure. The fifth component skill involves cognitive strategies used before, during, and after reading.

Prior Knowledge of Topic.   The purpose of assessing prior knowledge of topic is to determine the reader's knowledge of topics pertinent to reading material he or she is likely to encounter, the ability to apply prior knowledge during reading to improve comprehension, and the ability to learn new information and apply this new information during reading. The major source of information about the student's prior knowledge is likely to be diagnostic teaching, though school records may provide limited information.

The diagnostic teaching lesson illustrates how prior knowledge of topic can be assessed in a mini-lesson, although such mini-lessons provide considerably greater information about ability to learn new information and apply it during reading than about the reader's current knowledge of text topic.

Vocabulary Knowledge.   The chief purpose for assessing vocabulary is to determine knowledge of vocabulary in relation to the breadth and depth of vocabulary expected of students at their age and grade level. The major source of this information is norm-referenced reading diagnosis tests, such as the Woodcock-Johnson and Gates-MacGinitie, and norm-referenced vocabulary tests, such as the Peabody Picture Vocabulary Test and Word Test. A common criterion-referenced test is the cloze procedure, in which the student's vocabulary knowledge is correlated with the student's ability to identify semantically and syntactically appropriate words that have been systematically omitted in a brief passage.

The secondary purpose for assessing vocabulary is to evaluate the reader's ability to learn new vocabulary words prior to reading. For this purpose, the source of information is diagnostic teaching (as shown in the lesson).

Knowledge of Text Structure.   The purpose of assessing text structure knowledge is to determine if the student has internalized the structure of typical narrative and expository text and can use this text schema for enhancing comprehension. Norm-referenced tests such as the Stanford and Test of Reading Comprehension include subtests that assess text structure knowledge, but the most comprehensive source of this information is diagnostic teaching.

The diagnostic teaching lesson provides an example of how to assess knowledge of story structure within a lesson by asking questions that highlight the setting, initiating event, characters' actions and reactions, consequences of actions, and ending. Other approaches for assessing knowledge of story structure involve asking the student to tell a story, write a story, or retell a story after reading and then comparing the story structure components the student includes with the components of a well-formed story.

Knowledge of Sentence Structure.   The purpose of assessing knowledge of sentence structure is to determine if syntax presents any barriers to comprehension. The sources of this information are norm-referenced reading tests such as the Test of Reading Comprehension, norm-referenced language tests such as the Test of Language Development, criterion-referenced tests such as the cloze procedure, and diagnostic teaching.

54

CHAPTER 2

Assessment:
Putting the Reader
at the Center
of the Reading
Program

The diagnostic lesson provides an example for assessing sentence structure knowledge; however, such mini-lessons cannot provide comprehensive information about the student's syntactic knowledge.

Cognitive Strategies.   The purpose of assessing cognitive strategies is to determine the ways in which the reader consciously monitors comprehension and adapts strategies to improve comprehension before, during, and after reading. Further, assessment includes the student's ability to learn new cognitive strategies.

The sources of information for cognitive strategies are predominantly criterion- and norm-referenced tests, such as the tests listed in Table 2.1, and diagnostic teaching. Given the range of cognitive strategies, no single test or diagnostic lesson will provide comprehensive information on the student's ability to set goals, overview, activate prior knowledge, predict, note relationships between ideas in text, distinguish important information from less or unimportant information, infer, interpret, realize when understanding breaks down, recognize problems in concentration and pacing, recognize inconsistencies in text, recognize discrepancies between predictions and new information, pace appropriately, self-question, visualize, paraphrase, and think deeply and critically. With this in mind, the diagnostic teaching lesson illustrates the assessment of a few of these cognitive strategies.

Attitude and Interests

The fifth step in the assessment process is to determine the student's attitude toward reading and interests in genre, topics, and authors. The sources for this information include observations and interviews/questionnaires. For observations, the teacher observes the student during classroom activities, free time as well as reading instruction. During the observations, you should ask yourself the following questions:

Does the student:
- approach reading with enthusiasm?
- demonstrate confidence about reading abilities?
- participate willingly in reading activities?
- read material thoroughly?
- use books and other written material as resources?
- read a variety of genres?
- read independently?

Is the student:
- relaxed when reading?
- able to concentrate?
- able to read for more than a few minutes?

The second source of information about attitude and interests is questionnaires and interviews. You can develop your own format with questions such as the following, or you can use one of the published questionnaires or interview formats shown in Table 2.1.

55

CHAPTER 2

*Assessment:
Putting the Reader
at the Center
of the Reading
Program*

1. I think reading is . . .
2. My favorite place to read is . . .
3. When my mom or dad reads to me . . .
4. When my teacher reads to me . . .
5. My parents read because . . .
6. My favorite kind of reading is . . .
7. I would rather read than . . .
8. The reasons that people read are . . .
9. The reason that I read is . . .
10. The hardest thing about reading is . . .
11. The easiest thing about reading is . . .
12. If I got a book for a present, I would . . .
13. My friends think that reading is . . .
14. When I am grown-up . . .
15. If I were the teacher, I would teach reading by . . .

At-Risk Factors

The sixth step in the assessment process is to determine if any other factors may be associated with the student's reading ability. As discussed in Chapter 1, the factors most likely to influence reading ability include cognitive, linguistic, social and cultural, emotional, educational, and physical factors.

Diagnosis of cognitive, physical, and linguistic factors is not the primary responsibility of the classroom teacher. If you suspect the presence of any of these at-risk factors, you should refer the student for assessment by a qualified professional

There is an important distinction between understanding the influence of any at-risk factor on the student's reading ability and determining where to focus instruction. Although an at-risk factor should be taken into account in planning a reading program, the factor itself is not the target of instruction. As Kibby (1995a) noted, "The objectives of reading instruction are always reading and reading strategies—*not* correcting a child's limitations" (p. 48).

The current Response to Intervention (RTI) model that is mandated in the 2004 Reauthorization of the Individuals with Disabilities Education Act reflects current concerns that too much emphasis has been placed on within-student factors when diagnosing students as learning disabled and too little on appropriate instruction in reading when students struggle with reading (Fuchs, Fuchs, & Speece, 2002). RTI "requires educators to provide early intervention, match instruction to the academic needs of students, and

56

CHAPTER 2

*Assessment:
Putting the Reader
at the Center
of the Reading
Program*

monitor student progress with ongoing data-based decision making" (Vaughn, Linan-Thompson, & Hickman, 2003, p. 392). Though RTI is intended to be used specifically as a preintervention strategy with students suspected of having a learning disability, focusing on instructional needs versus the reader's at-risk factors should be applied to teaching all students. Indeed, differentiating instruction based on what you have learned in your assessment of each student is the approach presented in this book.

In the discussion of lesson models and teaching strategies in the next chapters, the particular issues that may emerge from an at-risk factor will be identified and how you can adapt instruction to meet the learning needs of the reader will be discussed.

Ongoing Assessment

When the student's reading abilities have been assessed, you can use the information gathered from observations, recollections, tests, artifacts, diagnostic teaching, and extant information to make professional judgments about what should be included in the reading program for the struggling reader. Once the program is developed, ongoing assessment provides you with information about the student's progress and enables you to modify and adjust instruction when a lesson plan model, instructional strategy, or teaching technique is not working effectively. In order for ongoing assessment to be meaningful, you must be willing to reconsider instructional decisions and shift approaches.

The two most common types of ongoing assessment are curriculum-based assessment and alternative assessment (which includes assessment that is referred to as performance assessment, authentic assessment, and portfolio assessment). It is important to recognize that these types of assessment are not discretely different from each other, and most classroom teachers use a combination of approaches to gather information about the reader's progress.

In *curriculum-based assessment*, the skills delineated in the reading curriculum are assessed regularly according to benchmark goals set in the curriculum. The student's performance is compared specifically to progress on these benchmark goals and not compared to the abilities of peers or other norms. When conducting curriculum-based assessment, you seek to figure out what the student knows, what the student can do, how the student thinks, how the student approaches what he or she is unsure of, and what you should do (Burns, MacQuarrie, & Campbell, 1999). According to Gravois and Gickling (2002), seven essential dimensions of reading should guide assessment and instruction in curriculum-based assessment. For each of these dimensions, ask yourself the following questions:

1. *Language/prior knowledge*: Does the student have adequate language, conceptual knowledge, and previous experiences to comprehend the material?

2. *Word recognition*: Does the student possess a sufficient sight word vocabulary to read the material?

3. *Word study*: What strategies does the student use for identifying unknown words?

4. *Fluency*: Can the student read at an adequate rate and with appropriate expression orally? Can the student read at an adequate rate silently?

5. *Response*: Can the student retell effectively and accurately, both orally and in writing?

6. *Comprehension*: Does the student understand the author's meaning?

7. *Metacognition*: Does the student use strategies for monitoring comprehension and learning?

57

CHAPTER 2

*Assessment:
Putting the Reader
at the Center
of the Reading
Program*

Alternative assessment involves approaches that are not standardized or norm-referenced. You might be thinking that curriculum-based assessments also involve approaches that are not standardized or norm-referenced, and you would be correct. Indeed, curriculum-based assessment might be considered under the umbrella of alternative assessment approaches. These approaches are considered alternatives to assessment that relies on forced-choice questions typical of norm-referenced tests.

One type of alternative assessment is *performance assessment*. Any assessment requiring the student to carry out a task can be seen as a performance assessment. Meaningful performance assessment involves tasks that are directly related to what is taught, identification of standards of acceptable performance, criteria for judging performance, feedback, and self-assessment (Spinelli, 2006).

Performance assessment becomes *authentic assessment* when it involves the application of knowledge, skills, or behavior in a real-world setting or simulation using a real-world activity. Writing an essay might be viewed as performance assessment. Writing an essay that the student submits as a letter-to-the-editor in the local newspaper is authentic assessment. Boyd-Batstone (2004) defines authentic assessment "by the active role the teacher plays in classroom-based assessment of actual literacy experiences" (p. 230).

In *portfolio assessment*, artifacts reflecting the student's strengths, growth, and goals are collected. In order for portfolio assessment to be effective, the approach must be systematic and continuous. You decide in advance which areas of instruction and student performance will be assessed, which items can provide information about the student's current strengths, and which items can illustrate growth in learning over time. Taken as a whole, the artifacts in a portfolio must connect directly to the student's reading goals. Examples of portfolio artifacts include the following:

- *Observations*. The informal *kidwatching* that teachers do when students are engaged in reading activities, as well as planned observations, can be notated in a notebook. The first step is to systematically seek information on word recognition, fluency, comprehension, and attitude

58

CHAPTER 2

Assessment:
Putting the Reader
at the Center
of the Reading
Program

and interests during observations. The second step is to analyze the information periodically to identify trends and patterns.

- *Recollections.* Conferences with students are a second source of ongoing assessment information in portfolio assessment. During conferences, you can review recently completed tests and projects, discuss a story or book the student is reading, and probe for information that reflects reading strengths and weaknesses. Notations on conferences can be kept in the same notebook as observations and should be analyzed periodically, just as observations are.

- *Tests.* Recent tests are important artifacts because they reflect the reader's current abilities. Past tests reflect growth in learning and can also provide you with feedback about which skills are being assessed through tests. For example, if word recognition and comprehension are regularly tested but fluency is not, either fluency needs to be tested or you need to ensure that fluency is being assessed regularly through another means.

- *Artifacts.* Artifacts are the essential component of portfolio assessment and include items from observations, recollections, tests, and diagnostic teaching. Artifacts can also include items such as a list of books or stories the student has read independently, reports or stories the student has written, and projects the student has completed.

- *Diagnostic Teaching.* In ongoing assessment, diagnostic teaching can be any lesson and should be every lesson. For portfolio assessment specifically, you can periodically record information about the reader's performance in word recognition, fluency, and comprehension (such as the diagnostic teaching lesson).

- *Extant Information.* Portfolio assessment generally includes only information gathered from the time the student is placed in your classroom. However, for students on IEPs, it is crucial to incorporate IEP goals into the portfolio. Documentation of the student's progress in meeting these goals is required and can be provided in part within the context of a portfolio.

Case Studies

Throughout this book, case studies will be used to illustrate how to apply the ideas to students who struggle with reading. Because your process in developing a reading program for the struggling reader begins with assessment, the discussion of each of the case studies will begin with each child's assessment (see the Case Study Children box). The teachers introduced to you at the beginning of this book were asked by their instructor to post their assessments on the online course bulletin board. The teachers described not only what they did but their thought processes from step to step. The online instructor

(text continues on page 66)

Case Study Children

....

Adani

Adani is 7 years old and attends first grade in her neighborhood school. She lives at home with her mother. English is not the primary language spoken at home. Adani just moved to the neighborhood and received Title I services at her last school. When her teacher, Ms. Edberg, examined the school files that were transferred with Adani, she found that Adani's previous first-grade teacher commented that Adani was performing poorly in reading but that she had a good relationship with her teachers and classmates, and her work habits were good. The teacher particularly remarked that Adani works slowly but completes her work. The teacher noted that reading was integrated throughout the curriculum and so Adani's slow progress in reading was affecting her achievement in other subjects. No standardized test information was provided in the cumulative file.

> **Child Background/ At-Risk Factors**

With the help of her student teacher, Ms. Edberg was able to spend one-on-one time with Adani to assess her reading abilities. She started by talking with her about books to get a sense of Adani's attitude toward reading. She found that Adani was enthusiastic and positive about reading. She told Ms. Edberg that she's a good reader and that the other kids in the class were good readers, too. When Ms. Edberg asked what makes a good reader, Adani said that her idea of a good reader is someone who goes to school and learns from reading groups. She was able to name her favorite book and brought it to school to show Ms. Edberg. During storytelling time, Ms. Edberg noticed that Adani clearly enjoyed being read to. She listened attentively and often made comments or asked questions.

> **Attitude and Interests**

Ms. Edberg used the Standardized Reading Inventory with Adani. Based on the background information she had gathered, Ms. Edberg predicted that the grade 1 passage would be at Adani's instructional level, which was confirmed. Oral reading showed that Adani relied heavily on phonics to identify unknown words. She attended to the beginning and ending sounds but not usually medial vowel sounds. She rarely used semantic or syntactic cues from context. When Ms. Edberg asked her what she does when she encounters an unknown word, Adani indicated that she sounds it out or asks for help. Given Adani's relatively successful use of the phonic skills she knew, Ms. Edberg did not assess phonemic awareness. Ms. Edberg asked Adani to read several brief stories with the Dolch words and found that she recognized instantly most of them through the first-grade list. At this point in the assessment, Ms. Edberg believed that Adani had

> **Phonic Analysis/ Context**

> **Phonemic Awareness**

> **Automatic Word Recognition**

(continued)

Phonic Analysis/ Context

Analogy/ Structural Analysis

difficulty with identifying unknown words because she did not use phonic analysis to map all of the letter-sound relationships within a word or she did not use context very effectively. She was uncertain about Adani's ability to use analogy and structural analysis.

Comprehension

Prior Knowledge of Topic

Cognitive Strategies

Sight Words

Cognitive Strategies

Ms. Edberg decided to use diagnostic teaching. For the first lesson, she asked Adani to read a preprimer story silently as a nondirected reading activity (otherwise known as sustained silent reading). When she was finished, Ms. Edberg asked her to retell the story. After the retelling, Ms. Edberg posed several questions and asked Adani to show the places in the story that supported her answers. For the second lesson, Ms. Edberg developed a lesson plan that followed a directed reading thinking activity. She began by talking about the title and what the story would be about. She asked several questions to determine Adani's knowledge about the topic. She then asked Adani what questions she had about the story. Ms. Edberg taught six new sight words that Adani would encounter in the story. She showed each on a flash card and reviewed them several times. She asked Adani what she thought would happen at the beginning of the story. She then asked Adani to read the first page silently. When Adani finished, Ms. Edberg asked her whether her prediction turned out to be correct. She then asked another question designed to determine if Adani had recognized one of the sight words. Each one-page segment was read similarly. Adani made a prediction and when she was finished reading, they discussed her prediction. The other questions Ms. Edberg asked were designed to determine the word recognition strategies that Adani was using. Ms. Edberg often asked Adani to read aloud the sentence or two that answered the question. Thus, she could determine the strategies Adani was using to identify unknown words, as well as which new sight words she was retaining. Once during the lesson, Ms. Edberg taught a brief lesson about a prefix in an unknown word. Another time, she taught a brief lesson on using context to figure out an unknown word. At the end of the story, Ms. Edberg asked questions that highlighted the major story structure components. She also asked questions requiring Adani to think beyond the literal.

Sight Words

Comprehension

Word Recognition

Structural Analysis

Context

Story Structure

Cognitive Strategies

Story Structure

Cognitive Strategies

Vocabulary Knowledge

Cognitive Strategies

Ms. Edberg noticed that Adani's retelling relied heavily on the text and reflected the sequence of events in the story. She pulled exact sentences from the story to support her retelling. Her predictions were very concrete and made sense. She recalled important details, comprehended the vocabulary, and had some difficulty with questions requiring inferences and synthesis of ideas. Both in her retelling of the first story and answers to questions of the second story, she clearly understood that a story is made up of characters, problems, and solutions. However, she ignored the setting in her retelling and she struggled with answering a question about setting. Several of Ms. Edberg's questions indicated that Adani had difficulty with some English sentence structures. Adani was able to learn the new sight words, retained a couple of them during reading, and was quickly reminded of the others. She appeared to benefit from the brief lessons on structural analysis and context. She clearly relied most heavily on phonic analysis when encountering an unknown word though was often unsuccessful in correctly identifying the word.

> Story Structure

> Sentence Structure

> Sight Words

> Structural Analysis/ Context/Phonic Analysis

Ms. Edberg concluded that Adani would benefit from concentrated instruction in the word recognition strategies of phonic analysis, analogy, word analysis, and context along with building her sight vocabulary. She also concluded that Adani's poor performance in reading at her previous school might be related to Adani's being an English language learner. Ms. Edberg realized that she would need to consider ways to enrich Adani's oral English language development along with her reading development.

> Goals for Instruction

Maria

Maria is 11 years old and in the fifth grade. She has been identified by her school district as having a learning disability and has been attending a special class for math and reading for a year. Mr. Ginnetti talked with the special education teacher and was told that Maria is reading 2 years below grade level. The special education teacher also told Mr. Ginnetti that Maria is very pleasant and personable but she tends to be inattentive and to turn in incomplete work. She also commented that Maria appears to have difficulty with tracking across the page and sequencing. When Mr. Ginnetti examined her cumulative file, he found that her previous classroom teacher noted her independent reading level to be first grade, instructional reading level to be second grade, and frustration level to be third grade.

> Child Background/ At-Risk Factors

Mr. Ginnetti met with Maria's parents and they expressed concern about her academic progress. When Mr. Ginnetti talked with Maria, she said that she does not like to discuss her reading difficulties but she is aware that reading is a struggle for her. She told him that she doesn't enjoy reading and rarely reads at home. When he asked for her definition of an effective reader, she said it is someone who sounds out words and asks the teacher or parent for help when sounding out doesn't work.

> Attitude and Interests

Mr. Ginnetti administered the first-, second-, and third-grade levels of the Burns-Roe Reading Inventory. Results confirmed the information he had found in the cumulative file that Maria's independent level was first grade and her instructional level was second grade. He found large discrepancies between her oral and silent reading comprehension. Maria was much more

> Comprehension

(continued)

Cognitive Strategies

successful answering comprehension questions when she read the material aloud. She had equal difficulty with questions requiring inference and factual recollection. Her answers often did not relate to the question. When Mr. Ginnetti prompted her and provided suggestions for answers in the text, she was able to respond correctly. She relied heavily on phonic analysis for

Phonic Analysis

Structural Analysis/ Analogy/Context

word recognition and had most difficulty with sounds in the medial position. She did not appear to use structural analysis, analogy, or context.

Comprehension

At this point in the assessment, Mr. Ginnetti knew he needed to learn more about Maria's comprehension and the relationship between comprehension and vocabulary knowledge. He realized that she also appeared to

Vocabulary Knowledge

have some difficulty with word recognition and wanted to learn more about her strengths and weaknesses in this area. Thus, he decided to develop a

Word Recognition

diagnostic reading lesson using the format of a directed reading activity with a story at the first-grade readability level.

Mr. Ginnetti began by presenting several vocabulary words from the story that he thought would be new to Maria. For each, he used a semantic

Vocabulary Knowledge

map. He put the word in the center and put three circles around it. The first circle asked for the word's meaning. The second circle asked for words with similar meanings. And the third circle asked for words with opposite meanings. He started with the definition and if Maria didn't know it, he explained the meaning. He then offered a word with a similar meaning and asked Maria if she knew any others. He did the same with the third circle on opposite meanings. The activity offered a lot of opportunity to discuss each word.

Prior Knowledge of Topic

Mr. Ginnetti then showed Maria the story and they discussed what the story was probably going to be about. He had divided the story into segments and, for each segment, he asked a question that he wanted her to

Cognitive Strategies

think about while she read. After reading each segment, he posed the question and several others. At least once for each segment, he asked Maria to read aloud the sentences that answered a question. He noticed that she was able to answer questions indicating that she remembered the meaning

Vocabulary Knowledge

of the new vocabulary words. He also noticed that her lack of knowledge of several other vocabulary words negatively affected her comprehension. Mr.

Comprehension

Ginnetti observed that Maria often did not recognize automatically words with prefixes and suffixes that she probably knew as root words. So he

Structural Analysis

taught a couple of brief lessons on separating roots from prefixes and suffixes when she asked for help during oral reading.

Goals for Instruction

Mr. Ginnetti concluded that he should emphasize vocabulary instruction, which he could combine with sight word instruction by teaching the written word and its meaning simultaneously. By including word study of roots, prefixes, and suffixes in his vocabulary instruction, he could add a valuable word recognition strategy to Maria's repertoire. Knowing that the special education teacher was emphasizing phonics, he decided not to concentrate on this skill in his class. He did decide to include the cognitive strategies of inferring and monitoring comprehension. He was particularly interested in helping Maria realize when she did not comprehend and to figure out what she needed to do.

Ellison

Ellison is a 14-year-old eighth grader. At the fall parent-teacher conference with his English/language arts teacher, Mrs. Hong, his mother expressed concern about Ellison's reading. She reported that he has always had trouble with reading. He seldom reads at home and tells her that he doesn't like to read. She also told Mrs. Hong that he had been prescribed Ritalin for ADHD but she had stopped administering it after 2 years because she felt that he had been taking it too long and it was ineffective. Mrs. Hong asked her about the kinds of reading she does at home. She said that she likes to read the newspaper and sometimes tells Ellison about an article, particularly if it's about agriculture, because he wants to go into farming.

Child Background/At-Risk Factors

Attitude and Interests

Mrs. Hong examined Ellison's cumulative file and found that he was identified as having a developmental disability in first grade. He spent part of each day in a resource room throughout elementary school and subsequently was seen by a special education teacher once or twice a week. His IEPs throughout middle school have included goals in functional reading and math. According to his most recent scores on the Stanford Achievement Test, Ellison is reading at approximately the fourth-grade level.

Child Background/At-Risk Factors

Mrs. Hong talked with Ellison during class independent project time. She administered the Motivation to Read Profile, which uses a conversational interview format, and asked Ellison to complete the Reader Self-Perception Scale. Ellison expressed interest in reading about flowers, plants, gardening, and animals. His responses indicated a predominantly negative attitude toward reading. For example, he said that he does not like to visit the library, go to a bookstore, or read at home.

Attitude and Interests

Mrs. Hong administered the Woodcock-Johnson III Diagnostic Reading Battery. Ellison's total reading score placed him at the fourth-grade level, with subtest scores showing greatest strength in word attack and most difficulty in reading vocabulary and passage comprehension. Mrs. Hong presented 20 randomly selected words from Fry's 300 Instant Sight Words and Ellison missed just 3. At this point in the assessment, Mrs. Hong believed that Ellison had relatively good word recognition skills and a very negative attitude toward reading. Mrs. Hong decided to assess Ellison's fluency through the Oral Reading Fluency Scale. She found that Ellison

Word Analysis

Vocabulary Knowledge

Comprehension

Sight Words

Attitude and Interests

(continued)

read with good phrasing with third-grade material but his reading rate was quite low at 88 words per minute. With fourth-grade material, he read primarily word by word.

Mrs. Hong decided to teach a diagnostic reading lesson using the reciprocal teaching lesson plan model. She chose a short story at the fourth-grade readability level. She added one step, which was to teach several vocabulary words using the concept wheel approach. She drew a circle and divided the circle into four parts. In one part she wrote the word. She and Ellison discussed the word and then she asked Ellison to think of three words that would help him remember the new vocabulary word. He wrote these in the other quadrants. Mrs. Hong kept these on the board

during the lesson. Mrs. Hong asked Ellison to predict what would happen in the story. She then asked Ellison to read the story silently during free time or

at home that evening. The next day, Mrs. Hong asked Ellison to describe the main idea of the story. She asked a few questions and encouraged Ellison

to ask his own questions. She often asked Ellison to read aloud segments to clarify something he didn't understand. Mrs. Hong found that Ellison had

difficulty identifying main ideas and determining sequences of events. In oral

reading, he did not use context cues for identifying unknown words and many of his word substitutions did not make sense semantically.

Mrs. Hong concluded that Ellison's major difficulties involved vocabulary, fluency, and comprehension of main idea. Ellison referred to the concept wheels during reading, which indicated the benefit of this strategy for

learning new vocabulary words. Given that Ellison tended to devote too much attention to identifying each word, which slowed his rate considerably and seemed to cause comprehension problems, Mrs. Hong decided to focus on fluency and comprehension in her instruction. She also realized that success with reading would improve Ellison's attitude and if his attitude improved, he might be more willing to do independent reading, which in turn might further improve his reading ability. She considered the influence of Ellison's developmental disability on his reading difficulties but decided to suspend judgment on Ellison's capacity to become a skilled reader. Rather, she decided to attempt strategies that could at least incrementally improve his abilities and attitude and, at best, help him make significant gains.

Marek

Marek is 9 years old and nearing the end of third grade. His family moved to the area a month ago. His teacher, Mr. Rumrill, found Marek to be a cooperative and cheerful child who made friends easily. When he examined

Marek's cumulative file, he found that when Marek was 5 years old, his doctor had discovered that he suffered from lead poisoning. After successful treatment, his speech improved considerably though he attended a special education kindergarten for 2 years before placement in a regular first-grade classroom. Marek had been evaluated each year by the speech-language pathologist and the reports indicated that he showed delays in language development. Progress reports indicated that Marek is currently reading at the late first-grade level and that he has limited sight words and poor word attack skills.

Mr. Rumrill asked Marek to complete the Elementary Reading Attitude Survey. His scores indicated that he enjoys reading for pleasure, does not particularly enjoy reading school material, and thinks reading is too hard. Given Marek's language development issues, Mr. Rumrill decided to assess Marek's vocabulary with the Peabody Picture Vocabulary Test. His score indicated above average vocabulary ability for his age. Given the information in Marek's file indicating his weak word recognition skills, Mr. Rumrill decided to determine if these difficulties might be related to Marek's phonemic awareness skills. He administered the Yopp-Singer Phoneme Segmentation Test. Marek appeared to understand the task of listening to a word and reproducing the individual sounds in order but he was only able to provide four correct responses before becoming frustrated.

Mr. Rumrill decided to administer the Gray Oral Reading Test. On the primer passage, Marek recognized most of the words but when he misidentified a word, it was usually semantically unacceptable and he rarely self-corrected. His comprehension score indicated that the primer passage was at his independent level. On the first-grade passage, he showed much difficulty with the middle and ending sounds in words. Again, few of his miscues were semantically appropriate and he seldom self-corrected. His oral reading rate was very slow. Mr. Rumrill then carried out a cloze procedure. He gave Marek a first-grade passage of 300 words with a line replacing every fifth word except within the first and last sentences. Marek was able to provide contextually appropriate words for most of the blanks but found the task very frustrating.

Mr. Rumrill decided to use a language experience story as a diagnostic reading lesson. The class had been studying the Lewis and Clark expedition and had just watched a video. Mr. Rumrill asked Marek to tell him a story about the expedition. Mr. Rumrill wrote Marek's sentences onto the computer, which they could both see simultaneously. Sometimes he used a synonym instead of Marek's actual word. When each sentence was written,

Attitude and Interests

Vocabulary Knowledge

Word Recognition

Phonemic Awareness

Automatic Word Recognition/Phonic Analysis/Context

Fluency

Context

Vocabulary Knowledge

Sentence Structure

Prior Knowledge of Topic

Vocabulary Knowledge

(continued)

Phonic Analysis/ Analogy

Fluency

Goals for Instruction

he and Marek read it aloud together. When Marek hesitated on a word, Mr. Rumrill highlighted the sounds or onset-rime in the word and helped Marek figure it out. When the story was complete, Marek read it aloud. Mr. Rumrill assisted when he needed help with a word. Mr. Rumrill then asked Marek to read it a second time aloud. Marek read with greater fluency in the second reading.

Mr. Rumrill concluded that Marek's reading difficulties were connected with his weak phonemic awareness skills. Marek's language delay appeared to be less a factor in his struggle with reading than word recognition, particularly his use of phonic analysis, analogy, and context for identifying words. His ability to carry out the cloze task indicated that context would be less of a factor once he could effectively utilize phonic analysis and analogy. Mr. Rumrill's assessment had not shed light on Marek's ability to use structural analysis for word recognition. And he had spent little time assessing cognitive strategies for comprehension because it seemed more urgent to understand Marek's difficulties with word recognition. Mr. Rumrill decided to assess comprehension as part of the ongoing assessment during reading instruction and to focus his instruction on phonemic awareness and word recognition.

added notations to the right of the case descriptions to identify which reading skills were being addressed so that the teachers could see whether they had, indeed, gathered all of the pertinent information about each student's reading ability.

The teachers describe their assessments as if they were assessing each reader individually. However, almost all of their assessments were actually conducted with a small group of students, just as your assessments can be conducted with small, and sometimes large, groups of students. These teachers certainly needed to keep track of differing responses from the students, which is clearly much more challenging than if they could have assessed the students individually. And sometimes they could assess individually while the students were carrying out seat work or when a paraprofessional or literacy coach was available. The point to remember is that most assessments can be conducted with small groups of students and some can be conducted with the whole class. When individual assessment is needed, you can employ techniques that you use for classroom management in general, which is to make sure the students all have independent activities to carry out while you work with an individual student.

Table 2.2 summarizes the information that each teacher learned during the assessment. You will find this information helpful in subsequent chapters as you learn about the reading instructional models and strategies that the teachers selected to use with these students.

(text continues on page 70)

TABLE 2.2 Summary of Case Studies

	Adani	Maria	Ellison	Marek
Child's Teacher	Ms. Edberg	Mr. Ginnetti	Mrs. Hong	Mr. Rumrill
Age	7 years old	11 years old	14 years old	9 years old
Grade	1	5	8	3
Instructional reading level	1st	2nd	4th	1st
At-risk factors	English proficiency	Learning disability	Developmental disability; ADHD	Lead poisoning
Home language	Not English			
Previous educational experience and reading instruction	Received Title I services in first grade at last school; reading integrated throughout curriculum	Special class for math and reading for the past year	Resource room instruction for part of each day throughout elementary school and subsequently seen by special education teacher one to two times per week	Special education kindergarten for 2 years; regular classrooms first grade and beyond
Previous test results and specialist reports	No standardized test information	Reading 2 years below grade level; difficulty tracking across the page and sequencing	Previously on Ritalin	Delays in language development
School progress reports	Performed poorly in reading; good relationship with teachers and classmates; good work habits; worked slowly but thoroughly	Is pleasant and personable but tends to be inattentive and turns in incomplete work	Always has had trouble with reading	Limited sight words and poor word attack skills
IEPs and other special programs	Title I services	Resource room instruction in math and reading by special education teacher	IEP goals in functional reading and math; itinerant special education teacher instruction	None at present

(continued)

TABLE 2.2 continued

	Adani	Maria	Ellison	Marek
Word recognition				
Strengths	Phonic analysis (beginning and ending sounds but not medial); recognizing the Dolch words through first grade list; learning new sight words; learning structural analysis and context cues	Phonic analysis with beginning and ending sounds	Word analysis; sight vocabulary	Sight vocabulary at primer level
Weaknesses	Using semantic or syntactic context cues	Applying phonic analysis to medial sounds; using structural analysis, analogy, or context; automatic word recognition	Using context cues	Attending to phonemic awareness tasks; phonic analysis of middle and ending sounds; using context; weak sight vocabulary at first grade level
Unknown	Analogy and structural analysis skills			Analogy and structural analysis skills
Fluency	Fluency unknown	Fluency unknown	Good phrasing but low reading rate with independent level material; reads primarily word-by-word with instructional level material	Slow oral reading rate

TABLE 2.2 continued

	Adani	Maria	Ellison	Marek
Comprehension				
Strengths	Story structure knowledge for characters, problems, and solutions; sequencing; prior knowledge of topic; predicting concrete events; noting important details; vocabulary knowledge.	Reading aloud for comprehension; learning new vocabulary		Vocabulary ability
Weaknesses	Story structure knowledge for setting; sentence structure knowledge; making inferences and synthesizing ideas	Making inferences; recalling factual information; understanding questions; vocabulary knowledge	Vocabulary knowledge; identifying main idea, determining sequence of events	
Unknown		Text structure knowledge	Cognitive strategies	Text structure and sentence structure knowledge; cognitive strategies
Attitude and motivation	Enthusiastic and positive	Does not enjoy reading; rarely reads at home; views reading as a struggle	Negative attitude toward reading; seldom reads at home; interested in farming (flowers, plants, gardening, animals)	Cooperative and cheerful; enjoys reading for pleasure but not school reading; thinks reading is too hard
Instructional goals	1. Phonic analysis, analogy, word analysis, and context for word recognition 2. Sight vocabulary 3. Oral language development	1. Vocabulary development (including word study of roots, prefixes, suffixes) combined with sight vocabulary instruction 2. Inferring and monitoring comprehension 3. Phonic analysis by the special education teacher	1. Fluency 2. Comprehension, particularly main idea and sequencing 3. Vocabulary development	1. Phonemic awareness 2. Phonic analysis, analogy, structural analysis, and context for word recognition

70

CHAPTER 2

Assessment:
Putting the Reader
at the Center
of the Reading
Program

Next Step

Assessment provides substantial information about the struggling reader's abilities, along with the factors that can influence these abilities, including at-risk factors, interest, and motivation. As the case studies illustrate, the particular techniques used for assessing the reader vary depending on what is learned at each point of the assessment. The results of the assessment reveal the reader's strengths on which to build and the weaknesses that instruction should address.

The next step is putting together a reading program based on the information gained in the assessment. The next chapter will describe a framework for developing a reading program that includes how to choose instructional lesson models and reading materials.

QUESTIONS FOR REFLECTION AND APPLICATION

1. How can you ensure that when you interpret assessment information, you are exerting objective and accurate professional judgment?

2. Why should teachers have to gather assessment information for various stakeholders if some of this information will not directly and immediately improve classroom instruction?

3. How can you carry out a comprehensive assessment on each reader when there are 20, 25, or more students in the classroom?

4. How helpful is the assessment information developed by the teachers of the case study children and how does it compare to the kind of assessment information that teachers usually receive from a student's previous teacher?

SUGGESTED RESOURCES FOR ADDITIONAL READING

Afflerbach, Peter. (2007). *Understanding and Using Reading Assessment, K–12.* Newark, DE: International Reading Association.

Kopriva, Rebecca J. (2008). *Improving Testing for English Language Learners.* London, England: Taylor and Francis.

Lipson, Marjorie Y., & Wixson, Karen K. (2009). *Assessment and Instruction of Reading and Writing Difficulties: An Interactive Approach* (4th ed.). Columbus, OH: Allyn & Bacon/Merrill.

McKenna, Michael C., & Stahl, Katherine A. D. (2009). *Assessment for Reading Instruction* (2nd ed.). New York: Guilford.

Salvia, John, Ysseldyke, James E., & Bolt, Sara. (2007). *Assessment in Special and Inclusive Education* (10th ed.). Boston: Houghton Mifflin.

Framework for Developing a Reading Program for the Struggling Reader

1 The Reading Process: The Task and the Reader

2 Assessment: Putting the Reader at the Center of the Reading Program

3 Framework for Developing a Reading Program for the Struggling Reader

4 Before-Reading Strategies: Prereading and Planning

This chapter will describe a framework for putting together a reading program based on information gained during assessment. The framework will include how to choose reading models and reading materials. Several models will be described in depth. This chapter will also discuss the readability of reading materials as a key factor in identifying appropriate materials for instruction.

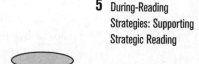

5 During-Reading Strategies: Supporting Strategic Reading

8 Families: Partnering with Parents

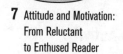

6 After-Reading Strategies: Synthesizing and Extending

7 Attitude and Motivation: From Reluctant to Enthused Reader

A reading program consists essentially of a model, set of materials, and collection of instructional strategies. The model provides the framework for the reading program as a lesson structure. This lesson structure remains stable while the materials and instructional strategies vary. Models are differentiated by the reading tasks that are emphasized and the amount of teacher support

72

CHAPTER 3

*Framework for
Developing a
Reading Program
for the Struggling
Reader*

built in. Models at one end of the continuum provide substantial support to assist children at the earlier stages of reading development and students struggling with reading. Models along the remainder of the continuum offer increasingly less teacher support as students become more proficient readers.

The choice of model depends on what is learned during the assessment. For example, if the student needs considerable instruction and help with word recognition, fluency, and comprehension, the appropriate model will be at the end of the continuum in which you provide substantial support in each area. If the student is relatively skilled in word recognition and fluency but has some difficulty in using cognitive strategies for comprehension, the appropriate model will be at the point on the continuum in which you provide little support in word recognition and fluency, limited support in using prior knowledge, and significant support in developing and using cognitive strategies. Following this approach enables you to differentiate instruction that meets the needs of all your students.

Models

To choose a model, you must match the student's needs with reading tasks that are emphasized in the model. If the student needs substantial support in learning word recognition strategies, the model chosen must incorporate opportunity for this instruction. If the student needs support in one reading task but not the others, you have to consider the benefits and drawbacks of choosing a model that requires substantial support (and thus your time and attention) for tasks in which the student is already skilled.

The following models are presented in a general progression from more to less teacher support. Figure 3.1 displays the continuum of models discussed in this chapter. Table 3.1 provides a synopsis of only those models that can be adapted for classroom use without purchasing a published program or reading series. (In this diagram, the models are listed in alphabetical order rather than according to levels of teacher support.) This figure also designates the reading tasks that are emphasized within each model so that you can choose the model that provides the maximum opportunity to address the goals identified in your assessment.

Directed Reading Activity/ Directed Reading Thinking Activity

The *Directed Reading Activity* (DRA) was first suggested by Betts (1946). It was adopted as the basic lesson format by most basal reading series in preference to the older and questionable round-robin format. With more than a half century of changes and adjustments, the DRA continues to be used widely with young and struggling readers because its framework enables the teacher

Substantial Teacher Support			**Substantial Student Independence**

DRA/ DRTA	Early Steps	Reciprocal Teaching	Book Club
Scaffolded Reading Experiences	Reading Recovery	Collaborative Strategic Reading	Reading Workshop
Direct Instruction	Success for All/CIRC	Guided Reading	
Integrated Skills Method	Language Experience Approach		

to focus heavily on word recognition and comprehension. The DRA includes the following steps:

1. *Concept Development.* This step is variously called prereading activities, preparation, and background building. In this step, the teacher activates and builds the student's knowledge of the topic so that connections to new information in the material can be made. This step includes presenting and teaching new vocabulary in the material.

2. *Sight Words.* In this step, the teacher introduces words for the students to learn to recognize instantly. For children at the earliest stages of reading development, two to three words may be introduced; for those at later stages of development, six to eight words may be introduced each day. The selected words should be familiar to the student in speech (in other words, the student knows the meaning of each word) but not in print, and should be encountered in the passage to be read that day.

3. *Guided Reading.* In this step, the teacher divides the story or chapter into segments for silent reading. For less skilled readers, a segment might be a sentence, a few sentences, or a paragraph. For more skilled readers, a segment might be one or two pages. If the student could read the complete story or chapter with no guidance from the teacher and the material is at the student's instructional reading level, the DRA is not the most appropriate model to be using. For each segment, the teacher sets a purpose, asks the students to read the segment silently, encourages them to discuss the purpose-setting question and

(text continues on page 78)

TABLE 3.1 Synopsis of Reading Models

Reading Model	Reading Abilities		
	Word Recognition	*Fluency*	*Comprehension*
Book Club			• Reading strategies and vocabulary may be taught during the Community Share step. • Students discuss what they have read during the Book Club step. • Students engage in sustained reading daily.
Cooperative Integrated Reading and Composition (CIRC)	• Strategies for identifying unknown words during reading are reviewed in teacher-led reading groups. • Rapid and repetitive oral reading of vocabulary takes place during teacher-led reading groups. • New and difficult words are practiced until they are read automatically during the word mastery list activity.	• Each story is read silently and then orally in partner reading. Partners correct each other's errors.	• Students engage in discussion of previously read material and predict what will happen in upcoming passages. • The teacher sets a purpose for the reading. • The teacher teaches new vocabulary prior to reading and the students are given words for extensive vocabulary development. • Story structure is addressed through discussion after reading and treasure hunt questions. • Students retell the story to partners. • Direct instruction in reading comprehension skills is provided weekly.

TABLE 3.1 continued

Reading Model	Reading Abilities		
	Word Recognition	*Fluency*	*Comprehension*
Directed Reading Activity/ Directed Reading Thinking Activity/ Scaffolded Reading Experiences	• New sight words are presented before reading. • Word analysis skills and using context for word recognition are practiced during silent reading and monitored during purposeful oral rereading. • Word recognition skills are practiced after reading in the skills development step.	• Purposeful oral rereading provides opportunity for fluency development. Fluency can also be an enrichment activity after reading.	• Knowledge of topic is built and activated before reading. • New vocabulary words are taught before reading and can be practiced in the skills development step. • Text structure can be addressed in the discussion step through questions or as a skills development activity. • Sentence structure abilities are monitored during purposeful oral rereading and can be practiced in the skills development step. • Cognitive strategies are addressed during guided reading and discussion, and can be included in an enrichment activity. • In the Scaffolded Reading Experiences model, comprehension is addressed through prereading activities (activating background knowledge, teaching vocabulary and new concepts, predicting, and suggesting comprehension strategies) and postreading activities (e.g., questioning, discussion, and writing).

(continued)

TABLE 3.1 continued

	Reading Abilities		
Reading Model	*Word Recognition*	*Fluency*	*Comprehension*
Early Steps	• The word study step provides direct and systematic instruction in letter sounds and spelling patterns. The reading steps and writing step provide practice in word recognition skills and lead to increased sight vocabulary.	• Stories are reread until fluency is attained.	• Comprehension strategies are taught in the reading steps.
Guided Reading	• During silent reading, the teacher provides support with word recognition difficulties.	• Passages can be reread with partners and books can be reread independently.	• Topic and vocabulary are discussed before reading. • Comprehension is addressed during discussion after reading. Text is revisited for evidence of interpretations and for problem solving.
Integrated Skills Method	• Phonemic awareness is addressed through auditory awareness activities. • Phonic analysis and analogies are taught daily through carefully sequenced letter sound and pattern decoding activities. • Sight words are taught and practiced until mastery is attained.	• Sentences and stories are reread until fluency is attained.	

TABLE 3.1 continued

Reading Model	Reading Abilities		
	Word Recognition	*Fluency*	*Comprehension*
Language Experience Approach	• Story vocabulary emerges from the children's experiences. • The teacher points to each word during oral reading. • New words are underlined and written on word cards for each child's word bank.	• The story is reread until fluency is attained.	
Reading Recovery	• Letter-sound relationships and analogies are taught in the context of reading text.	• Stories are reread until fluency is attained.	• Comprehension strategies are taught in the context of reading text.
Reading Workshop			• Mini-lessons on literary craft, conventions of writing, and reading strategies are taught at the outset of each workshop. • Students engage in extended reading, respond in a reading journal, conference with the teacher, and share their reading with classmates.
Reciprocal Teaching/ Collaborative Strategic Reading			• Students predict what will happen, generate and answer questions, clarify information not understood, and summarize. • In the Collaborative Strategic Reading modification of the model, students preview the material, identify information they know and information they don't know during reading, apply fix-up strategies for comprehension breakdowns, and identify the key ideas during reading and the main idea after reading.

78

....

CHAPTER 3

*Framework for
Developing a
Reading Program
for the Struggling
Reader*

several other comprehension questions, and asks each student to reread orally relevant sentences or paragraphs to clarify answers.

   a. *Purpose Setting.* In this part of the guided reading step, the teacher sets a purpose, either through a question (such as "What kind of picture does Stacy choose to bring to school for the baby picture bulletin board?") or through a statement (such as "Find out the kind of picture Stacy chooses to bring to school for the baby picture bulletin board").

   b. *Silent Reading.* The students are then directed to read the segment silently.

   c. *Questions.* When the students have completed reading the segment silently, the teacher draws their attention back to the purpose by reiterating the purpose-setting question or statement. The teacher also asks one or two other questions, usually about salient details but sometimes about inferences.

   d. *Purposeful Oral Rereading.* When the student answers a question, whether correctly or incorrectly, the teacher can ask, "What part of the story made you think of that answer?" and then ask the student to read that passage aloud. For the reader, the purpose is to share more information about an answer. For the teacher, the purpose is to identify problems with word recognition or comprehension, to help the student develop fluency, or to encourage oral expression.

4. *Discussion.* When the cycle of purpose setting, silent reading, questions, and purposeful oral rereading is complete, questions are asked to stimulate discussion about the central story line (such as questions designed to highlight story structure components) and to engage the students in higher level and critical thinking.

5. *Skills Development.* Skill-building activities offer practice in a skill that was needed in the story or chapter that the students just read such as applying a phonics principle to new words, adding sight words and vocabulary to a personal dictionary, or identifying the main idea.

6. *Enrichment.* In this step, the teacher creates opportunities for the students to extend their comprehension through activities such as field trips, dramatizations, art projects, writing, viewing a video, independent reading by each student, and read-aloud by the teacher.

The *Directed Reading Thinking Activity* (*DRTA*) was developed by Stauffer (1969). The difference between the DRA and DRTA lies in purpose setting and questioning. Instead of having a purpose set by the teacher, the students make predictions about what they think will happen in the upcoming segment. After silent reading, instead of asking questions, the teacher directs them back to their predictions. The students are then asked to create new predictions for the upcoming segment.

Two types of questions are typically asked in a DRTA. The first are asked before reading a segment and require speculation and prediction ("What do you think?" "Why do you think so?" "What makes you think that?"). The second are questions asked after reading a segment and require support for conclusions ("What makes you think that?" "Why?" "How do you know that?").

The DRA and DRTA are highly supportive for the reader and, thus, time intensive for the teacher. The model is commonly used with small reading groups in which the teacher carries out steps 1 through 4 with one group while the other groups are engaged in step 5 or another activity such as writing or independent reading. As shown in Table 3.1, the model provides support in virtually all of the reading tasks including prior knowledge of topic (step 1), vocabulary knowledge (steps 1 and 5), automatic word recognition (steps 2 and 5), phonic analysis (steps 3 and 5), structural analysis (steps 3 and 5), context (steps 3 and 5), text structure (step 4 and 5), sentence structure (steps 3 and 5), and cognitive strategies (steps 3, 4, and 6).

Scaffolded Reading Experiences

Scaffolded Reading Experiences (Graves & Braaten, 1996; Graves & Graves, 2007) is very similar to the DRA and DRTA but this model offers greater flexibility to the teacher in choosing prereading, during-reading, and postreading strategies and activities. The term *scaffolded* is used to indicate the temporary and adjustable nature of the support needed to enable the reader to be successful. Scaffolded Reading Experiences give the teacher the option of offering less intrusive instruction than the DRA/DRTA require but this model is still at the high-teacher-support end of the continuum. The model involves three basic steps.

1. *Prereading Activities.* In this step, the teacher prepares the student to read the upcoming material. Options include relating the topic to the students' lives, motivating, activating background knowledge of the topic and content, teaching vocabulary for known concepts, teaching new concepts, using questions and predictions to help students identify key ideas in the text, and suggesting strategies they should use during reading.

2. *During Reading Activities.* The teacher chooses from among several strategies for reading the material including reading it aloud to the students as they follow along in their own copy of the passage, having the students read it silently, or using guided reading.

3. *Postreading Activities.* In this step, the teacher provides opportunity for the students to analyze and synthesize ideas, evaluate the text and their understanding, and respond to the material. Options include questioning, discussion, writing, drama, nonverbal activities such as artistic and graphic responses, and application and outreach activities such as field trips. The teacher might also reteach a skill or strategy, ask the students to reread a segment, or present a brief lesson on a difficult part of the text.

The DRA or DRTA would be an excellent choice as an instructional model for Maria. As you can see from her assessment, summarized in Table 2.2,

80

....

CHAPTER 3

*Framework for
Developing a
Reading Program
for the Struggling
Reader*

although she is in the fifth grade, she is reading instructionally at the second-grade level and independently at the first-grade level. Mr. Ginnetti's assessment indicated that she needs much teacher support during instruction. The model offers particular support in areas that Mr. Ginnetti identified as goals for Maria. For example, he could combine teaching new vocabulary in the concept development step with teaching these new vocabulary words as sight words. During guided reading, he could make sure to ask comprehension questions that checked on whether Maria had understood the new vocabulary and, if not, he could remind her of the vocabulary lesson or make a note to himself to find another strategy to use later for teaching the new concepts and words. After reading, he could ask questions that encouraged Maria to make inferences and to know when she did and did not understand what she had read. Although Mr. Ginnetti had decided not to focus specifically on the skills of phonic analysis, structural analysis, analogy, and context for word recognition at this time, DRA and DRTA provide opportunity to learn and practice these skills, which the assessment showed that Maria needs to strengthen.

Maria is not the only student reading instructionally at the second-grade level who would benefit from the degree of support provided by the DRA or DRTA instructional model. Mr. Ginnetti could put a small reading group together from his own class or even put a group together with students from other classes if his school uses a block scheduling approach.

Direct Instruction

Direct Instruction (*DI*) is a highly structured approach of curriculum materials and instructional sequences that move students through mastery of basic skills to higher level processing (Adams & Engelmann, 1996; Carnine et al., 2004; Carnine et al., 2006). Published primarily by SRA/McGraw-Hill, the goal of Direct Instruction is to accelerate learning through rapid pacing and active student engagement of carefully sequenced tasks that lead to automaticity and generalization of skills. Lessons are scripted to ensure success of the instructional procedure and to diminish the amount of teacher talk.

Direct Instruction is teacher intensive and requires substantial training. Materials must be fully decodable and sequenced so that only the phonic skills and sight words that have been taught systematically appear in the material. If your district is using Corrective Reading, Ravenscourt Books, Reading Mastery, or Open Court, then Direct Instruction is the model of reading instruction.

Although the principles of DI (e.g., systematic and explicit skills instruction) can be applied to other instructional models presented in this chapter, Direct Instruction is generally implemented as a schoolwide or remedial program. Ms. Edberg, Mr. Ginnetti, Mrs. Hong, and Mr. Rumrill are not in a DI school, have never been trained to use the approach, and did not have the program materials that would enable them to use DI appropriately, so they could not select it as a model for their students.

Integrated Skills Method

81

CHAPTER 3

*Framework for
Developing a
Reading Program
for the Struggling
Reader*

The *Integrated Skills Method* was originally developed by Richardson and
Bradley (1975) to provide an individualized, remedial program for students
with a reading disability, particularly those who have not advanced beyond
the first-grade reading level. According to DiBenedetto (1996), the model can
be used with small groups of students within 20- to 30-minute daily lessons
that involve the following steps.

1. *Preparation.* The teacher develops a sequence of onsets, rimes, pattern
   words (i.e., analogies), and sight words. (Teacher resources such as
   Cunningham [2009] and Bear, Helman, Templeton, Invernizzi, and
   Johnston [2007], listed at the end of this chapter, provide lots of examples from which the teacher can choose.) Each is written on an
   index card. A sentence is developed for each set so that one sentence
   incorporates an onset, rime, pattern word, and sight word. Each
   sentence is also written on an index card.

2. *Auditory Awareness.* The teacher begins each lesson with a brief activity
   that involves the students in distinguishing consonant sounds, vowel
   sounds, rhymes, or blending.

3. *Letter Sounds.* The teacher selects 7 cards from the onset-rime pack,
   presents them to the student, and discards each as the student masters
   it.

4. *Pattern Decoding.* The teacher shows 10 cards in the pattern decoding
   pack, presents them to the student, and discards each as the student
   masters it.

5. *Sight Words.* The teacher shows 9 cards in the sight word pack (some
   words should be ones that the student will need for reading the upcoming story and some words should be ones the teacher will need
   for composing sentences). The teacher shows these cards quickly, providing the word if the student does not recognize it instantly, and re-
   peats the activity until the student recognizes all the words instantly.

6. *Sentences.* The teacher shows five or six sentence cards, which have
   been chosen from the sentence pack plus sentences from the upcoming story. When reading the sentences, the teacher provides instruction
   in letter-sound components, pattern decoding, and use of context. The
   student is asked to read each sentence until fluency is attained. The
   meaning of each sentence is also discussed.

7. *Games.* The teacher creates six short sentences or phrases from as
   many of the sight words as possible. The teacher makes copies of the
   sentences and engages the student in a card game such as Concentration, Go Fish, or Old Maid.

8. *Spelling and Writing.* The teacher dictates pattern words and sight
   words for the student to write in a notebook. When the student is able
   to write the words with no difficulty, the teacher can modify this step

82
....

CHAPTER 3

*Framework for
Developing a
Reading Program
for the Struggling
Reader*

by dictating brief sentences or asking the student to compose his or her own sentences. Invented spelling (i.e., spelling based on the child's best guess from his or her current state of knowledge about the spelling system) is not used in this activity. If the student does not spell a word correctly, the teacher provides the correct spelling.

9. *Reading for Meaning and Pleasure.* The teacher and the students in the reading group take turns reading orally. During reading, the teacher points out the role of punctuation for expression. The story is reread until the students attain fluency.

The Integrated Skills Method is highly supportive for the reader and requires substantial teacher time both for the preparation and delivery of instruction. As shown in Table 3.1, the model provides extensive support in word recognition and fluency. Based on Mr. Rumrill's assessment (summarized in Table 2.2), the model is well suited for Marek, who is in grade 3, reading at a grade 1 level, and needs instruction to focus on phonic analysis, analogy, structural analysis, and context for identifying words. If Mr. Rumrill is able to devote time to preparing the materials for onset-rime, pattern decoding, sight word, and sentence activities, integrating ISM into instruction with Marek's reading group would not be more time-consuming than most of the other models, particularly as a relatively short-duration intervention until the students gain needed skills in phonemic awareness, phonic analysis, analogy, and automatic word recognition.

Early Steps

Early Steps is one of several tutorial programs designed for children in the early grades who are identified as at risk for reading difficulties. (Reading Recovery is one of the best known of these tutorial programs. Another is Success for All, which includes one-to-one tutoring as a major component of its schoolwide program.) Early Steps was developed by Morris (1995), who also developed the Howard Street Tutorial Program. Whereas Howard Street uses primarily volunteers, Early Steps was designed to be used by teachers.

In Early Steps, the lowest 20th percentile of students in first grade are provided with daily 30-minute lessons. The teachers who conduct the tutoring sessions and the classroom teachers both receive yearlong training. Lessons are divided into the following four main sections:

1. *Reading.* The student rereads a book or story introduced the previous lesson. The goal is fluency and comprehension.

2. *Word Study.* The tutor provides instruction in a phonemic awareness and word recognition skill. The direct, systematic study of letter sounds and spelling patterns is isolated from the context of actual reading in this step to ensure that the student is devoting full attention to the pattern being taught.

3. *Writing.* The student writes his or her own sentences, the tutor rewrites each sentence, the tutor then takes apart the sentence, and the student puts the sentence together into the original form. When writing each sentence, the student is asked to speak each word aloud and to focus on the letters that comprise each word.

4. *New Reading.* The tutor introduces a new book or story that is slightly more difficult than the previous book. The student is encouraged to predict the main idea by using pictures, title, and other cues. During reading, the tutor encourages the student to use the word recognition skills and comprehension strategies previously taught and to self-correct.

Early Steps was developed more recently than Reading Recovery and Success for All and differs most dramatically by the step involving direct and systematic word study instruction, the training of classroom teachers as well as tutors, and the use of typical reading material rather than special decodable text (Morris, Tyner, & Perney, 2000; Santa & Hoien, 1999). Early Steps is time intensive as a tutoring model but can be adapted for small-group classroom instruction. As shown in Table 3.1, the model is particularly supportive for word recognition skills and fluency. Although the model is intended to be supplementary to classroom reading instruction, a classroom teacher could employ it as the major instructional model and supplement it with another model or vice versa.

Adani's teacher might choose Early Steps because Adani's goals in word recognition are a good match to the reading tasks that are emphasized in the model. As a first grader who is at risk for reading difficulty, even if one-to-one tutoring is not available in Adani's school, Ms. Edberg could group her with the other children at the lowest 20th percentile in her class. Early Steps does not require that the teacher use specially designed material so Ms. Edberg can use material she already has in her classroom. Given the importance of using material that gradually increases in difficulty, she will need to assess the readability of her reading materials and sequence them carefully, or use leveled material available from publishers. Assessing readability is described later in this chapter.

Reading Recovery

Reading Recovery is a preventive tutoring program originally developed by Marie Clay (1985) in New Zealand and brought to the United States in the mid-1980s by Pinnell and other researchers at The Ohio State University. As designated by Clay, the children chosen to receive Reading Recovery are those in the lowest 20th percentile reading-achievement group in the first-grade classrooms. The tutors are certified teachers who have received intensive training for a full academic year. Each day the children are tutored for 30 minutes until they either reach the level of performance of their classmates in the middle reading group or until they receive 60 lessons without achieving this level of performance, at which point they are often referred for special education

84

....

CHAPTER 3

*Framework for
Developing a
Reading Program
for the Struggling
Reader*

services. The average length of program is 12 to 20 weeks. Reading Recovery lessons include the following four steps:

1. *Rereading a Familiar Book.* The student rereads a familiar book or story with the goal of reading for fluency and focusing on comprehension.
2. *Reading Yesterday's Book.* The student reads aloud a book that was new the previous day as the teacher takes a running record by marking errors and substitutions, noting self-corrections, and monitoring behaviors.
3. *Writing a Story and Working with Letters.* The student writes a message or story. The teacher rewrites it onto sentence strips, cuts the strips, and asks the student to reassemble and read the story. During this step, the teacher also uses magnetic letters and other techniques to work on letters and sounds.
4. *Reading a New Book.* The teacher introduces a new book by talking about it and looking at the pictures. The student is then asked to read the book.

Reading Recovery is difficult for the classroom teacher to implement unless the model is modified for small group instruction. Although it is not intended to be used by teachers who have not undergone yearlong training, the steps themselves can certainly be adapted by classroom teachers. One example is the format suggested by Hedrick and Pearish (1999). They suggested seven steps in a 30-minute period: (a) 2 minutes of read-aloud by the teacher; (b) 6 minutes of phonics and word study; (c) 2 minutes of shared reading using a story chart; (d) 10 minutes of read-aloud by the students with guidance from the teacher; (e) 2 minutes of writing by the teacher, breaking the sentences apart, and asking the student to put them back together; (f) 3 minutes of writing by the student with guidance from the teacher; and (g) 5 minutes of independent reading. In another modification, Lee and Neal (1992/1993) suggested combining the Reading Recovery model with the Language Experience Approach (which will be described later in this chapter) so that the material the student reads, rereads, and writes emerges from the student's dictated stories.

As Table 3.1 shows, Reading Recovery provides particular support in word recognition and fluency. As with Early Steps, the model is intended to be supplementary to classroom reading instruction. The steps themselves, however, could form the nucleus of the main instructional model. Adani's teacher could choose Reading Recovery but because Early Steps provides more intensive word study instruction, the Early Steps model appears more appropriate for Adani.

Success for All

Success for All is a comprehensive schoolwide program designed for schools with large number of students living in poverty (Slavin & Madden, 2000). Success for All emphasizes prekindergarten and kindergarten approaches, one-to-one tutoring for first graders who are at at risk for reading failure, family support services, and instruction in math, science, social studies, and literacy (Borman et al., 2007; Duffy-Hester, 1999; Madden, Slavin, Wasik, & Dolan, 1997). The reading program is implemented in three phases starting with children in preschool or the first semester of kindergarten. The second phase begins in the second semester of kindergarten and continues until the children attain the primer reading level. The third phase begins when the students are reading on a first-grade level and continues until fifth or sixth grade. Students are assessed every 8 weeks to monitor progress, identify which students can be accelerated, and determine which students should receive and which students no longer need tutoring. Students are grouped for reading so that each reading class contains one reading level only. One-to-one tutoring is provided for 20 minutes daily during times outside of reading and math periods to students having difficulty. The tutor works on the same skills being taught by the classroom reading teacher but uses different instructional strategies. During classroom reading instruction, tutors serve as extra reading teachers.

Success for All is a school reform program that requires the restructuring of school instruction. It is not intended to be used by a lone teacher in a school. Unless you are in a Success for All school, you would not be able to implement the full instructional model. Next in this section, Cooperative Integrated Reading and Composition (CIRC) will be described, which is one of the reading models used in Success for All. CIRC can be applied as an instructional model whether or not the teacher is in a Success for All school.

Cooperative Integrated Reading and Composition (CIRC)

Cooperative Integrated Reading and Composition (CIRC) can be used as a stand-alone program for students in grades 2 through 6 or as a component of Success for All (Slavin, Madden, Farnish, & Stevens, 1995). The four principal elements of the program are story-related activities, explicit instruction in reading comprehension, integrated writing/language arts, and independent reading. The first element includes the following 10 story-related activities:

1. *Teacher-Led Reading Groups.* Students are assigned to reading groups based on reading achievement levels. The teacher spends 20 minutes daily with each group. The materials are stories from a basal reading series or anthology of stories. The teacher engages the students in discussion of previously read material, sets a purpose for the reading, reviews old vocabulary, and introduces new vocabulary. During vocabulary instruction, the teacher makes sure that each student understands all word meanings, reviews methods for identifying unknown words during reading, and provides practice for rapid and repetitive oral reading of vocabulary. Before reading, the students predict what the story will be about from the title and vocabulary they just learned. After reading, the teacher engages them in discussion about the story, emphasizing the story problem and how the characters changed.

86

....

CHAPTER 3

*Framework for
Developing a
Reading Program
for the Struggling
Reader*

2. *Partner Reading.* The students read the story, first silently and then orally with a partner by taking turns for each paragraph. The listener follows along and corrects the reader's errors.

3. *Treasure Hunt Questions.* The students are given questions that emphasize story structure, which they answer during partner reading.

4. *Word Mastery List.* The students practice new or difficult words from the story with partners until they can read the words automatically.

5. *Word Meaning.* The students are given words for extensive vocabulary development. They look these words up in a dictionary, paraphrase the definitions, write a sentence for each reflecting the word's meaning, and practice them with partners.

6. *Story Retell.* After reading and discussing the story in the reading group, the students summarize the story to their partners.

7. *Story-Related Writing.* The teacher asks the students to write a few paragraphs on an open-ended topic, such as writing a new ending to the story.

8. *Spelling.* The students pretest each other on a list of spelling words each day of the week, gradually creating new lists of missed words until all words are mastered.

9. *Partner Checking.* Students sign off on each other's forms confirming the completion of tasks and achievement of criterion levels of performance that the teacher set for each student.

10. *Tests.* Approximately every 3 days, the students are given a comprehension test on the story, a test on writing meaningful sentences for specific vocabulary words, and a test of oral reading of words from the word mastery list.

The other three elements of CIRC involve the following: (a) One day each week the teacher uses a step-by-step curriculum for explicit instruction in reading comprehension. After each lesson, the students work in heterogeneous groups on comprehension activities and games; (b) The teacher uses a process approach for writing instruction (i.e., writing-revising-editing steps with peer feedback and editing, teacher-directed instruction of skills, and team practice on language arts skills) for the integrated writing/language arts curriculum; and (c) Students read a book of their choice every evening for at least 20 minutes and write a book report every 2 weeks. Parent signatures verifying nightly reading and book reports contribute to team scores.

As shown in Table 3.1, CIRC addresses all of the major reading skills and provides particular support in vocabulary development, fluency, and comprehension. Ellison has relatively good word recognition skills but poor fluency, weak vocabulary, and difficulty identifying main ideas, determining sequences of events, and using semantic context cues for identifying unknown words. Given that the model addresses the areas that are goals for Ellison, it could be very effective for him, as well as the other students in Ellison's reading group. Recognizing that she will need access to the published curriculum materials, Mrs. Hong will discuss the curriculum with other teachers in her building, and perhaps even ask the curriculum specialist if there is interest in pursuing the possibility of purchasing the curriculum and participating in the 2 days of required training.

Language Experience Approach (LEA)

In the *Language Experience Approach* (*LEA*), students dictate ideas or experiences to the teacher, the teacher records their dictation in the form of an experience story, and the story becomes the instructional reading material. Originally developed by Stauffer (1970), the LEA is usually taught with a small group of students but can be individualized or even used with a full class. Given that the students create their own stories, the language of the stories directly reflects their linguistic and vocabulary levels. Thus, the syntactic structures and vocabulary are familiar to the readers and the topic is one about which they are knowledgeable and interested. The steps in the LEA are typically the following:

1. *Introduction of Stimulus.* The teacher provides a stimulus for the story. It can be an object, animal, field trip, video, art project, celebration, or anything else that is likely to stimulate a discussion.

2. *Story Dictation.* The students dictate their thoughts or impressions about the experience. The teacher writes their words onto a large sheet of paper, overhead transparency, whiteboard, or computer. The teacher can guide the discussion, ask for clarification, and offer suggestions. In order for the story to emerge with the structure of an actual story, the teacher may need to ask leading questions. As Heller (1988) noted, "Group dictated stories that are recorded verbatim often lack the continuity that distinguishes a story from lists of sentences" (p. 130).

3. *Read-Aloud.* The students read the story aloud while the teacher points to each word. The story is reread until fluency is attained. New words are underlined and later written on word cards for each reader's word bank. Sentence strips can also be created for practice in reading sentences and sequencing.

4. *Story Writing.* The students copy the story or the teacher makes a copy for each student's notebook (or anthology), which they can illustrate.

5. *Story Rereading.* The stories are reread periodically to the teacher, peers, and parents. Words are continuously added to the word bank and used for activities such as games and new story writing.

One of the challenges in using the LEA arises when the student's dictated story differs noticeably from Standard English (the variety of English that is generally used in school because it is viewed as the model of speech and writing for educated individuals). If the teacher writes the story as dictated, the text may be a poor model of written English. If the teacher modifies the syntax,

88

CHAPTER 3

*Framework for
Developing a
Reading Program
for the Struggling
Reader*

the implicit message is that the student's language is inferior or flawed. Also, one of the benefits may be lost if the student has difficulty with sentence patterns that do not match his or her own expressive language. Gillet and Gentry (1983) proposed that the teacher write two stories. The first should reflect the student's language as dictated and the second should be written in Standard English. The second story can be introduced as another story about the same topic and both stories used in the conventional LEA activities.

A second challenge in using the LEA involves revising stories so that the students are not led to believe that the first draft and final draft of a story are identical. Karnowski (1989) advised teachers to engage students in discussion that encourages ongoing revision just as they urge the students to revise in other writing activities.

If Mr. Rumrill chooses the Integrated Skills Method as the major instructional reading model for Marek, the LEA might be an appropriate supplementary model. Indeed, he had used the LEA as a diagnostic reading lesson and found it worked well with Marek. The LEA provides ample opportunity to focus on word recognition skills and yet might be viewed much more positively by Marek than the traditional school reading that he dislikes because in the LEA, he is reading his own stories.

Reciprocal Teaching/Collaborative Strategic Reading

Reciprocal Teaching is a model developed by Palincsar and Brown (1986, 1988) for enhancing reading comprehension through dialogue that encourages collaborative problem solving between teachers and students. In Reciprocal Teaching, the following four activities form the basis of the dialogue:

1. *Prediction.* The students predict what will happen in the upcoming passage.
2. *Question Generating.* The teacher, who initially is the classroom teacher and later is one of the students taking over the role of teacher, asks questions after the passage is read.
3. *Clarifying.* The questions lead to clarifications that are needed by any of the students. This step involves monitoring comprehension and using repair strategies when comprehension has broken down.
4. *Summarizing.* The teacher summarizes the passage and asks for modifications to the summary, or the teacher asks one of the students to summarize the passage. Again, clarifications can be sought when the students differ about the main ideas and salient details included in the summary.

The model typically begins with a review of the four activities. The lesson then follows the four steps and ends with the students' making predictions about the passage to be read the next day. Initially, the teacher leads the dialogue, but gradually the teacher transfers responsibility for initiating and sustaining dialogue to the students. The teacher continues to provide feedback and coach the students. Reciprocal Teaching represents a kind of intermediate point between highly teacher-structured models, such DRA/DRTA and Direct Instruction, and models that call for the teacher to be less of a "sage on the stage" and more of a "guide on the side" (as you can see in Figure 3.1).

Collaborative Strategic Reading is a modification of Reciprocal Teaching (Klingner & Vaughn, 1999; Klingner, Vaughn, Arguelles, Hughes, & Leftwich, 2004; Klingner, Vaughn, Dimino, Schumm, & Bryant, 2001). First, students at mixed reading and achievement levels are grouped so that they can engage in cooperative learning. Second, the approach is used with content area reading material. And third, the four activities are modified as the following:

1. *Preview.* The students scan the material for clues about the topic. The goal is to generate interest and questions about the material, activate background knowledge, and encourage their predictions.

2. *Click and Clunk.* The students "click" when they identify information they already know and "clunk" when they identify difficult words, concepts, or ideas. They can write the words that represent clicks and clunks or use different-colored sticky notes to mark the words. The goal is to monitor comprehension and to use fix-up strategies when comprehension has broken down. The teacher provides instruction in "declunking" and writes these fix-up strategies on clunk cards that the students can reference during reading. Examples of fix-up strategies include rereading the sentence with the clunk, looking for clues in the sentences before and after the sentence with the clunk, looking for a prefix or suffix in the word, breaking the word apart into smaller parts, using a picture, and asking for help.

3. *Get the Gist.* The students identify the main idea or most important information in a paragraph or passage during reading and restate it in a few words.

4. *Wrap-Up.* The students generate questions and answers after reading the passage and summarize the most important ideas.

As shown in Table 3.1, Reciprocal Teaching emphasizes comprehension. Ellison's strengths in word recognition and his goals in comprehension indicate that the model might be a good choice. Indeed, his particular weaknesses in main idea and sequencing story events could be well served in the summarizing and clarifying steps of the Reciprocal Teaching model and the Get the Gist and Wrap-Up steps of the Collaborative Strategic Reading version, particularly if Mrs. Hong is unable to obtain the materials and training for CIRC. However, Mrs. Hong would have to modify the format to add fluency instruction and vocabulary development for Ellison.

Another advantage to Reciprocal Teaching and Collaborative Strategic Reading is that these are models that middle school teachers have found to be effective in improving comprehension of content area material (Bryant, Vaughn, Linan-Thompson, Ugel, & Hamff, 2000; Hashey & Connors, 2003).

90
....

CHAPTER 3

*Framework for
Developing a
Reading Program
for the Struggling
Reader*

Certainly, Ellison would benefit from this type of reading instruction, which is aimed at moving the student from dependence on the teacher to independence in applying comprehension strategies.

Guided Reading

Guided Reading was developed by Fountas and Pinnell (1996) as a model for supporting independent and fluent reading of students from kindergarten through grade 4. The term *guided reading* can be confused with the guided reading step of the DRA and DRTA. As with the DRA and DRTA, students of similar reading levels are placed in small reading groups. Guided Reading also shares some of the steps of the DRA and DRTA models, though it incorporates considerably less teacher-led instruction, as the following steps show:

1. *Selection of Leveled Books.* The teacher selects a book that the students can read with greater than 90 percent accuracy but is not so easy that there is no opportunity to build problem-solving strategies. As discussed in the section on reading materials later in the chapter, Guided Reading requires that a selection of books along a continuum of difficulty levels has been identified. Each student is provided with a copy of the book to be read.

2. *Introduction of Book.* The teacher introduces the book by having the students look at the cover, read the title and author, and talk about the topic. Vocabulary words crucial to understanding the story are briefly discussed but the teacher does not carry out vocabulary instruction per se and does not teach new sight words.

3. *Silent Reading.* The students read the book independently and silently. Some students may subvocalize while reading. Indeed, silent reading seems to be a skill that begins with subvocalizing and, with less skilled readers, is related to the demands of the material (Wright, Sherman, & Jones, 2004). The teacher observes, notes student behaviors during reading, and provides support with word recognition, understanding unfamiliar sentence structures, and comprehension when needed.

4. *Discussion.* After reading, the students discuss the book. The teacher has them revisit the text to find evidence of interpretations and to discuss strategies for problem solving. The students might also be asked to reread a passage independently or with a partner.

Guided Reading provides support that can be characterized as incidental rather than direct because the teacher's role is to respond to difficulties the student is having as these emerge in the context of reading. As shown in Table 3.1, most of the support centers on comprehension. The model does not incorporate the kinds of concentrated and systematic instruction that struggling readers typically need at the early stages of development, which is why it was not selected for any of the case study children. One study, however, has shown that Guided Reading is effective with deaf students when modified to include explicit and systematic teaching of new words that the students would encounter in their reading material (Schirmer & Schaffer, 2008). Though this is the only research evidence on a modified Guided Reading approach, it is often recommended that it be adapted or combined with at least one other model that provides support with word recognition skills.

In one example, Avalos, Plasencia, Chavez, and Rascón (2007) developed a modified guided reading lesson format for English language learners. They extended the amount of instructional time spent per story; incorporated a step for preteaching vocabulary, figurative language, and homophones; and focused strategy instruction on complex syntax and text structure features. An example of putting Guided Reading together with another model is the *Literacy Collaborative Framework* of The Ohio State University (2008), which combines Guided Reading with *Shared Reading* and *Interactive Writing*. In Shared Reading, the teacher points to each word during group read-aloud of big books or enlarged text. Interactive Writing is similar to the Language Experience Approach except the teacher and student share the writing. When writing each word, the teacher helps the student identify the sounds and connect these sounds to letters and letter combinations. Yet another example of combining Guided Reading with another model for word recognition is the *Four Blocks*, which was developed by Cunningham, Hall, and Sigmon (1999). In Four Blocks, the Working with Words block incorporates activities to help the student read and spell high-frequency words and to use word analysis for reading and spelling other words (the other three blocks are Guided Reading, Self-Selected Reading, and Writing). Several of the Working with Words strategies are discussed in Chapter 4.

The leveled books of Guided Reading comprise the component of the model most valuable to the struggling reader. Having an easily available set of books of increasing difficulty enables the teacher to make an appropriate match between the student's reading level and the level of the material. Leveled books can be used effectively with any instructional model and are discussed more fully later in this chapter.

Book Club

Raphael and her associates (Goatley, Brock, & Raphael, 1995; Raphael & McMahon, 1994; Raphael, Pardo, & Highfield, 2002) developed *Book Club* as a student led, discussion rich model. Book Club includes four components, which the authors refer to as contexts for reading instruction.

1. *Community Share.* The Community Share context is the only component of the model involving teacher-directed instruction. Topics may include reading strategies, writing strategies, vocabulary, writing conventions, connections between books the students are reading or have read, and attributes of good discussions. The teacher might use Community Share to read aloud, preview new books, or encourage students to share what they are reading.

92

CHAPTER 3

*Framework for
Developing a
Reading Program
for the Struggling
Reader*

2. *Book Club.* The central feature of the model is the Book Club discussions. Students in small heterogeneous groups meet to discuss material chosen by the teacher that they have all read.

3. *Reading.* At least 15 minutes each day, the students engage in sustained reading. The teacher can vary the activity by having the students read individually, with partners, or in small groups. Another option is for the teacher or one of the students to read aloud to the class. During this time, the teacher can provide instruction to individual students or small groups on a needed skill or strategy.

4. *Writing.* Brief or extended periods of time are allotted for the students to engage in writing, such as making entries in reading logs or writing stories.

Book Club is appropriate for students who have strong word recognition skills, are relatively strategic readers, and can participate effectively in discussions with peers. The limited instruction in reading skills and strategies built into the model (as shown in Table 3.1) makes it an unlikely choice for struggling readers, which is why it was not selected by Ms. Edberg, Mr. Ginnetti, Mrs. Hong, or Mr. Rumrill.

Reading Workshop

Reading Workshop is based on the premise that students need time to engage in reading, develop ownership over what they read, and find opportunity to respond in ways that they find meaningful. The model involves three key components (Atwell, 1998; Serafini, 2001).

1. *Mini-lessons.* The first 5 to 20 minutes of class time are spent in direct teacher instruction of an aspect of reading that the teacher has identified as important to the students. Atwell offered four categories of mini-lessons: (a) workshop procedures; (b) literary craft, which involves techniques, styles, genres, authors, and particular works of literature; (c) conventions of writing; and (d) reading strategies.

2. *Reading.* The greatest proportion of the reading instruction period is devoted to independent reading of a self-selected book. The students are encouraged to discontinue a book if they do not like it, reread a favorite book, skim or skip parts if they are bored, and seek suggestions for new books to read.

3. *Response.* The students write in a reading journal regularly to express their ideas, feelings, experiences, and questions. So that she wouldn't have to respond to every journal, Atwell asked students to write a letter to a classmate or the teacher at least once each week. The person receiving the letter is asked to respond within a day.

4. *Conferences.* The student and teacher meet regularly, usually once each week, to discuss the student's reading.

5. *Sharing.* A few students daily take turns leading a brief discussion. Each student tells the title and author, summarizes the story, and asks for questions and comments.

On the continuum from highly teacher-directed reading instruction for students needing significant and ongoing support in the early stages of reading development, to teacher-facilitated instruction for students who are relatively autonomous and proficient readers, DRA/DRTA and Reading Workshop are at opposite ends. As Table 3.1 shows, Reading Workshop instruction is aimed at comprehension and involves higher order concepts of craft, conventions, and strategies. It is unlikely that this model would meet the needs of struggling readers, though this view is not shared by Roller (1996), who noted that the ample opportunities provided to teachers for observing and analyzing the students' performance makes it highly appropriate. However, given that the model incorporates little opportunity for systematic skills and strategy instruction, Reading Workshop was not used with the case study children.

Reading Materials

As the selection of instructional model emerges from the struggling reader's assessment, so does the choice of reading materials. Some models, such as Direct Instruction and the Language Experience Approach, mandate the materials. Most of the models leave the choice to you. The two principal types of materials for reading instruction are basal readers and trade books.

A *basal reader* is a book in a basal reading series. *Basal reading series* were traditionally characterized by controlled vocabulary, progressive difficulty, and detailed teaching instructions. Basal texts were referred to as contrived because in order to create basals in an easy to progressively more difficult sequence, authors traditionally developed stories and passages in which sentence length and complexity were monitored, vocabulary was controlled, and content selection was limited. Except for a few series such as Open Court, which uses decodable text, contemporary basal publishers incorporate literature selections and publishers highlight the literature content by referring to these series as anthologies rather than basals.

A *trade book* is simply a book published for a general audience. In reading programs, a trade book refers to any commercial book other than a basal that is used for reading instruction (Harris & Hodges, 1995). Educators have argued about the benefits and drawbacks of basals versus trade books for decades. As publishers incorporated literature into basal reader selections and developed reading packages and theme collections of children's literature, the distinction between published reading programs and literature-based instruction blurred. Teachers are now offered a range of materials, from book excerpts to full novels.

Whether you use trade books, basal readers, or publishers' collections, you must carefully evaluate the materials to determine how appropriate they

94
....
CHAPTER 3

*Framework for
Developing a
Reading Program
for the Struggling
Reader*

are for your students (Gunning, 2003). Two major approaches are available. The first is to assess the *readability* of text (i.e., difficulty level of the material) and match the readability level to the student's reading level. The second is to use leveled books, a cornerstone of the Guided Reading model, and choose the level that matches the student's reading level. Both approaches enable you to distinguish between materials at the reader's independent, instructional, and frustration levels.

Independent materials are those that the student can read with essentially no support. These materials are aimed at the student's current developmental level. *Instructional materials* are those that the student can read only with support. These materials are aimed at the student's *zone of proximal development* (Vygotsky, 1978)—the distance between the student's current developmental level as indicated by independent problem solving and potential developmental level as indicated by problem solving with guidance from an adult or in collaboration with a more capable peer. *Frustration materials* are those that the student cannot read regardless of the support provided. These materials represent the reader's zone of distal development, the distance between his or her current developmental level and furthest potential developmental level. Even with significant support from the teacher, the student is unable to read materials within the zone of distal development. Materials at the reader's frustration level make appropriate read-alouds by the teacher.

The term *instructional materials* is used purposefully because these are the materials used for instruction. The student's reading abilities develop as a result of learning to read materials that are challenging and that present opportunities for applying newly learned skills and strategies. You know that the student is developing as a reader when instructional materials become independent materials, and frustration materials become instructional materials.

Readability

A number of factors, within texts and within readers, contribute to readability. Within-text factors include content, structure, cohesiveness, format, typography, literary form and style, vocabulary difficulty, sentence complexity, idea or proposition density, level of abstractness, and organization. Within readers, attitude, motivation, purpose for the reading, cultural background, knowledge of vocabulary, extent of background knowledge of the topic, knowledge of text structure, and ability to identify words contribute to the ease with which the text will be comprehended (Irwin & Davis, 1980; Zakaluk and Samuels, 1988).

The most frequently used tool for determining readability is a *readability formula*. Most formulas rely on two factors. Some use average sentence length and vocabulary difficulty, such as Spache (grades 1 to 4) and Dale-Chall (grades 4 to adult); others use average sentence length and number of syllables, such as Fry (elementary to adult) and Flesch-Kincaid (upper elementary to secondary). Clearly, these factors do not exhaust all of the possible variables that influence text readability. When used as probability statements or estimates though, formulas can provide predictive information regarding how easily a text will be understood by the average reader (Fry, 1989). But they will not predict precisely whether a given reader will interact successfully with a particular text.

The use of readability formulas is simple and straightforward, and computer technology has made the process relatively quick. Software is available for most of the formulas and virtually all word-processing programs incorporate readability measures. However, formulas cannot be used in isolation. Although it may be tempting to rely solely on computer software with its aura of scientific validity, formulas must be augmented with other measures for estimating the readability of text (Kotula, 2003).

One approach is for teachers to read the target text themselves, using their own knowledge and understanding of their students to compare against the demands of the text (Dreyer, 1984). A second approach is to give a selection of the text to the student for a trial reading (Rush, 1985). If the student is able to read 98 percent of the words automatically, with good phrasing and strong comprehension, the material is independent. If the student is able to read 90 percent or fewer of the words automatically, uses word-by-word reading, and has weak comprehension, the material is frustration. Instructional material lies between these two points. A third approach is to use a cloze procedure, in which the student is given a reproduced portion of the text from which words have been systematically deleted, usually every fifth word except for the first and last sentences. A fourth suggestion is to use a checklist that includes within reader and within text factors, such as the checklist presented in Figure 3.2.

A sixth approach was developed by Chall, Bissex, Conard, and Harris-Sharples (1996) that they termed *qualitative assessment of text difficulty*. They created six sets of exemplars, one each for literature, popular fiction, life sciences, physical sciences, narrative, social studies, and expository social studies. Each set consists of exemplar passages at different reading levels, from easiest to hardest. To use this measurement tool, the teacher compares the text being assessed to the exemplar passages and determines readability by choosing the passage that seems to represent the closest match.

Leveled Books

Leveled books are a collection of books organized according to characteristics reflecting easy to difficult challenges for developing readers. The list originally developed by Fountas and Pinnell (2005) has become an ever increasing list as new titles are added regularly and posted on their website (2008). Four main criteria are used in the leveling process.

- *Book and print features* include length (number of pages, words, and lines per page), print (font type, font size, and spaces between words and lines), layout (placement of phrases, sentences, print, and pictures; consistency of layout; use of chapters, headings, and other organizational features), range of punctuation, and illustrations (number and relation to print).

FIGURE 3.2 Readability Checklist

Book Title: _____

Author(s): _____

Other Readability Data: _____

EVALUATION: (Circle your rating along the 5-point scale)

Readability Factors within Texts

Word Frequency	(few new words)	1 2 3 4 5	(many new words)
Concept Density	(few new concepts)	1 2 3 4 5	(many new concepts)
Level of Abstraction	(low level of abstraction)	1 2 3 4 5	(high level of abstraction)
Organization	(clearly organized)	1 2 3 4 5	(complexly or poorly organized)
Cohesiveness	(highly cohesive)	1 2 3 4 5	(not cohesive)
Clarity in Presentation of Ideas	(very clear)	1 2 3 4 5	(not clear)
Format/Design/Typography (e.g., print size, length of line of print, length of paragraph, color, typeface, punctuation)	(typical for level)	1 2 3 4 5	(not typical for level)
Use of Illustrations	(many, good illustrations)	1 2 3 4 5	(few and/or poor illustrations)
Sentence Complexity	(simple sentence structures)	1 2 3 4 5	(complex sentence structures)
Vocabulary Difficulty	(simple vocabulary)	1 2 3 4 5	(difficult vocabulary)
Literary Form and Style	(familiar form and style)	1 2 3 4 5	(unfamiliar form and style)
Textual Structure	(familiar and consistent)	1 2 3 4 5	(unfamiliar or inconsistent)

Readability Factors within Readers

Attitude	(positive toward reading)	1 2 3 4 5	(negative toward reading)
Motivation	(high motivation)	1 2 3 4 5	(low motivation)
Extent of Background Knowledge	(considerable)	1 2 3 4 5	(limited)
Vocabulary Knowledge	(extensive)	1 2 3 4 5	(narrow)
Knowledge of Text Structure	(thorough)	1 2 3 4 5	(incomplete)
Purpose for the Reading	(clear and important)	1 2 3 4 5	(unclear or unimportant)

ADDITIONAL COMMENTS:

RECOMMENDATION:
_____ Appropriate as independent reading material
_____ Appropriate as instructional reading material
_____ Appropriate as reading material for teacher read-aloud
_____ Not appropriate

- *Content, theme, and ideas* include familiarity with content, technical nature of content, sophistication of theme, and complexity of ideas.

- *Text structure* includes narrative text (predictability of story structure, description of setting, character development, plot complexity, genre, structure of episodes) and expository text (presentation, organization, and level of information and ideas).

- *Language and literary features* include perspective of author and characters, structure of phrases and sentences, structure of paragraphs and chapters, use of words or phrases as literary devices, and vocabulary (variety of words, number and range of high frequency and interest words, number of multisyllabic words, and word difficulty).

Several options are available for teachers who are not using the Fountas and Pinnell leveled books. Fawson and Reutzel (2000) suggest adapting basal readers. Teachers can work together in using Fountas and Pinnell's criteria to level the basal stories in their reading series or use Fawson and Reutzel's text leveling of several popular basal reading series (including Harcourt Brace, Silver Burdett Ginn, Houghton Mifflin, Scott Foresman, and Scholastic).

Another option is to use the increasingly popular publishers' leveling of their reading packages and theme collections. Some of these publishers use Fountas and Pinnell's leveling and some use their own algorithms.

When using a published leveling system, it is important to recognize that the particular criteria used in leveling may not result in a good match between the book's level and your students' instructional reading needs. For example, Cunningham and his colleagues (2005) analyzed books leveled by Reading Recovery and found that although Reading Recovery lessons incorporate the study of high-frequency words and phonics instruction using onset-rime patterns, "the books they select for their program provide little support for these two instructional components, and the way they level the books provides none at all" (p. 45).

Whatever system you use to determine the readability of the material you select for reading instruction, it is up to you to determine whether the leveling system makes sense in light of the instructional strategies and skills you will be teaching and, if not, to feel free to modify the levels using the other readability measures discussed in this section.

Next Step

The intent of this book is to provide you with a unifying framework for developing a coherent reading program that will enable struggling readers to become proficient readers. The expectation is that you will be able to situate your current knowledge about the components of teaching reading into this framework. This chapter provided a process and graphic representation for selecting a reading model. The model you choose is based directly on knowledge of which aspects of the reading process present difficulty to the student. This chapter has also provided an explanation of how to select reading materials targeted at the student's instructional level.

The next step is choosing strategies to teach before, during, and after reading. These strategies are essentially slotted into the steps of the reading model. The next chapter will present strategies that you can use during the prereading or planning phase of reading.

Questions for Reflection and Application

1. How do you know whether a particular reading model is the most appropriate for a certain student?

2. When is it time to change from a model incorporating a great deal of teacher support to one that offers more autonomy to the reader?

3. What, if any, are the differences between reading models used with struggling readers and reading models used with students who are not experiencing difficulties in learning to read?

4. If you were a newly hired teacher and were given the opportunity to purchase reading materials for your classroom, what factors would you consider?

Suggested Resources for Additional Reading

Bear, Donald R., Helman, Lori, Templeton, Shane, Invernizzi, Marcia, & Johnston, Francine. (2007). *Words Their Way with English Learners: Word Study for Phonics, Vocabulary, and Spelling Instruction.* Upper Saddle River, NJ: Merrill/Prentice Hall.

Carnine, Douglas W., Silbert, Jerry, Tarver, Sara G., Archer, Anita L., & Kame'enui, Edward J. (2009). *Direct Instruction* (5th ed.). Columbus, OH: Allyn & Bacon/Merrill.

Cunningham, Patricia M. (2009). *Phonics They Use: Words for Reading and Writing* (5th ed.). Columbus, OH: Allyn & Bacon/Merrill.

Fountas, Irene C., & Pinnell, Gay Su. (1996). *Guided Reading: Good First Teaching for All Children.* Portsmouth, NH: Heinemann.

Graves, Michael F., & Fitzgerald, Jill. (2004). *Scaffolded Reading Experiences for English Language Learners.* Norwood, MA: Christopher-Gordon.

Klingner, Janette K., Vaughn, Sharon, Dimino, Joseph, Schumm, Jeanne S., & Bryant, Diane. (2002). *Collaborative Strategic Reading.* Frederick, CO: Sopris West.

Nessel, Denise D., & Nixon, Carol N. (2008). *Using the Language Experience Approach with English Language Learners.* Thousand Oaks, CA: Corwin.

Oczkus, Lori D. (2003). *Reciprocal Teaching at Work: Strategies for Improving Reading Comprehension.* Newark, DE: International Reading Association.

Orehovec, Barbara, & Alley, Marybeth. (2003). *Revisiting Reading Workshop: Management, Mini-Lessons, and Strategies.* New York: Scholastic.

Raphael, Taffy E., Pardo, Laura S., & Highfield, Kathryn A. (2002). *Book Club: A Literature Based Curriculum.* Newark, DE: International Reading Association.

Before-Reading Strategies
Prereading and Planning

1 The Reading Process: The Task and the Reader

2 Assessment: Putting the Reader at the Center of the Reading Program

3 Framework for Developing a Reading Program for the Struggling Reader

4 Before-Reading Strategies: Prereading and Planning

This chapter will present reading strategies that the student can use during the prereading or planning stage of reading, such as identifying words, building background knowledge for the topic, learning new vocabulary, and having a purpose or goal for reading the material.

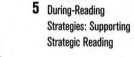

5 During-Reading Strategies: Supporting Strategic Reading

8 Families: Partnering with Parents

7 Attitude and Motivation: From Reluctant to Enthused Reader

6 After-Reading Strategies: Synthesizing and Extending

*C*hapter 3 provided a framework for developing a reading program for the struggling reader. This framework includes models ranging along a continuum of high to low teacher support in the areas of word recognition, fluency, and comprehension. A reading program also consists of a set of materials, and Chapter 3 explained how to select instructional reading materials. Instructional strategies comprise the third component of a reading program, and this chapter will focus on the first decision point for choosing

100

CHAPTER 4

*Before-Reading
Strategies:
Prereading and
Planning*

instructional strategies, which is the prereading and planning phase. Regardless of the model, you must decide what to teach about literacy before the student begins to read the material.

Two tactics to choosing instructional strategies are available. The first tactic is to look through files or index boxes of teaching strategies gathered from preservice and inservice coursework, education journals, magazines, websites, books, and other teachers. The second tactic, and the one presented in this chapter, is to connect pertinent and evidence-based strategies to the instructional model and materials.

Prereading and planning strategies involve building the student's knowledge of the words, sentence structures, vocabulary, and content so that the student has the background knowledge needed to read and comprehend the material with support from the teacher. Each of the reading word recognition and comprehension tasks described in Chapter 1 can be the aim of prereading instruction, though of course no one lesson would include them all. If the strategies are chosen well and taught appropriately, the student will be ready to interact meaningfully with the material.

The strategies presented in this chapter are summarized in Table 4.1. Indeed, all of the strategies are summarized in parallel fashion in this chapter and the next two chapters, with before-reading strategies presented in Table 4.1, during-reading strategies in Table 5.1, and after-reading strategies in Table 6.1. When you put these three figures together, you have a summary of evidence-based strategies for teaching word recognition, fluency, and comprehension.

Word Recognition before Reading

Four of the models discussed in Chapter 3 include a prereading step for word recognition (as summarized in Table 3.1).

In the Directed Reading Activity/Directed Reading Thinking Activity, new sight words are presented before reading. The Integrated Skills Method includes auditory awareness activities, daily letter sound and pattern decoding activities, and sight word instruction. In Early Steps, the Word Study step provides direct and systematic instruction in letter sounds and spelling patterns. Cooperative Integrated Reading and Composition includes the teaching of strategies for identifying unknown words. Not surprisingly, these four models are those at the higher-teacher-support end of the continuum.

The key difference between instruction in word recognition for students who are struggling with reading and other readers is the emphasis on explicit and systematic teaching of skills and strategies. Though all students may benefit from instruction in word recognition skills, for the struggling reader this instruction is essential. As Foorman and Torgesen (2003) noted, "The primary

TABLE 4.1 Instructional Strategies before Reading

Strategies	Reading Abilities		
	Word Recognition	*Fluency*	*Comprehension*
Phonemic awareness instruction	• Listening games • Rhyming activities • Syllable awareness • Detecting and identifying sounds activities • Blending, segmenting, and deleting sounds activities • Letter-sound activities		

Phonics, analogy, and structural analysis instruction	• Systematic phonics
	  • Most common sounds for consonants and vowels in vowel-consonant and consonant-vowel-consonant words with regular spelling
	  • Common generalizations
	  • Reading material with words spelled with the letters students just learned and creation of student sentences
	  • Consonant clusters and digraphs, vowel digraphs and diphthongs
	• Analogy instruction
	  • Word Study
	  • Making Words
	  • Using Words You Know
	  • Word-Building
	  • Cubes and Tiles
	  • Making and Writing Words and Making and Writing Words Using Letter Patterns
	  • Benchmark School Word ID Programs
	• Structural analysis instruction
	  • Roots, prefixes, and suffixes
	• Chunk Strategy		

(continued)

TABLE 4.1 continued

Strategies	Reading Abilities		
	Word Recognition	*Fluency*	*Comprehension*
Context strategy instruction	• Cloze activity		
Automatic word recognition instruction	• Flash card approach • Games • Word walls • Reading material at child's instructional level • Criteria for number and kind of sight words to preteach	• Practice until automatic word recognition	

Vocabulary instruction			• Definition-based approaches
			  • Traditional approach
			  • Possible Sentences
			  • Contextual Redefinition
			  • Rivet
			• Concept-based approaches
			  • Semantic Mapping
			  • Semantic Feature Analysis
			  • Concept Attainment
			  • Concept Wheel

Key concept instruction			• Reconciled Reading Lesson
			• ReQuest
			• Text Walk
			• K-W-L
			• PReP
			• Organizers and Overviews
			  • Previews
			  • Thematic Organizers
			  • Structured Overviews
			  • Anticipation Guides

Purpose setting			• Question or statement about key idea in upcoming passage

differences between instruction appropriate for all children in the classroom and that required by children at risk for reading difficulties are related to the manner in which instruction is provided. Specifically, instruction for children who have difficulties learning to read must be more explicit and comprehensive, more intensive, and more supportive than the instruction required by the majority of children" (p. 206).

103

CHAPTER 4

*Before-Reading
Strategies:
Prereading and
Planning*

If the model you selected for a group of students incorporates a step for word recognition, and your students need explicit instruction in some or even all of the tasks involved in word recognition (i.e., phonemic awareness, phonic analysis, analogy, structural analysis, context, and automatic word recognition), then you should consider the evidence-based strategies presented in this chapter for teaching these skills before reading. You should select those strategies that address the goals you identified in your assessment of each student so that each day you are teaching the word recognition skills needed by the students.

Some of the models dictate specific word recognition strategies, and others simply leave it open to you which strategies would be most appropriate. The strategies presented in the next sections have been shown to be effective, but that does not mean they are the only strategies available. From this corpus of strategies, you can add others that you learn about in the professional literature, from other teachers, and through professional development activities. Having a wide range of strategies available also allows you to vary the strategies you use. This is also true for fluency and comprehension strategies.

Teaching Phonemic Awareness

If assessment of the student's reading ability indicates that phonemic awareness is an area of weakness, then phonemic awareness instruction must comprise one component of the reading program. This was true of Marek. Given that Mr. Rumrill is using the Integrated Skills Method, which includes a step for auditory awareness activities, he has a lesson plan slot that incorporates daily opportunity for direct and systematic instruction in phonemic awareness. If Mr. Rumrill had selected a different model that did not incorporate a step for phonemic awareness, he could modify the model to add this step if he knew from his assessment that it was important to Marek's reading development.

No one model will be perfect for each reader, and certainly not perfect for each reading group. You need to be ready to modify the steps of the model you are using to meet the instructional needs of your students. Of course, if you notice that you have modified the model to the point at which it no longer matches the qualities found to be evidence based, you need to find a model that more closely matches the goals you identified from your assessment of the student and that you can, therefore, use with greater fidelity.

104

CHAPTER 4

*Before-Reading
Strategies:
Prereading and
Planning*

Converging evidence from the research (Adams, Foorman, Lundberg, & Beeler, 1998; Ehri et al., 2001; Smith, Simmons, & Kame'enui, 1998) indicates that the sequence of instruction in phonemic awareness should involve the following:

1. Phonological awareness activities
   - Listening games
   - Rhyming
   - Awareness of syllables
2. Simple and complex phonological units
   - Initial sounds: detecting and identifying
   - Final sounds: detecting and identifying
   - Medial sounds: detecting and identifying
   - Phoneme blending, segmenting, and deleting
   - Increasingly complex phonological units
3. Mapping sounds to letters and application to decoding words

The aspects of teaching that appear to be crucial in phonemic awareness instruction (Smith, Simmons, Gleason, et al., 2001; Smith et al., 1998) include the following:

- Direct teaching of phoneme detection and manipulation
- Teacher modeling
- Student producing specific sounds
- Support during initial learning with practice
- Short and regular instructional sessions of 15 to 20 minutes daily

Mr. Rumrill had targeted the Integrated Skills Method as the primary instructional model to use with Marek and the Language Experience Approach as a supplementary model. In the Integrated Skills Method, the Auditory Awareness step involves brief auditory awareness activities involving consonant sounds, vowel sounds, rhyming, or blending. Given the sequence of instruction in phonemic awareness, Mr. Rumrill will begin with listening games and then move to rhyming activities, word tasks, syllable awareness activities, sound activities for initial and final sounds and then medial sounds, phoneme blending and segmenting activities, and phoneme deletion activities. Once Marek is successful with these phonemic awareness activities, Mr. Rumrill will use his teaching time to move to the Letter Sounds step in the model and focus on activities that connect letters and sounds. The Integrated Skills Model is a 20- to 30-minute daily lesson that consists of nine steps; however, in the first few weeks, Mr. Rumrill plans to focus on phonemic awareness activities almost exclusively during instructional time in order to assure that Marek has this skill base before including the steps of pattern decoding, sight words, sentences, games, and spelling and writing. However,

Marek is also involved in writing Language Experience stories as well as other literacy related activities, such as Mr. Rumrill's read-aloud time, during the school day so his literacy instruction will not be limited to one aspect of reading and writing development.

Though phonemic awareness activities can be integrated into other instructional activities, the need for systematic and explicit teaching of these phonemic awareness skills emphasizes the importance of short but focused instructional daily time given to these activities. The following are examples of activities in the sequential order of skills that is currently considered best practice in building phonemic awareness. However, ensuring that all the activities shown to correlate with early reading achievement are carried out is a daunting task for the teacher. Indeed, Smith et al. (2001) found that four commercial basal reading programs published in the early 1990s failed to integrate critical dimensions of phonemic awareness and did not provide sufficient tasks, materials, or teacher support. With this in mind, you might consider one of the published phonemic awareness programs as central or supplementary to your phonemic awareness activities.

105

CHAPTER 4
*Before-Reading
Strategies:
Prereading and
Planning*

Listening Games

The purpose of listening games is to engage students in listening attentively and analytically to everyday sounds. Typical activities include tape recordings of common sounds such as birds chirping, water dripping, leaves blowing, babies crying, dogs barking, telephones ringing, and jet engines roaring. Everyday environmental sounds can also be generated in the classroom, such as closing a door, cutting paper with scissors, eating a crunchy food, turning on the water tap, and sharpening a pencil. Adams et al. (1998) suggested that the activities be sequenced from first identifying the kind of sound, to identifying a sequence of sounds, to identifying the source of the sound, and finally to identifying one sound among several presented simultaneously. For students who are deaf or hard of hearing, it is crucial to be aware of the relationship between their degree of hearing loss and the sounds they are capable of discerning.

Rhyming Activities

Rhyming involves differentiating words that have the same ending sounds. It is considered one of the easiest of phonemic awareness skills. Rhyming activities for younger children typically involve nursery rhymes, jump-rope chants, rhyming books, poems, and songs. For older students, rhyming activities can involve song lyrics, raps, and rhymed poetry. Rhyming objects and pictures can be sorted, students can be asked to complete the last word in rhyming lines, provide examples of words that rhyme with a target word, and distinguish the one of a group of objects or words that does not rhyme.

106

CHAPTER 4

*Before-Reading
Strategies:
Prereading and
Planning*

Syllable Awareness Activities

Phonological awareness involves being aware of word syllables. Syllable awareness activities typically include clapping the syllables of names during daily opening activities and words during storybook reading and games. Cunningham (2009) suggested following up clapping activities with writing the words on differently sized sentence strips to show the students that a word with more syllables, or beats, often takes more letters.

Detecting and Identifying Sounds Activities

Simple phonological activities involve detecting and identifying initial, final, and medial sounds. Letter weeks that highlight words and names that begin with a particular letter each week, looking through magazines or picture cards for pictures that begin or end with the same sound, distinguishing an object or picture that does not belong because it does not have the same target sound, and saying words and asking the students to identify the sounds at the beginning, middle, or end are common activities for young children. Tongue twisters are popular with older students as are guessing games such as asking them to guess a word based on clues as in, "a food that is lots of little pieces and is white and begins with *r* or ends in *ice.*" Drawing the students' attention to how their lips and tongue make the sound appears to be helpful in making a connection between auditory perception and kinesthetic movement for each sound (Gunning, 2006).

Blending, Segmenting, and Deleting Sounds Activities

Elkonin boxes, sometimes referred to as sound boxes, are used to help students segment words into sounds (Elkonin, 1973). An Elkonin box includes a picture of a word alongside boxes representing the number of sounds in the word. The boxes are drawn on paper. As the student says the word, one sound at a time, he or she places a mark on or token into the appropriate box. For example, for a word with three sounds such as *man*, the student would mark or move a token into the first box for the initial sound of *m*, second box for the medial sound of *a*, and third box for the final sound of *n*. Gradually, the picture cards and tokens are removed and the student is asked how many sounds are in the word and which is first, second, and so on.

Onset-rime activities are intended to focus the student's attention on phoneme blending, segmenting, and deleting. Activities for young children include using pieces of paper to make word chains, with onsets on half the pieces and rimes on the other half; creating egg words using plastic eggs by writing onsets on one side of each egg and onsets on the other side; or asking the children to think of words with the same onset or rime as the teacher's example and listing those on a chart, whiteboard, or projected computer screen (Fox, 2008). Activities for older students can include tongue twister books and mystery bags, which involve placing an object in a bag and providing clues related to the word's onset or rime (Gunning, 2006).

One activity for blending is called *Sandpaper Words* (Fox, 2008). The teacher creates words using letters cut from fine-grade pieces of sandpaper. The teacher models and then asks the student to trace his or her finger from one letter to the next, saying the sound of each letter and blending to the next letter as the finger glides from one letter to the next. At first, the teacher's voice leads the student's, but as the student gains skill, the teacher's voice aligns with the student's until the student is able to carry out the activity without the teacher's voice.

Another activity for blending is a guessing game in which the teacher either asks the students to guess a word the teacher is thinking, such as the name of a color, or to guess the name of an object hidden in a bag (Cunningham, 2009). For blending, the teacher says the sounds as in *r-e-d* or *r-ed*, or the teacher can say either the onset or rime and ask the students to guess the word.

There is some disagreement whether sound deletion is more difficult or easier than blending and segmenting (Adams et al., 1998; Cooper & Kiger, 2009; Reutzel & Cooter, 2007). Sound deletion activities often involve sound substitution. In one type of activity, teachers ask the students to delete or substitute sounds in familiar rhymes, songs, and story refrains even when the deletion or substitution creates a nonsense word, as in the Name Game Song in which the first letter of the name is replaced with a *B*, *F*, or *M* (*Barbara Barbara Bo Arbara; Banana Fanna Fo Farbara; Fe Fi Mo Marbara; Barbara!*). In another type of activity, the teacher calls out a word and asks the students to substitute a sound to make a new word.

The *Making Words* activity involves the students in looking for patterns in words (Cunningham, 2003). The students are given the letters of a secret word in mixed-up order and asked to make 10–15 words, some of which the teacher knows are easy and hard, some of which are morphemically related, and some of which are rhymes. The teacher gives them the first, short word and then guides them to add and substitute letters to make the other words. In the next step of the lesson, the teacher asks the students to identify morphemically related words or words with the same root, prefix, or suffix. The teacher then asks them to sort the words that rhyme. In the final step, the students are given new words and asked to place them in groups under the words with which they rhyme.

Letter-Sound Activities

Phonemic awareness enables the reader to distinguish the phonemes in spoken words. The student must first be aware of the individual phonemes or sounds in order to phonologically code written words. Letter-sound activities bridge phonemic awareness with phonic analysis, enabling the student to see the relationship between letters and sounds. As Adams et al. (1998) note, letter-sound activities prepare students for phonic analysis instruction by introducing the concept that each phoneme is represented by a letter or letters.

Many of the activities used for identifying, blending, segmenting, and deleting sounds are appropriate for letter-sound activities by including the

108

CHAPTER 4

*Before-Reading
Strategies:
Prereading and
Planning*

additional step of focusing the student's attention on the written word. *Mediated scaffolding* is a strategy for moving students from phonemic awareness to decoding words through phonic analysis (Carnine et al., 2004; Coyne, Kame'enui, & Carnine, 2007). From Scaffold One to Four, the lesson structure evolves from the teacher's saying the sounds in a word while pointing to each letter (Model), to the student's saying the sounds in a word while the teacher is pointing to each letter (Overt Sound Out), to the student's saying the sounds "in his or her head" while the teacher is pointing to each letter (Internal Sound Out), to the student's sounding out the word independently while the teacher is pointing to the word (Whole Word Reading). The transfer of responsibility from Scaffold One to Four takes place over a series of lessons.

Teaching Phonics, Analogy, and Structural Analysis

If assessment of the student's reading ability indicates that phonic analysis, analogy, and/or structural analysis are areas of weakness, then instruction in these word recognition strategies must comprise one component of daily reading instruction. As you know from the assessments of the case study children in Chapter 2, Marek, Maria, and Adani showed difficulties with these word recognition strategies.

In addition to difficulty related to phonemic awareness, Marek showed problems with phonic analysis and analogy for word recognition. His ability to use structural analysis was not determined during the assessment. The Integrated Skills Method that Mr. Rumrill may use as Marek's primary model includes a step for Pattern Decoding before reading, which will provide opportunity to focus on phonic analysis and analogy. It also includes a step for Sentences, during which Mr. Rumrill can provide instruction in letter-sound components and pattern decoding. The Language Experience Approach that Mr. Rumrill is planning to use as a supplementary approach does not offer a step during the prereading or planning stage but does allow for word recognition strategies to be taught during and after reading, which will be discussed in the next two chapters.

Maria's assessment showed that although she relied heavily on phonic analysis, she had difficulty with medial sounds and she did not appear to use analogy and structural analysis. Maria's teacher, Mr. Ginnetti, planned to use the Directed Reading Thinking Activity as the primary instructional model. Given that the special education teacher was emphasizing phonics and that sight word instruction is one of the prereading steps in the DRTA, Mr. Ginnetti decided to use this step in the model to provide opportunity to focus Maria's attention when presenting new sight words on the letter-sound relationships, analogies, and roots and affixes that the special education teacher was presenting in pull-out instruction.

Adani's goals included concentrated instruction in phonic analysis, analogy, and word analysis. In Early Steps, the model that Ms. Edberg chose to use with Adani, the Word Study step provides direct, systematic study of letter sounds and spelling patterns isolated from the context of actual reading. In the model, the Word Study step comes after the rereading of a previously read book and before the steps involving writing and reading a new book. Thus, it can be viewed as a postreading phase when viewed from the perspective of previously read material and as a prereading phase when viewed from the perspective of new material.

Phonic Analysis Instruction

Phonic analysis has been variously described as using letter-sound relationships, grapheme-phoneme relationships, sound-symbol relationships, and sound-spelling relationships to identify an unknown word. It has been referred to as the glue that holds sight words in short term memory because letter-sound correspondences and spelling patterns are already secured in memory (Ehri, 1992; Share, 1999).

Systematic phonics involves the delineation and explicit teaching of a sequential set of phonic elements. Systematic phonics typically emphasizes a synthetic approach in which students are taught to map letters and letter combinations to sounds and to pronounce the word by blending the sounds together ("sounding out") to form a recognizable word in the student's vocabulary. *Incidental phonics*, sometimes referred to as *embedded phonics*, involves highlighting phonics elements opportunistically as they appear in text. Incidental phonics typically emphasizes an analytic approach in which students are taught first to recognize the word as a whole ("sight word") and then to analyze the letter-sound relationships in the word.

Research indicates that a systematic phonics approach is more effective than an incidental phonics approach for young readers, and even more so for students who struggle with reading (Pressley, Roehrig, Bogner, Raphael, & Dolezal, 2002). Certainly systematic phonics instruction is essential. But you can do both by explicitly teaching phonics skills before reading and reinforcing these skills incidentally when encountering an unknown word during reading.

Lists of phonics rules are incorporated into all introductory reading texts, and most states have developed scope-and-sequence charts as part of state expectations for literacy instruction. Commercially and locally developed lists of reading skills almost always include the following as the most important phonics patterns to be taught (Hendricks & Rinsky, 2007; Oldrieve, 1997; Reutzel & Cooter, 2009): (a) beginning consonant sounds in words (most consistent consonants are *b, d, h, l, m, n, p, r, t, v*); (b) the C rule (this letter does not have a sound of its own but rather typically has the *k* sound, or hard *c* sound, when followed by *a, o,* or *u* and the *s,* or soft *c* sound, when followed by *e, i,* or *y*); (c) the G rule (this letter sound follows the same rules as the *c* sound); (d) CVC pattern (when a vowel appears between two consonants, it usually has a short vowel sound) and CVVC pattern (when two vowels come together, referred to as a vowel digraph, the long sound of the first vowel is usually used; sometimes described as "when two vowels go a-walking, the

110

CHAPTER 4

*Before-Reading
Strategies:
Prereading and
Planning*

first vowel does the talking"); (e) final silent *E* (when two vowels appear in a vowel-consonant-vowel pattern and the final vowel is an *e*, the first vowel is usually long and the final *e* is silent); (f) CV pattern (in two-letter words or two-letter syllables beginning with a consonant, the vowel sound is usually long); (g) *R*- and *L*-controlled vowels (when vowels appear before the letter *r* and *l*, the *r* and *l* control the sound of the vowel); (h) diphthongs, blends, and clusters (two vowels, two consonants, and vowel-consonant combinations often produce a sound different from the vowels or consonants individually); and (i) schwa (the letters *a*, *e*, and *o* sometimes produce a sound that sounds like *uh* in English).

Though there is currently no compelling research evidence to indicate which constituent elements of phonics should be taught sequentially, the following guidelines seem to make sense based on what is currently known (Chard & Osborn, 1999; Gunning, 2006; Torgeson et al., 2001):

1. Most common sounds for consonants and vowels in vowel-consonant and consonant-vowel-consonant words with regular spelling should be presented first. Also, letters that are visually or auditorily dissimilar and more useful letters should be presented earlier. As sounds are presented that involve variability in spelling patterns, common generalizations should be taught and, rather than teaching exceptions to the "rules," flexibility in applying generalizations should be encouraged.

2. Words spelled with the letters students have just learned should appear in their reading material and the students should create their own sentences with these words. As they encounter words they do not recognize, the students should be encouraged to break the words into syllables and the syllables into letter-sound parts, and then to blend the parts to pronounce meaningful words.

3. *Consonant clusters* (pairs of consonant letters that blend together such as the *bl* in *black* and the *st* in *stop*), *consonant digraphs* (pairs of consonant letters that represent one sound such as *sh* in *shake* and *th* in *think* and *the*), *vowel digraphs* (pairs of vowel letters that represent one sound such as the *oo* in *shook*), and *vowel diphthongs* (blend of two vowel sounds or a vowel and semivowel sound such as *oy* in *boy* and *ow* in *howl*) should be added as the students gain skill and words with these sounds appear in their reading material.

Analogy Instruction

Whether analogy instruction is referred to as onset-rime instruction, analogy phonics, or spelling-based approach, the principle for word recognition is essentially the same. The student is taught to recognize an unfamiliar word by connecting it to a familiar word with the same rime but different onset. The student uses phonics to identify the onset and then blends it with the known rime.

Word Study is one analogy strategy (Bear et al., 2007; Bear, Invernizzi, Templeton, & Johnston, 2008). In Word Study, readers examine and categorize words through several types of sorting activities that draw their attention to the patterns in English. Bear and his associates identify three kinds of sorts and note that they are as effective for English language learners as for students whose native language is English. The three main types of sorts are sound sorts, pattern sorts, and concept or meaning sorts. In sound sorts, the students compare commonalities and differences in the sounds they hear when pronouncing words. In pattern sorts, they compare patterns in letters and letter groups. In concept or meaning sorts, the students compare patterns in meaning-spelling relationships. Sorts can be carried out as (a) teacher-directed (the teacher selects the categories and explains why each picture or word belongs in a particular category) or student-centered sorts (the students create their own categories with known words); (b) guess my category sorts (the teacher demonstrates a sort and the students figure out the label for the category) or brainstorming (the teacher provides a category and the students brainstorm as many examples as possible); and (c) writing sorts (the teacher calls out words and the students write them into categories) or word and picture hunts (the students search for examples of categories in books, magazines, and in the environment). Speed sorting is done after the students have gained accuracy with the words and the goal is to sort as quickly as possible.

The *Making Words* strategy described earlier for phonemic awareness is also used as an analogy strategy. When used for analogy instruction, the step in which the students sort the rhyming words is particularly important (Cunningham, 2009; Cunningham & Cunningham, 1992). The students sort the words by beginning sounds or onsets, and then they sort the words into rhymes. At that point, the teacher adds new rhyming words and the students use the rhymes to decode them. The teacher then says new rhyming words and the students use the known rhyming words to spell the new ones. Finally, all the words are lined up under their rhyming category.

Using Words You Know was developed by Cunningham (2009) to guide students in using known words to decode and spell other words. The teacher provides a set of words, each in its own column, which the students write on their own papers. Each word has a different rime, which the teacher points out. In the first activity, the teacher presents words on index cards and the students write them in the column of words with the same rime (and also the same spelling pattern). In the second activity, the teacher says the words and the students again write them in the correct column. In the last activity, the teacher shows the students some longer words and the students say them, spell them, and add them to the correct column.

The *Word Building* lesson developed by Gunning (2006) incorporates six steps. Step one is *Adding the Onset*. The teacher writes a vowel, such as *o*, says a word, such as *go*, and asks the students to identify the name of the letter that is needed. This is repeated for five or six words ending with the same rime. Step two is *Adding the Rime*. This step is the same as the previous one

112

....

CHAPTER 4

*Before-Reading
Strategies:
Prereading and
Planning*

except the teacher writes the consonant onset. Step three is *Providing Mixed Practice* and involves adding word patterns from previous lessons. Step four is *Introducing the Model Word* which is a permanent chart in the classroom depicting model words for onsets and rimes. Each time a new pattern is taught, a model word is added to the chart. Step five, *Guided Practice*, involves practicing new patterns in sentences and step six, *Application*, involves reading a passage containing several words that fit the target pattern.

Several other activities capitalize on onset-rime patterns. For younger children, onsets and rimes can be practiced with cubes and tiles (Vacca et al., 2009). For older students who are struggling readers, *Making and Writing Words* and *Making and Writing Words Using Letter Patterns* is a variation of the Making Words strategy. In Making and Writing Words (Rasinski, 1999a), the student uses a blank form for writing letters and words instead of using cards preprinted with letters. In Making and Writing Words Using Letter Patterns (Rasinski, 1999b), onsets, rimes, prefixes, suffixes, and other more complex word patterns are used and the target word is always a multisyllabic word.

The *Benchmark School Word Identification* programs (Gaskins, 2000; Gaskins, Ehri, Cress, O'Hara, & Donnelly, 1996–1997) were developed specifically for students with difficulties learning to read. They are designed to be used as one aspect of a literacy program that should also include guided reading, strategy lessons, independent reading, writing, and teacher read-aloud. The programs are divided into Beginning, Transition, and Intermediate levels plus a program for middle and high school students who are struggling readers. The basis of the program is a set of key words that represent the most common rimes in English. These key words are used to decode unknown words. Students are taught to follow the process of looking for spelling patterns within the word, thinking of known words (from the key words they have been taught) that have the same spelling pattern as those in the unknown word, and then to use the known words to decode the unknown word.

Structural Analysis Instruction

The research on structural analysis instruction is highly limited and some of these studies focus on structural analysis as a vocabulary tool rather than a word recognition tool (Baumann et al., 2002; Nagy, Diakidoy, & Anderson, 1993). Indeed, the two functions often go hand-in-hand with the reader for whom new words in print are also new vocabulary words.

Durkin (1976) considered structural analysis to be a natural accompaniment to phonic analysis because considering the word's structure enables the student to identify the root, and once the root is identified, the reader can apply letter-sound relationships to figure out the word's pronunciation, thus triggering it as a word the student knows. If the reader does not know the root word, the other structural information, such as the prefix *un* in *unsafe* and the suffix *s* in *friends*, may provide clues to its meaning.

Structural analysis instruction involves focusing the reader's attention on morphemes. As explained in Chapter 1, every word consists of at least one free morpheme. Compound words have two or more free morphemes and many words include bound morphemes as prefixes and suffixes. The strategies for teaching onsets and rimes discussed previously are also effective for teaching structural analysis.

Focusing on a selected list of common prefixes and suffixes is recommended practice (Almasi, 2003). The most frequently appearing prefixes are *un, re, dis,* and *in* (meaning "not") and the most frequently appearing suffixes are *s, ed, ing, ly,* and *er.* Activities can include creating a chart of prefixes and suffixes and adding words under each as they appear in reading, revising sentences based on adding and taking away prefixes and suffixes, and playing games such as Concentration with prefixes and roots (Crawley & Merritt, 2000).

Fox (2008) used the term *Chunk Strategy* to describe the reader's use of meaningful units to assist in pronouncing and understanding the meaning of words during reading. Chunks include prefixes, suffixes, Greek and Latin roots, compound words, and contractions. Flexibility in chunking words is key to the approach, so Fox suggested that students be taught to chunk, rechunk and reblend, and then try analogy or letter-sound relationships.

Teaching Context Strategies

The use of context during reading has been found to be a strategy more often relied on by poorer readers. Although skilled readers use context to facilitate comprehension, they tend to rely on phonic analysis and analogy rather than context when encountering an unknown word in text (Ehri, 1991; Juel, 1991).

Adani, Marek, and Maria all showed difficulties with using context for word recognition. Adani rarely used semantic or syntactic cues from context to identify unknown words though she benefited from brief lessons during the assessment that Ms. Edberg conducted. During Marek's assessment, he often provided a semantically unacceptable word when miscuing and found the cloze task to be very frustrating. Although Maria did not appear to use context for word recognition during the assessment of her reading abilities, it was not a skill that Mr. Ginnetti had decided to target right away because some of her other apparent difficulties and strengths warranted different instruction.

Both Adani and Marek would benefit from instruction in using context for word recognition; however, the instructional models their teachers are using either do not offer or offer limited opportunity for teaching contextual analysis before reading. (The Early Steps model that Ms. Edberg is using with Adani includes a step for teaching letter sounds and spelling patterns but no step for teaching context skills. In the Integrated Skills Method, the Sentences step provides an opportunity for Mr. Rumrill to provide instruction in the use of context, though with five or six sentence cards daily, the amount of instruction is clearly limited.)

114

CHAPTER 4

*Before-Reading
Strategies:
Prereading and
Planning*

The cloze activity can be done any time during the day to teach and reinforce the use of context skills. To create the material, the teacher systematically deletes words from a passage that the student has not previously read. The system that the teacher uses depends on the goal for that particular lesson, but common systems include deleting every nth word. Usually every 5th word is deleted; however, Gipe (2006) noted that although this is appropriate when cloze is used as an assessment technique, every 10th or 15th word is more appropriate when used as a teaching technique. An alternative to deleting every so many words is to delete every word of a particular syntactic class—usually a noun, verb, adjective, or adverb.

When creating a cloze, first and last sentences are generally excluded. For each omitted word, lines of equal length, a line that represents the word length, or dashes to represent the number of letters in the word can be placed in lieu of the word.

Maze is a variation of cloze in which choices are listed, usually three words of the same syntactic class. Another variation is to provide clues, such as the first letter or letter blend, final letter or suffix, all the consonants, all the vowels, or other pattern. For younger or less skilled readers, cloze can be introduced as an oral activity (Leu & Kinzer, 2003).

When context is taught as a stand-alone activity such as cloze, the key is to focus attention on the question that students should ask themselves during reading when identifying an unknown word: "Does this make sense?" For the struggling reader, this question is key to applying all of the word recognition strategies successfully. If the word makes sense in the context of the reading passage, it means that the student is focusing on comprehension, which, of course, is the goal of being able to read each word accurately.

Teaching Sight Words

The research on the importance of phonemic awareness and phonic analysis in learning to read, and the national attention on including these skills in reading instruction, has tended to obscure the role of automaticity in word recognition. All of the strategies intended to assist students in figuring out the identity of unknown words are designed to lead ultimately to enabling them to recognize instantly almost every word they encounter by sight. As Samuels (2002b) noted, "Automatic word recognition allows the reader to concentrate on constructing meaning from the text" (p. 42).

Although some educators use the term *sight words* to refer exclusively to high-frequency words that are taught to readers as "whole words," that is not how the term is used here. Sight word instruction refers to teaching students to become automatic in the recognition of words so that when these words are encountered in reading, they are read quickly and accurately. The goal is for most of the words encountered to be "sight" words because the more attention the reader gives to using phonics, analogy, structural analysis, and context, the less attention is available for comprehension (Samuels, 2002a). If you think about how many words you actually have to decode when you read the newspaper or a book versus how many you read instantly, you will realize how powerful automaticity is to your reading ability and enjoyment.

Automatic word recognition is an instructional goal for Maria, Adani, and Marek. For Maria, Mr. Ginnetti plans to combine sight word instruction alongside vocabulary instruction by teaching the written word and its meaning simultaneously. Sight word instruction is one of the prereading steps in the Directed Reading Thinking Activity model that Mr. Ginnetti is planning to use. Given that Maria is reading instructionally at the second-grade level, Mr. Ginnetti will preteach five to six words each day that Maria will encounter in the text. When presenting each word, he will point out letter-sound relationships, analogies, and roots and affixes that are relevant to the word and, whenever possible, connect to his other lessons in phonics, analogies, and structure (in other words, he will combine systematic and incidental phonics instruction). He will also discuss the meaning, bring in pictures or props, or provide an experience in advance to help Maria understand the concept of each word. He is planning to use the word in a sentence or ask Maria to think of a sentence so that the meaning of the word is further clarified. The word cards will be flashed a few times for speed and accuracy, first in the order in which he presented them initially and then shuffled. With only five or six words, these activities should take no more than 10 minutes, which will allow Maria to engage in reading some or the entire story that day because preteaching sight words is most effective when the student immediately encounters the words in connected text.

Ms. Edberg is planning to use the Early Steps model with Adani. In the first step, Reading, Adani will reread a book that Ms. Edberg introduced the previous day. The goal is fluency and comprehension, which focuses directly on automatic word recognition. For the second step, Word Study, Ms. Edberg plans to follow up the explicit, systematic study of letter sounds and spelling patterns with brief practice in recognizing the new words automatically so that when Adani encounters them in the new story, she will recognize them instantly.

The Integrated Skills Method that Mr. Rumrill plans to use with Marek includes a step for teaching sight words. Nine words are chosen based on the sequence of sight words plus several words that Marek will need for reading an upcoming story and words that Mr. Rumrill will need for composing sentences. Mr. Rumrill will show these words on cards several times, providing the word if Marek does not remember it. In the Sentences step, Marek will read the sentences until fluency is attained, thus assuring automatic recognition of the sight words included in the sentences. Sight word learning is again reinforced in the Games step and yet again in the Spelling and Writing steps.

The *Flash Card* approach is the approach typically used to teach and practice sight word recognition. In this approach, sight words are written on cards, as Ms. Edberg and Mr. Rumrill did, and shown word by word, first for scrutiny and then for increasing speed. Manzo and Manzo (2008) developed the New Eclectic Sight Word Strategy as a step-by-step approach. First, the

116

CHAPTER 4

*Before-Reading
Strategies:
Prereading and
Planning*

teacher presents a high-frequency word on a flash card and asks the students to look at it and then say it together. The teacher responds, "That's correct!" Second, the teacher asks the students to say the word five times while looking at the flash card. The teacher praises them and asks them to say it louder with each reading. Third, the teacher shows the students three other word cards and tells them to say, "No!" when they see a word that is not the target word and to say the target word in a whisper. Fourth, the teacher asks the students to close their eyes and picture the written word, say it in a whisper, spell it aloud together, and then write it in the air while saying each letter. Fifth, the teacher asks the students to describe the written word (not the word's meaning). Finally, the teacher asks the students to say it again loudly. For the rest of the day and for homework, the students are asked to find the word in the materials they encounter.

Sight word instruction lends itself to many games, such as Concentration, Bingo, Lotto, Go Fish, Hangman, Wheel of Fortune, and Dominoes, that serve to reinforce automatic word recognition. Reinforcement activities also include student *word banks*, which the student can return to again and again for review, writing, and practice at home (Bender & Larkin, 2003). The students can also practice peer to peer, each using their own words if a picture or sentence on the reverse side of the card gives a clue to the word's identity for the peer tutor.

Word walls are used for word study and so the strategy cuts across all of the word recognition skills (Wagstaff, 1999). It seems particularly useful for assisting with sight word recognition because the words on the wall serve as a constant reminder to the students. Word walls are typically developed as columns of words on large sheets of paper displayed prominently. An ABC word wall would focus on words that begin with a certain letter, phonic walls on words with certain letter sounds, pattern walls on words with certain onsets and rimes, and high-frequency walls for words that appear most frequently in written language. Cunningham (2009) recommends seven types of word walls as having the highest utility: (a) most frequent words, (b) words for each consonant, (c) most common blends, (d) most common vowel-spelling patterns, (e) most common rimes, (f) most common contractions, and (g) words that students use frequently in their writing. Though word walls are typically used with younger readers, they have been used successfully with middle and high school readers (Staires, 2007; Whitaker, 2008).

There is an important relationship between the sight words you preteach and the instructional material the students will be reading. As discussed in Chapter 3, the student's reading abilities develop as a result of learning to read material that he or she could not read independently. These materials are aimed at the reader's zone of proximal development. It is through support from the teacher or in collaboration with a more capable peer, which some authors refer to as scaffolding or mediated scaffolding (e.g., Dickson, Collins, Simmons, & Kame'enui, 1998), that the student is able to read these materials and to develop the knowledge and skills to progress as a strategic reader. The rule of thumb is that instructional material contains 5 to 10 unknown words for every 100 running words (independent material contains 2 to 5 unknown words and frustration material contains more than 10). Conversely, the student should be able to read automatically 90 to 95 of every 100 running words for instructional material. Given the student's knowledge of previously learned sight words, the teacher should be able preteach enough sight words (2 to 3 for less skilled readers and up to 8 for more skilled readers) so that the student will be able to read 90 to 95 running words quickly and effortlessly.

In other words, the material to be read should contain a few words that the teacher can preteach as sight words and still contain a few more words per running 100 for which the student will need to apply phonic analysis, analogy, and context strategies during reading. Material that is described as predictable (because words and phrases are repeated) and books as decodable (because new words are presented systematically) can be particularly facilitative for sight word learning.

The most important criterion for choosing the words to be presented for sight word instruction is that the words appear in the reading material to be read that day. In addition, high-frequency words, words crucial to the key ideas in the material, words with phonic irregularities, words the students will likely find interesting, and words that contain a pattern or structure that will enable the student to read other words in the material are also considerations in choosing daily sight words.

Comprehension before Reading

Most of the models discussed in Chapter 3 include a prereading step for comprehension. The two that do not, Book Club and Reading Workshop, are those at the low-teacher-support end of the continuum. In the Directed Reading Activity/Directed Reading Thinking Activity, the Concept Development step includes activating and building the student's knowledge of topic and teaching new vocabulary. The DRA/DRTA also includes a Purpose Setting step prior to the student reading each text segment. In Early Steps, the New Reading step begins with the teacher's introducing a new book and encouraging the student to predict the main idea by using pictures, title, and other cues. Reading Recovery similarly includes a teacher introduction through discussion and looking at the pictures in the Reading a New Book step. The Language Experience Approach is based on the student's own background experience, usually an experience created by the teacher. During the Teacher-Led Reading Groups activity of the Cooperative Integrated Reading and Composition model, the teacher sets a purpose for the reading, reviews old vocabulary, and introduces new vocabulary. Before reading, the students also predict what the story will be about from the title and vocabulary they just learned. The first of the four steps in Reciprocal Teaching is Predicting, in

118
....

CHAPTER 4

*Before-Reading
Strategies:
Prereading and
Planning*

which the students predict what will happen in the upcoming passage. Guided Reading lessons begin with the teacher's introducing the book by having the students look at the cover, read the title and author's name, and talk about the topic. The teacher also briefly discusses vocabulary words crucial to understanding the story.

In addition to the specific prereading activity incorporated into the model you are using, you can add other activities that focus on comprehension skills needed by your struggling reader, as well as the other students in their reading groups.

Teaching Vocabulary

In spite of the direct relationship between vocabulary knowledge and reading comprehension and the positive relationship between vocabulary instruction and comprehension, no particular instructional method or combination of methods has been found to be the most effective for teaching vocabulary (Graves, 1986; National Reading Panel, 2000; Stahl & Fairbanks, 1986). The common instructional denominator for students with weak vocabularies appears to be strong and systematic educational support that is designed to help them become independent word learners (Baker, Simmons, & Kame'enui, 1998).

Ellison's difficulty with vocabulary showed up during the assessment and in the diagnostic reading lesson that Mrs. Hong conducted, which showed that he benefited from explicit vocabulary instruction. Mrs. Hong was considering three instructional models to use with Ellison. The Cooperative Integrated Reading and Composition model provides a step for reviewing old vocabulary and introducing new vocabulary. The model does not specify the particular strategies the teacher should use but does presume that instruction will assure understanding of all word meanings before reading. Reciprocal Teaching offers no step for preteaching vocabulary; however, the Preview step in Collaborative Strategic Reading, which is a modification of Reciprocal Teaching, does provide an opening to teach new vocabulary when the students scan the material for clues about the topic.

Maria's assessment showed that vocabulary difficulty was negatively affecting her comprehension and, as with Ellison, she benefited from explicit vocabulary instruction. The Directed Reading Thinking Activity model that Mr. Ginnetti had chosen to use with her provided a step for vocabulary instruction as part of the Concept Development step. The model, however, does not stipulate the way vocabulary should be taught, leaving the choice of strategy to the teacher.

As you consider the kinds of teaching activities for vocabulary development, it is helpful to start with determining how closely the components of the activity match with what is known about instruction that works in building vocabulary.

Three qualities of effective vocabulary instruction have been identified (Blachowicz, Fisher, Ogle, & Watts-Taffe, 2006; Kibby, 1995b; National Reading Panel, 2000):

1. *Integration* involves relating new words to the reader's background knowledge.
2. *Repetition* involves providing the reader more than one encounter with the meanings and uses of new words.
3. *Meaningful use* involves developing rich conceptual frameworks for new words and providing opportunities for the reader to encounter new words in authentic text.

Two approaches to vocabulary instruction slot well into the prereading phase of a reading lesson: definition-based and concept-based approaches.

Definition-Based Approaches

Definition-based approaches commonly take two forms. In one form, the students are asked to look up the definitions of a list of words in the dictionary, copy them, and write a sentence for each word. In the other form, the teacher briefly discusses the meaning of the new words in an upcoming reading selection. Studies have shown that definition-based approaches can be effective when ample time is spent in teacher-student discussion about the new vocabulary (McKeown, 1993). It is through discussion that the word's meaning can be integrated with the student's background knowledge and that terminology unfamiliar in the dictionary definition per se can be explained. When definition-based approaches are followed by immediately encountering these words in the text selection and presenting reinforcement activities after reading (which will be discussed in Chapters 5 and 6), then the approach also incorporates repetition and meaningful use.

Variations of definition-based approaches include Possible Sentences, Contextual Redefinition, and Rivet. *Possible Sentences* involves teaching new concepts so that they are related to each other and to the overall topic of the text (Jansen & Duffelmeyer, 1996; Moore & Moore, 1986; Stahl & Kapinus, 1991). The teacher chooses six to eight words that would likely cause difficulty for the students and four to six words that are likely to be familiar to the students and writes them on the board, chart paper, overhead projector, or computer/LCD projector. The teacher provides a brief definition or asks if anyone knows a definition. The students are then asked to think of possible sentences in the passage that they will be reading, using at least two of the words in each sentence. The teacher writes their sentences on the board whether they are accurate or not. When all the words have been included in at least one sentence and the students have no further ideas, the students read the material. After reading, they discuss each sentence and decide if it could

120

CHAPTER 4

*Before-Reading
Strategies:
Prereading and
Planning*

or could not be true based on what they have just read. Sentences that could not be true are modified to make them true.

Developed by Bean, Readence, and Baldwin (2008), the strategy of *Contextual Redefinition* involves selecting unfamiliar words from an upcoming passage; presenting each word and asking the students to hypothesize about the definition based on familiarity with the whole or parts of the word; presenting each word to the students within a sentence that is either taken directly from the passage or contains enough contextual information to enable the students to glean some meaning from the word; asking the students to refine their original hypotheses about the meaning; and, finally, directing them to look the word up in the dictionary to verify its definition.

In the *Rivet* activity (Cunningham et al., 1999), the teacher begins by creating a numbered list and then drawing lines next to each number representing the number of letters each word has. The students are asked to do the same on their own papers. The teacher then fills in the letters of the first word, pausing after each letter and asking the students to guess what the word is. When a student has guessed correctly, the teacher asks him or her to finish spelling it, which the teacher does on the board and the students do on their papers. If a student has guessed incorrectly, the teacher continues writing letters until someone guesses correctly. The same procedure is carried out for the rest of the words. When all of the words have been correctly guessed, the students are asked to use them to predict what will happen in the upcoming passage.

Concept-Based Approaches

Concept-based approaches are grounded on the assumption that new knowledge is gained from finding new relationships in old knowledge and from relating new information to old information. Research indicates that concept-based approaches are more effective than definition-based approaches (Bos & Anders, 1992; Pittelman, Heimlich, Berglund, & French, 1991).

In *Semantic Mapping* for vocabulary development, the teacher starts by writing a word that represents a key concept and drawing a circle or box around it. The students are asked to think of words that relate to the key word. These words are grouped around the key word in categories, either preset by the teacher or created by the students. The teacher then suggests new words and encourages a discussion about where these words might fit into the map (Duffelmeyer & Banwart, 1993). For example, a semantic map for "sports" might include preset categories for "benefits," "problems," "kinds," and "related concepts." Schwartz and Raphael (1985) suggested that semantic maps can be used as a visual display of a word's definition by placing the word in the center and having three questions form the categories: What is it? What is it like? What are some examples? This variation of Semantic Mapping is sometimes referred to as *Word Mapping*.

In a *Semantic Feature Analysis* (Fisher & Blachowicz, 2007; Johnson & Pearson, 1984), the teacher chooses a word or phrase that represents a major topic or category about which the students will read. In a column, the teacher lists some words related to the topic. In a row, the teacher lists some features shared by some of the words already listed in the column. At the intersection of row and column, the teacher asks the students to put a plus (+) if the word possesses the feature or minus (–) if the word does not possess the feature (or a scale from 0 to 5 can be used). The students are also asked to add words to the column and features to the row. An example is a semantic feature analysis for "musical instruments." The teacher might begin by writing several instruments in a column such as "guitar," "flute," and "drum" and several features in a row such as "strings," "blow into," and "hit." A variation of this strategy is *Vocabulary Venns* (Nagy, 1988; Stahl, 1999). A Venn diagram is an intersection of two circles. In Vocabulary Venns, the unique features are listed along the outer parts of each circle and common features are listed in the intersection area. Another variation is *Semantic Scales* (McKenna, 2002), which consist of a straight line demonstrating ends of a continuum. For vocabulary instruction, two contrasting words or antonyms are written by the teacher at the two ends of the scale and the students place related words along the continuum.

When using *Concept Attainment*, the teacher begins by presenting examples and nonexamples of a key word. The teacher then encourages the students to identify critical or relevant attributes of the concept (in other words, the attributes or characteristics important to the meaning of the word). The students are encouraged to separate the relevant attributes from the irrelevant attributes. The teacher can then ask the students for subordinate terms (examples of the concept), superordinate terms (more general concepts), and coordinate terms (concepts that share some of the same attributes as the targeted concept). Or the teacher can ask for further examples and nonexamples of the key word (Boulware & Crowe, 2008; McNeil, 1992; Wixson, 1986).

In using a *Concept Wheel*, the teacher starts by asking the students to brainstorm all the things that come to mind about a given word. The teacher writes all their ideas on the board and directs the students to a page in their books in which the word is written and also to the glossary that provides a definition. The teacher asks the students to decide on three words from their list that will help them remember the target word. The words are written inside a circle that has been divided into quarters. Because each reader may have a different list of three words, the concept wheels are individualized. According to Rupley, Logan, and Nichols (1999), the steps can be reversed, with the students given the concept wheel first and asked to supply the name of the wheel.

Yopp and Yopp (2003, 2007) developed strategies they called *Ten Important Words* and *Ten Important Words Plus* for content area reading. The students identify 10 words (or fewer if the passage is relatively brief) that they feel are the most important words in the expository materials they are reading and

122

CHAPTER 4

*Before-Reading
Strategies:
Prereading and
Planning*

write each word on a yellow sticky. The students then work together at the board to group sticky notes with the same words into columns. The resulting bar graph is the prompt for teacher-led discussion about why particular words were most and least popular. The students can then be asked to use the words in writing a one-sentence summary of the passage. The *plus* of the strategy involves prompts as an additional step to enhance word learning. These prompts are written on differently colored cards that direct the students to use the words in sentences, identify synonyms or antonyms, find other words with parts that are the same as the target word, create a semantic map, and other such activities. Students with the same-colored cards meet together to generate as many ideas as possible and then share their ideas with the full class.

Concept-based approaches are more likely than definition-based approaches to embody the three qualities of effective vocabulary instruction. Semantic Mapping provides integration because the map is built on the students' background knowledge and involves discussion; meaningful use is dependent on encountering the word in text and repetition through revisiting the map again after reading. Semantic Feature Analysis also provides integration because the map is built on the students' background knowledge and involves discussion that may be more intense than that provoked by Semantic Mapping because the students have to come to consensus. Meaningful use is dependent on encountering the word in text during reading and repetition through adding more examples and features to the chart after reading. Concept Attainment provides integration as well because the discussion draws on the students' background knowledge. Also similar to the other two strategies, meaningful use is dependent on encountering the word in text during reading and repetition through adding attributes or characteristics, subordinate terms, superordinate terms, and coordinate terms after reading. The Concept Wheel provides integration because first, the students share their background knowledge of the target word in the brainstorming activity and second, the student chooses his or her own three words that are most evocative for remembering the target word. As with the other strategies, meaningful use is dependent on encountering the word in text and repetition through revisiting the Concept Wheel again after reading. Ten Important Words incorporates integration as the students initially develop their own lists of the most important words in the passage, meaningful use when the students write their one-sentence summaries, and repetition in the "plus" step of finding related words.

Teaching Key Concepts

There is ample evidence from the research literature that the reader's prior knowledge of topic has a direct relationship with reading comprehension but there is considerably less evidence that instructional strategies designed to improve comprehension through the elicitation and building of background knowledge are actually effective (National Reading Panel, 2000).

Though none of the case study children showed particular difficulty with prior knowledge of topic during their assessments, the delays in their reading development indicate that at least in the early period of reading instruction, their respective teachers might incorporate instruction in key concepts the students will encounter in their reading material. The Directed Reading Thinking Activity that Mr. Ginnetti will use with Maria includes a Concept Development step for activating and building the student's knowledge of the topic. The Early Steps model that Ms. Edberg will use with Adani includes a step for the teacher to introduce a new book daily by encouraging the student to predict the main idea using pictures, title, and other cues. Though not specified in the model, Ms. Edberg could expand this activity if Adani's knowledge of the topic appeared to be limited. The Collaborative Strategic Reading model that Mrs. Hong will use with Ellison includes a previewing step for activating background knowledge and encouraging student predictions. The Cooperative Integrated Reading and Composition that she will alternatively use includes a step for asking the students to predict what the story will be about from the title and vocabulary that she just taught. As with the Early Steps model, Mrs. Hong could expand this activity if Ellison's knowledge of the topic seemed to warrant a more thorough lesson on key concepts. The Integrated Skills Method that Mr. Rumrill will use with Marek includes no designated step for teaching key concepts because the reading material is based heavily on words the student has already spent considerable time studying, and the Language Experience Approach to be used as a supplemental model is based on the student's own personal experiences.

As discussed in Chapter 1, students who struggle with reading may experience four problems with prior knowledge of topic. The two that can be addressed before reading include (a) making sure that the student possesses the prior knowledge the author assumes the reader has and (b) helping the students become aware that they have relevant background knowledge about the upcoming reading material. The problems with prior knowledge of topic that must be addressed during reading include (c) drawing on background knowledge that is relevant toward understanding the material while reading and (d) flexibly tapping into pockets of background knowledge as appropriate to shifting topics within the text. The first two will be discussed in this chapter; the other two will be discussed in Chapter 5.

When students are relatively knowledgeable about the topic and the goal is to activate their knowledge, engaging them in a brief discussion is generally adequate. This type of discussion is the easiest and most efficient way to activate prior knowledge. However, it is simply too brief for building new knowledge, which the following activities are designed to do.

Reconciled Reading Lesson

Reutzel (1985a) noticed that some of the best ideas for prereading activities were those suggested for enrichment in the teacher's manuals of basal reading series. He proposed that an enrichment activity should be the first

124

CHAPTER 4

*Before-Reading
Strategies:
Prereading and
Planning*

step instead of the last step. In a *Reconciled Reading Lesson,* activities such as performing a play, writing a recipe, and viewing a video are conducted before rather than after the story. Furthermore, the students are engaged in a full discussion of the story prior to reading. For example, if the students were getting ready to read *The Diary of Anne Frank,* the teacher doing a typical background-building activity might engage the class in a discussion of the events involved in World War II and the Holocaust. If the teacher used a Reconciled Reading Lesson format, instead of simply having a discussion and drawing on the students' knowledge of these historical events, the teacher might show the movie of *The Diary of Anne Frank* or *Schindler's List* and then engage the class in a discussion of the book they would be reading.

The Reconciled Reading Lesson fits easily into instruction for teachers who routinely integrate content and reading instruction through unit themes. For example, *The Diary of Anne Frank* dovetails nicely with a unit that involves more than one discipline to examine the social, scientific, economic, and political issues and events during the mid-20th century. This approach to connecting reading with content area instruction is beneficial for several reasons. The common set of concepts explored in thematic study are expressed through a common set of vocabulary, the learning of this vocabulary becomes deeper as the nuances of meaning are examined and applied to a variety of contexts, and the use of common terminology from subject to subject makes it more likely that the struggling reader will be able to apply knowledge of vocabulary to comprehending the reading material.

ReQuest

In the *ReQuest* procedure (Manzo, 1969), the students read the title and sentence of a story and look at the picture. They then ask the teacher anything they want to know about the title, sentence, and picture. When the teacher finishes answering all of their questions, the procedure is repeated for the second sentence. If the students run out of questions to ask, the teacher can suggest questions. Teacher questions not only add to the students' understanding of the upcoming passage, but they also serve as a model for good questions. After all the questions are answered, the teacher asks the students what they think will happen in the passage. At that point, the students read the passage silently.

Text Walk

In a *Text Walk,* sometimes referred to as a *Picture Walk,* the teacher walks the students through the entire text by showing the photos, illustrations, and graphics in the material while telling them the major elements, ideas, concepts, and key vocabulary (Goldenberg, 1991). The technique can be used with narrative and expository text at any grade level (Cooper & Kiger, 2009) though is especially helpful in making content area material accessible to the struggling reader.

K-W-L

The *K-W-L* approach developed by Ogle (1986) emphasizes the reader's prior knowledge and is usually used with content material. The first step in this approach is Step K, which Ogle defined as accessing *what I know.* In the first part of this step, the teacher writes the topic on the board, and the students brainstorm what they know about it. In the second part of this step, the students are encouraged to develop categories for the ideas they brainstormed. The second step is Step W, determining *what I want to learn.* In this step, the students are encouraged to create questions and are asked to write down the ones that interest them the most. The final step is Step L, recalling *what I did learn* as a result of reading. In this step, the students write or discuss what they have learned with specific attention to their original questions.

Prereading Plan (PReP)

The *PreReading Plan* (PReP) involves engaging students in brainstorming and discussing their ideas about a topic prior to reading (Langer, 1981). The teacher presents a key concept using a stimulus picture, object, or word and asks the students for their ideas. All ideas are written on the board in the first step. In the second step, the students are asked what made them think of their ideas. The teacher can add new vocabulary and clarify misconceptions. In the third step, the teacher probes the students' ideas and encourages them to consider revisions, additions, and deletions to the list of ideas. The PReP technique largely activates background knowledge rather than builds new knowledge. However, the ideas generated by the students provide the teacher with information about which concepts the students need more explicit instruction prior to reading.

Organizers and Overviews

Organizers and overviews consist of written information presented to the student prior to reading the actual text, usually content subject matter. The information contained in an organizer or overview is intended to activate the reader's background knowledge and highlight key concepts in the material to be read. For some text material, the organizer or overview can be given to the students for independent reading prior to reading the text. For other text material, the teacher and students can create the organizer or overview together, drawing on their background knowledge plus adding new information to be learned prior to reading the text.

126

CHAPTER 4

*Before-Reading
Strategies:
Prereading and
Planning*

Previews for narrative material can range from brief, introductory statements to detailed information that includes a story synopsis and identification of each character (Graves, Cooke, & Laberge, 1983). Previews can also include questions for the students to consider as they are reading.

Thematic Organizers and *Advance Organizers* are terms that are used almost interchangeably in the literature to describe previews created for expository text. As developed by Ausubel (1960), an advance organizer is presented in advance of the actual text and provides the reader with concepts that are more general, abstract, and inclusive than the actual text. According to Lenz, Alley, and Schumaker (1987), advance organizers generally include topics and subtopics, background information, new concepts, examples, new or relevant vocabulary, the organization or sequence of the text information, and an explanation of why the material should be read. Alvarez (1983) modified the advance organizer strategy and coined the term *thematic organizer* to describe an organizer written at the student's reading ability level that included information specifically related to the text topic. According to Risko and Alvarez (1983), the following elements characterize a thematic organizer:

1. Each organizer has three paragraphs that define the implied thematic concept of the passage and relate this concept to prior knowledge and/or experiences of the reader.

2. The concept is defined by presenting its various attributes and nonattributes.

3. Examples of how the concept relates to real-life experiences and the ideas in the text are given to further illustrate the meaning of the concept.

4. Following the three paragraphs are a set of statements written on the interpretive level. The students are instructed to indicate whether they agree with these statements during and/or after their reading. (p. 85)

Structured Overviews have been variously called graphic organizers, graphic overviews, and conceptual maps, but the original term comes from Barron and Earle (Barron, 1969; Earle, 1969; Earle & Barron, 1973). A structured overview is a graphic representation of key concepts from the text presented in a hierarchical structure that shows the relationships among superordinate, coordinate, and subordinate concepts. The flow of the structured overview is not meant to reflect the sequence of ideas presented in the text but rather the relationship among ideas. Semantic maps are a variation of structured overviews. Whereas structure overviews show hierarchical relationships between ideas and are created by the teacher, semantic maps show categorical relationships between ideas and are created with the students.

An *Anticipation Guide* is a set of statements about a topic to which students must respond before reading about the topic. The responses are generally written as agree-disagree, likely-unlikely, or similar dichotomous formats. According to Duffelmeyer (1994), constructing an anticipation guide "entails four tasks: identifying the major ideas presented in the text; considering what beliefs your students are likely to have; creating statements to elicit those beliefs; and arranging the statements in a form that requires students to respond to each one either positively or negatively" (p. 453).

127

CHAPTER 4

*Before-Reading
Strategies:
Prereading and
Planning*

Purpose Setting and Predicting

When you examine the reading tasks identified in Chapter 1, you will see that the previous approaches for comprehension instruction before reading involve building knowledge—knowledge of vocabulary and prior knowledge of topic. Purpose setting and predicting focus on teaching cognitive strategies before reading.

Setting a purpose for reading provides motivation and direction for reading (Anderson, Pichert, & Shirey, 1983; Blanton, Wood, & Moorman, 1990). Few models actually incorporate a designated step for purpose or goal setting although many of the models incorporate activities for encouraging student predictions. Each segment of silent reading for the Directed Reading Activity begins with a purpose setting statement or question by the teacher, which is replaced in the Directed Reading Thinking Activity with student predictions. In the Teacher-Led Reading Groups step of Cooperative Integrated Reading and Composition, the teacher sets a purpose for the reading after engaging the students in a discussion of previously read material and introducing new vocabulary. And Reciprocal Teaching includes a step for students to predict what will happen in an upcoming passage.

Purpose can be defined as the information the reader is seeking in an upcoming segment. The purpose may vary from segment to segment, and the reader may have more than one purpose per segment, but the goal is generally the same for the whole text (Gunning, 2006). For example, if the students are reading *The Diary of Anne Frank*, the purpose for one segment might be whether the sirens will stop at the house where the Franks are hiding. The goal may be to understand the Holocaust or it might very well be to pass whatever test the teacher has developed for the book or to meet a state English language arts content standard.

Asking a question or directing the students to look for a particular action, character reaction, or consequence of a previous action is still considered to be the most effective way for setting a purpose (Cooper & Kiger, 2009; Tierney & Cunningham, 1984). Most important, purposes should lead the students to text information important to key ideas rather than superficial details or overly broad concepts. Predicting should encourage active processing of text that was just read.

128

CHAPTER 4

*Before-Reading
Strategies:
Prereading and
Planning*

Next Step

In this chapter, instructional strategies were organized around the framework of the reading model chosen by the teacher. Just as selection of the model is based on strengths and weaknesses identified in the assessment of the student's reading abilities, so is the choice of strategies based on the student's specific needs. The strategies discussed in this chapter are those that are taught before the student begins reading the material. The purpose is to provide the reader with the knowledge and skills to interact successfully with the material given the types of teacher support that will be provided during reading. These prereading strategies provide part of the scaffold the student needs; the rest of the scaffold comes during and after reading.

The next step is choosing strategies during reading. As with prereading strategies, these strategies are essentially slotted into the steps of the reading model. In the next chapter, strategies that you can use during reading to support the student's strategic reading will be presented.

QUESTIONS FOR REFLECTION AND APPLICATION

1. Why is it important to spend valuable class time on instruction before reading?

2. If a reading model does not incorporate a prereading step for a strategy needed by the student, when and how can it be taught?

3. What should you do if you have provided instruction on word recognition and comprehension strategies before reading but the student still has great difficulty with the material?

4. How will you know if the strategy instruction you have provided before reading has been helpful to the struggling reader?

SUGGESTED RESOURCES FOR ADDITIONAL READING

Algozzine, Bob, Marr, Mary Beth, Barnes, Emme, & McClanahan, Tina. (2008). *Strategies and Lessons for Improving Basic Early Literacy Skills.* Thousand Oaks, CA: Corwin.

Blachman, Benita A., Ball, Eileen W., Black, Rochelle, & Tangel, Darlene M. (2000). *Road to the Code.* Baltimore, MD: Brookes.

Blachowicz, Camille, & Fisher, Peter J. (2009). *Teaching Vocabulary in All Classrooms* (4th ed.). Columbus, OH: Allyn & Bacon/Merrill.

Hendricks, Cindy, & Rinsky, Lee Ann. (2007). *Teaching Word Recognition Skills* (7th ed.). Upper Saddle River, NJ: Merrill/Prentice Hall.

Klingner, Janette K., Vaughn, Sharon, & Boardman, Alison. (2007). *Teaching Reading Comprehension to Students with Learning Difficulties.* New York: Guilford.

Readence, John E., Moore, David W., & Rickelman, Robert J. (2000). *Prereading Activities for Content Area Reading and Learning* (3rd ed.). Newark, DE: International Reading Association.

During-Reading Strategies
Supporting Strategic Reading

1 The Reading Process: The Task and the Reader

2 Assessment: Putting the Reader at the Center of the Reading Program

3 Framework for Developing a Reading Program for the Struggling Reader

4 Before-Reading Strategies: Prereading and Planning

This chapter will present reading strategies that the student can use during reading for constructing meaning, monitoring comprehension, and improving comprehension.

5 During-Reading Strategies: Supporting Strategic Reading

8 Families: Partnering with Parents

6 After-Reading Strategies: Synthesizing and Extending

7 Attitude and Motivation: From Reluctant to Enthused Reader

Strategies that are taught during reading are focused quite deliberately on providing the support needed by the student to interact effectively with reading material while it is being read and simultaneously to help the reader internalize these strategies so that they can be applied independently with future reading material. For the struggling reader, the timing for teaching these strategies is key and it is no accident that they are taught during reading, when application to the reading process is immediate. Interrupting the student's reading to intervene with a question or a strategy lesson is certainly not a recommended practice for pleasure or independent reading but it is an effective practice for supporting the student during instructional reading.

On the continuum of more to less teacher support incorporated into each model, the ones that provide opportunity for instruction during reading

130

CHAPTER 5

*During-Reading
Strategies:
Supporting
Strategic Reading*

are those at the end of the continuum with greater teacher support. As you know, these are the models being used with the case study children and are likely to be the ones you use with your struggling readers.

In the Directed Reading Activity/Directed Reading Thinking Activity that will be used with Maria, the passage is divided into relatively brief segments ranging from a sentence to a couple of pages, depending on the skill level of the reader. The choice of strategies during stop points is left up to Mr. Ginnetti though the model assumes that he will ask questions, clarify information, and teach a brief lesson as he sees that Maria and the other students in her reading group need targeted instruction on a particular word recognition or comprehension skill. Most of the steps in the Integrated Skills Method that Mr. Rumrill will use with Marek are carried out before reading though in the Reading for Meaning and Pleasure step, Marek and Mr. Rumrill will read together orally by taking turns. In this during-reading step, the model suggests that the teacher point out the role of punctuation for expression. Because this model devotes so much attention to phonemic awareness and word recognition instruction before reading, the expectation is that the story will contain no unknown words and so instruction during reading is aimed at fluency.

In the Early Steps model that will be used with Adani, Ms. Edberg will encourage Adani to use the word recognition skills and comprehension strategies previously taught and to self-correct during the New Reading step. In the Language Experience Approach that will be used as a supplementary model with Marek, creating the experience on which the story will be based is the before-reading strategy; creating the story with the students is the during-reading strategy.

One of the models that may be used with Ellison, Cooperative Integrated Reading and Composition, involves, first, silent reading, and then reading with a partner, with the partners correcting each other's word recognition errors. The other model that Mrs. Hong may use with Ellison, Collaborative Strategic Reading, involves two strategies during reading; one is designed to encourage the students to monitor their comprehension and use fix-up strategies when comprehension has broken down, and the other to identify the main idea or most important information.

Among the models that have not been selected for the case study children, the Guided Reading model (not the Guided Reading step in the DRA/DRTA) includes no teacher instruction during reading though the teacher is expected to observe, note student behaviors, and provide support with word recognition, unfamiliar sentence structures, and comprehension when needed. The Book Club and Reading Workshop models both involve brief instructional sessions but these are conducted at times other than during actual reading and the instructional topics involve aspects of literacy that the teacher views as important to the students but which may, or may not, relate to strategies that they can apply immediately in the reading context.

The selection of strategies during reading depends on the answer to two questions. First, what opportunity does the model make available? For example, the DRA/DRTA is quite open-ended and you can slot many different strategies into the Guided Reading step whereas the Cooperative Integrated Reading and Composition model offers limited opportunity for slotting other strategies into the partner activities steps. Second, what skills and knowledge, based on the student's assessment, will the strategies target? For example, if Ellison's goals include fluency and comprehension, spending time on strategies for word recognition would not be particularly helpful for Ellison but main idea and sequencing would be very appropriate during reading.

The following strategies are grouped as word recognition and comprehension strategies. Fluency is almost always a postreading strategy and so will be discussed in Chapter 6. The strategies described are intended to be used by the teacher during reading. The summary provided in Table 5.1 follows the format first presented in the last chapter. If you put these charts together, you can select from among a range of strategies that you can slot into your reading model before and during reading. As you learn about new strategies that have been shown to be effective, you can add them to your repertoire.

Word Recognition during Reading

Fluency and comprehension depend on the relatively rapid and effortless identification of words in print. Any time the reader stops to decode a word, attention is drawn away from comprehension and so the goal is to minimize these times to just a few, which are opportunities to teach or reinforce a word recognition strategy, or explain the meaning of figurative language or a complex sentence structure.

Using Word Recognition Strategies

In order to know whether the student is successfully applying word recognition strategies during reading, the teacher must either ask a question that will reveal whether the words have been read accurately or ask the student to read aloud. The Guided Reading step of the Directed Reading Activity/Directed Reading Thinking Activity provides the clearest opportunity of any of the models for you to do both. If you determine that the student has not applied a word recognition strategy appropriately or skillfully, the opportunity for teaching or reinforcing the skill is presented.

Mr. Ginnetti planned to focus Maria's attention on letter-sound relationships, analogies, and roots and affixes before reading when presenting new sight words. During reading, the DRTA model he plans on using will enable him to ascertain whether she retained these sight words and, if not, to reteach through a strategy lesson or think-aloud as described in a section that follows. For Marek, who showed difficulty with phonic analysis and analogy in the assessment, the Language Experience Approach will provide Mr. Rumrill opportunity during reading to focus on these word recognition skills, also using a brief strategy lesson or think-aloud.

FIGURE 5.1 Instructional Strategies during Reading

Strategies	Reading Abilities		
	Word Recognition	*Fluency*	*Comprehension*
Phonemic awareness instruction			
Phonics, analogy, and structural analysis instruction	• Strategy lessons • Think-alouds		
Context strategy instruction	• Strategy lessons • Think-alouds		
Automatic word recognition instruction		• Read words in context	
Sentence structures and figurative language instruction			• Strategy lessons • Parsing, Questioning, Rephrasing (PQR)

Cognitive strategy instruction			• Predicting
			• Questioning and self-questioning
			  • Elaborative Interrogation
			• Mental imagery
			  • Sensory Imaging Strategy
			• Paraphrasing and getting the gist
			• Think-Pair-Share
			  • Linguistic Roulette
			• Yellow stickies

Vocabulary instruction			• Context-based approaches • SCANR • Strategy lessons • Facilitated peer dialogues

Automatic word recognition is a goal for Maria, Adani, and Marek. The DRTA model to be used with Maria, Early Steps model to be used with Adani, and Integrated Skills Method to be used with Marek all involve reading text that includes new sight words, thus building automatic word recognition. Indeed, both Early Steps and Integrated Skills entail the rereading of text, which further reinforces knowledge of sight words.

Strategy Lessons

Strategy lessons involve students in brief, clear, and concise explanations as needed when the student has difficulty identifying a word. If the difficulty is with a newly taught sight word, the flash card is brought out and reviewed. If the difficulty is with a new word, you can use a strategy lesson to point out previously taught letter-sound relationships, onset-rimes, root and affixes, or other features. The strategy lesson can also be a prime opportunity to assist the student with using context for identifying an unknown word by pointing out syntactic cues in the sentence and semantic cues from the words surrounding the unknown word.

These succinct lessons serve three important goals:

1. Strategy lessons enable you to focus on specific reading skills on an as-needed basis, when the skill is relevant to the student's current reading needs.

2. Strategy lessons explicitly let the student know that individual skills are important because they are applicable to the reading process and not because they are an end in themselves.

3. Strategy lessons implicitly communicate the message that the most important part of the lesson is actual reading, because the strategy lesson involves a considerably smaller proportion of time than that spent reading.

Think-Alouds

In *think-alouds* for word recognition, readers are asked to verbalize their thinking as they are trying to figure out an unknown word. According to Gunning (2006), the teacher should first offer neutral prompts that serve to encourage students to explain their thinking and then offer instructional prompts that encourage them to try a particular strategy. For example, a neutral prompt might be, "What are you thinking as you look at that word?" and an instructional prompt might be, "Does the ending look familiar to you?"

Think-alouds offer a change of pace to strategy lessons and are particularly appropriate when the student has a relatively strong base of knowledge on which to draw, allowing the teacher to play a more facilitative role in guiding the reader rather than the instructive role needed when teaching a strategy lesson.

134

CHAPTER 5

*During-Reading
Strategies:
Supporting
Strategic Reading*

Understanding Sentence Structures and Figurative Language

Though sentence structure is a comprehension task, understanding a string of words in complex sentence structures and within figurative language during reading is directly connected to being able to identify the individual words. For this reason, the strategies are presented here rather than in the section on comprehension during reading.

For students who are deaf or hard of hearing, who are not native speakers of English, or who have language learning difficulties, problems in understanding sentence structures and figurative language are common and impede fluency and comprehension. Of the case study students, English is not Adani's first language and her assessment showed that she did have difficulty with English sentence structures. The Early Steps model that Ms. Edberg is using provides two opportunities for focusing on sentence structures. In the Writing step, Adani will write her own sentences, Ms. Edberg (or her aide, volunteer, literacy coach, or student teacher) will rewrite each sentence and then take apart each sentence, and Adani will then put the sentence together. Repeating this activity over and over is designed to help Adani internalize the correct grammatical structures of written English. The New Reading step of the model does not mandate any particular teaching activity, so Ms. Edberg will focus on sentence structures that Adani is having difficulty understanding through the strategy lessons and PQR technique described next.

Strategy Lessons

Just as strategy lessons for word recognition involve brief, clear, and concise explanations, so do strategy lessons that focus on sentence structures and figurative language. The teacher takes the sentence or figurative expression out of context for scrutiny and analysis by placing the individual sentences on sentence strips or the computer/LCD. Sentence analysis usually involves pulling apart the component syntactic components whereas figurative expression analysis usually involves showing how the sum is greater than its component parts. For example, "He was so angry that he started to shake" can be analyzed as two clauses with a cause (he was so angry) and effect (he started to shake). However, "He was so angry that he exploded like a firecracker" only makes sense when the full expression is considered and the reader does not think that the character detonated.

Parsing, Questioning, Rephrasing (PQR)

The process of *parsing, questioning, and rephrasing (PQR)* is a technique developed by Flood, Lapp, and Fisher (2002) to assist students who are having difficulty with text syntax. The teacher identifies a chunk of text containing sentence structures likely to be difficult for the students. This chunk is usually just a few sentences in length. The first step involves parsing the text sentence by sentence using the following guide:

Subject (Who, What)—Verb (Is, Do)—Object or Descriptor (Who, What, When, Where, How).

For example, the chunk may include the complex sentence: "Samuel was so embarrassed when he realized that he didn't have enough money to pay for the present he had chosen for his mom." Together, the teacher and students might parse this sentence as the following:

Samuel—chose—a present for his mom. He—didn't have—enough money. He—felt—embarrassed.

The second step, questioning, and the third step, rephrasing, actually occur simultaneously with parsing. The teacher asks questions that help the students parse the text into simplified syntactic structures. These newly created simple active declarative sentences are rephrases of the actual text. Flood and her colleagues suggest sometimes adding a bonus step in which the teacher provides additional information that explains the meaning of the sentence being parsed or extends understanding of the concept presented in the sentence.

Comprehension during Reading

Instruction during reading can be particularly powerful in teaching struggling readers to monitor comprehension and use strategies for improving comprehension because the instruction is immediate and applicable to actual reading. Some of the strategies are viewed as so important to comprehension that they are built into the instructional model.

All of the case study children had difficulty with some aspects of comprehension. In the assessment, Maria demonstrated difficulty with factual and inferential comprehension when she read material silently, and weak vocabulary knowledge appeared to affect her comprehension adversely. Ellison showed difficulty identifying the main idea and determining sequences of events. Adani demonstrated good literal comprehension but some difficulty with making inferences and synthesizing ideas. Marek's word recognition problems made it impossible to isolate comprehension issues though given his substitution of semantically unacceptable words when miscuing, it would appear that he was not fully aware that reading involves constructing meaning.

Teaching Comprehension

During reading, instruction aimed at monitoring comprehension and improving understanding can certainly be planned, but the likelihood is that during any given lesson, unexpected issues will arise requiring impromptu teaching.

The following strategies can form the nucleus of strategies taught during reading, from which you can extend and elaborate when teachable moments arise.

Predicting

Predicting during reading assumes that the reading passage is segmented so that the student reads parts of it at a time under the direction of the teacher. The Directed Reading Thinking Activity, the model to be used with Maria, was specifically designed to encourage the student to predict before reading each passage in the Guided Reading step. This approach differs from Reciprocal Teaching, a model that may be used with Ellison, which also has a step for prediction but the student then reads the complete passage silently with no during-reading intervention by the teacher. Similarly, the other model being considered for Ellison, Cooperative Integrated Reading and Composition, includes prediction prior to reading but no opportunity to revisit predictions during reading. Early Steps, the model to be used with Adani, includes prediction during the New Reading step.

It is believed that good readers are constantly predicting, testing their hypotheses to confirm or disconfirm them, integrating information by separating important ideas from less important ideas, and interpreting the important ideas (Brown, 1980; McNeil, 1992). Hansen (1981) found that teaching readers to use their prior knowledge to predict upcoming story events improved their comprehension. If good readers engage in prediction, the strategy would likely be an important one to teach struggling readers. And it is certainly one of the easiest and least time-consuming strategies to incorporate into your instruction.

Teacher Questions

Comprehension questions can be used to assess comprehension or to extend comprehension. Assessment was discussed in Chapter 2. In this section, using questions to promote understanding text more deeply and to provide models of self-questions will be presented.

Levels of Questions. Comprehension taxonomies are widely used by teachers for constructing varying types of comprehension questions. The most frequently used taxonomy is Bloom's classification of the intellectual objectives of education into six lower-to-higher levels: knowledge, comprehension, application, analysis, synthesis, and evaluation (Bloom, Engelhart, Furst, Hill, & Krathwohl, 1956). This taxonomy has been so popular that researchers continue to develop revised versions that incorporate advances in cognitive psychology, such as Anderson et al. (2001) and Marzano and Kendall (2007). Another popular taxonomy is Barrett's (1976), which was specifically designed to distinguish among the cognitive and affective dimensions of reading comprehension through four major levels: literal, inferential, evaluative, and appreciative. These taxonomies are further divided into multiple subcategories that teachers can use in creating comprehension questions.

Tatham (1978) cautioned that taxonomies should be viewed as classification systems and not as developmental frameworks of comprehension skills. "These taxonomies are nothing more than efficient systems for organizing types of reading behavior under clearly defined labels. The labels can be very useful when teachers want categories in which to place comprehension questions from instructional materials in order to analyze the types of thinking these questions promote" (p. 193).

In 1978, Pearson and Johnson proposed what they referred to as a simple taxonomy of questions that was designed "to capture the relationship between information presented in a text and information that has to come from a reader's store of prior knowledge" (p. 157). Their taxonomy included three types of questions: textually explicit, textually implicit, and scriptally implicit. Textually explicit questions have answers that are obvious in the text. Textually implicit questions have answers in the text but the answers are not obvious. To answer a textually implicit question, the reader must use inference. Scriptally implicit questions have answers that come from the reader's prior knowledge; the answers are not in the text but the question is related to the text. "It is similar to textually implicit comprehension in that an inference is involved; however, it is different in that the data base for the inference is in the reader's head, not on the page" (p. 162).

The *Question-Answer Relationship* (QAR) program was developed by Raphael (1984, 1986; Raphael & Au, 2005; Raphael & Pearson, 1985) and based on the Pearson and Johnson question taxonomy. Raphael divided question-answer relationships into two primary categories: (a) In the Book and (b) In My Head. The *In the Book* category includes two types of QARs. The first is called *Right There* and is the appropriate strategy to use when the answer can be found explicitly stated within a single sentence of the text. The second is called *Think and Search* or *Putting It Together* and is the appropriate strategy to use when the answer can be found in the text but requires the reader to synthesize information from different parts of the text. The *In My Head* category also includes two types of QARs. The first is called *Author and You* and is the appropriate strategy when the reader needs to combine background knowledge with text information. The second is called *On My Own* and is the appropriate strategy when the answer cannot be found in the story and could even be answered if the story was not read. *On My Own* questions require the reader to rely completely on background knowledge.

From an instructional perspective, a major difference lies between using Bloom's and Barrett's taxonomies and using QARs. Bloom's and Barrett's taxonomies provide guidance for developing comprehension questions to ensure that the teacher asks some questions that promote higher order thinking along with the questions that require recall of factual information. When students struggle with reading, there may be a tendency to ask them questions that focus on story details. Yet the difficulties that students experience in thinking critically, creatively, and abstractly may be due to their lack of

137

CHAPTER 5
*During-Reading
Strategies:
Supporting
Strategic Reading*

138

CHAPTER 5

*During-Reading
Strategies:
Supporting
Strategic Reading*

experience with this kind of thinking. When readers have not been asked questions that encourage higher order thinking, it may be very hard for them at first to think at levels beyond the literal. Instead of giving up and assuming they cannot answer inferential, evaluative, and other higher level questions, these are precisely the kinds of questions they need to be asked. Indeed, Taylor, Pearson, Clark, and Walpole (2000) found that classroom teachers with the highest achieving first- through third-grade readers asked significantly more questions requiring their students to integrate text information with their own background knowledge.

QARs also serve the function of providing the teacher with a framework for asking questions that require different levels of thinking. However, their primary purpose is to encourage the reader to be metacognitive because they are designed to help students become aware of the relationship between the kind of question the teacher has asked and the source of information for the answer. In other words, it is meant to help the student become a strategic reader by reflecting on his or her comprehension and applying a strategy for improving comprehension.

Scope of Questions.   As important as levels of questions is the scope of questions that you ask. Scope used to be discussed concomitantly with sequence, as in scope-and-sequence. Although the notion that comprehension skills can be neatly sequenced is no longer well supported, addressing the full scope of comprehension skills is still viewed as valuable. While the following list of comprehension skills may not be exhaustive, it represents the major areas (Collins & Cheek, 1999; McKenna, 2002):

- Understand sentence structures and figurative language.
- Identify main idea and supporting details.
- Identify sequence of events.
- Recognize cause-effect relationships.
- Contrast-compare information and ideas.
- Identify and interpret character attributes and actions.
- Predict.
- Make inferences.
- Draw conclusions.
- Make generalizations.
- Recognize relationships.
- Understand mood, emotional reactions, and affect.
- Summarize.
- Understand author's purpose and point of view.
- Synthesize information and ideas.
- Distinguish relevant information.

- Recognize bias and propaganda.
- Evaluate quality of writing and knowledge of author.
- Differentiate fact from opinion, reality from fantasy.

139

CHAPTER 5
*During-Reading
Strategies:
Supporting
Strategic Reading*

Another source for scope of comprehension skills is the academic content standards that many states have developed.

Think Time.   One characteristic of comprehension questions that is easily forgotten is that wonderful questions will not enhance comprehension if students are not given time to think about their answers. It has been observed that teachers give students an average of 1 second to answer a question. After 1 second, teachers ordinarily repeat or rephrase the question, answer it themselves, call on another student, or ask another question (Gambrell, 1983; Rowe, 1974; Tobin, 1986).

What happens when teachers wait 3 seconds, 5 seconds, or longer before soliciting an answer? In Tobin's (1986) study of students in grades 6 and 7, he found that waiting between 3 and 5 seconds resulted in significantly fewer failures of students to respond, greater length of student responses, and better comprehension. In a review of studies involving wait time, Tobin (1987) found that a wait time of between 3 and 5 seconds seemed to be optimal for improving the quality of teacher and student discourse and for affecting higher cognitive-level achievement. In Gambrell's review of the literature (1980), she found evidence that a wait time of 5 seconds or more resulted in student responses that were longer, more appropriate, and demonstrated higher order thinking. She also found that when teachers increased their wait time, they tended to ask more varied questions and to stimulate greater student involvement. In reviewing her own series of studies on wait time in elementary and high school classrooms along with a review of the studies conducted by other researchers, Rowe (1986) found that wait time influenced students and teachers in a number of ways. When the interval between the end of a teacher question and the start of a student response was 3 to 5 seconds as compared to only 1 second:

- The length of student response increased 300 to 700 percent.
- Students were much more likely to use evidence and logical argument to support their inferences.
- Students engaged more often in speculative thinking.
- Students asked considerably more questions.
- Students paid more attention to each other.
- "I don't know" responses decreased dramatically.
- Off-task behavior decreased.
- Greater percentages of students participated, particularly from groups rated as poor performers.

140
....

CHAPTER 5

During-Reading
Strategies:
Supporting
Strategic Reading

- Student confidence increased.
- Test performance improved on cognitively more complex test items.
- Classroom discourse more closely resembled discussion than question-answer routines. (Question-answer routines are explained in the next chapter.)
- Teachers asked fewer questions, and those they asked tended to invite clarification and elaboration.
- Teacher expectation for student performance rose, particularly with students for whom they had previously held low expectations.

Wait time is clearly very important to struggling readers, who may need more time to consider the question and to formulate their answer. It is particularly pertinent to students who are deaf and receiving information from the teacher through a sign language interpreter. Because interpreting is not simultaneous with the teacher's utterances, unless the teacher waits between asking a question and soliciting answers, the student who is deaf may have no opportunity to answer and certainly no opportunity to think.

Question Generation

Question generation is defined as having readers generate their own questions during reading. Sometimes referred to as *self-questioning*, it is a strategy that has emerged from three bodies of research—active processing, metacognitive theory, and schema theory (Wong, 1985). According to the active-processing perspective, self-questioning is critical to the reader's active engagement in comprehension because the act of generating questions creates an interaction between the reader and the text. According to metacognitive theory, self-questioning is crucial to the reader's ability to focus on important information and to monitor his or her own comprehension. In schema theory, self-questioning grows out of the connection between background knowledge and the learning of new information. According to schema theory, self-questioning is seen as a fundamental strategy for the reader to use in activating relevant background knowledge.

Question generation has been found to be effective and is a strategy recommended by the National Reading Panel (2000); however, the strategy has not been found to consistently improve students' reading comprehension (Rosenshine, Meister, & Chapman, 1996; Therrien, Wickstrom, & Jones, 2006). The strategy appears to be most effective in enhancing comprehension when students are able to read most words effortlessly, are given explicit instruction in how to generate questions, and have ample time to think while reading (Griffey, Zigmond, & Leinhardt, 1988; Wong, 1985). Bergman (1992) suggested that students be taught to ask themselves the following questions:

- To get the gist—What is the story about? What is the problem? What is the solution? What makes me think so?

141

CHAPTER 5

*During-Reading
Strategies:
Supporting
Strategic Reading*

- To predict-verify-decide—What's going to happen next? Is my prediction still good? Do I need to change my prediction? What makes me think so?

- To visualize-verify-decide—What does this person, place, or thing look like? Is the picture in my mind still good? Do I need to change my picture? What makes me think so?

- To summarize—What's happened so far? What makes me think so?

- To think aloud—What am I thinking? Why?

- To solve problems or help when I don't understand—Shall I guess, ignore and read on, reread or look back? Why? (p. 599)

Questioning the Author is a variation of the question generation strategy (Beck & McKeown, 2007; McKeown & Beck, 2004). In this approach, the teacher uses open-ended questions designed to encourage the students to think about what the author is trying to communicate. To emphasize that the questions should encourage meaningful engagement with the material, Beck and McKeown use the term *queries* to distinguish between open-ended versus known-answer questions. Examples of queries include:

- "What is the author trying to say about . . . ?"
- "What do you think the author means by . . . ?"
- "Why does the author set up the scene this way?"
- "That's what the author says, but why does the author say it this way?"
- "What does the author want you to think about . . . ?"
- "Why does the author want you to know this now?"

Wood, Pressley, and Winne (1990) developed *Elaborative Interrogation* as a question generation strategy specifically designed to be used with expository text in content area instruction. The students read one page of text, choose a statement from the text and turn it into a why question, use their prior knowledge and experiences to answer the question, read the page again or read the next page to see if the question is answered, and share it during group discussion with the teacher and other students.

The *TWA* strategy was also designed to be used with expository text. TWA is intended to be taught as a mnemonic that reminds students to *T*, think before reading about the author's purpose, what you know, and what you want to learn; *W*, think while reading about reading speed, linking knowledge, and rereading parts; and *A*, think after reading about the main idea, summarizing information, and what you learned (Mason, Meadan, Hedin, & Corso, 2006; Mason, Snyder, Sukhram, & Kedem, 2006; Rogevich & Perin, 2008).

Question generation is intended to guide the reader in the strategic processing of text. If you are using Bloom's taxonomy and asking knowledge, comprehension, application, analysis, synthesis, and evaluation questions, these questions serve as archetypes of self-questions so that during reading,

142

CHAPTER 5
*During-Reading
Strategies:
Supporting
Strategic Reading*

the student will begin using his or her inner voice in asking questions aimed at distinguishing important details through evaluating the material. The same is true if you are using Barrett's taxonomy or QARs. So, in explicitly teaching your students to generate their own questions during reading, the questions you ask will implicitly show the kinds of questions they should ask themselves.

Beyond Questions

Questions are not the only way to enhance comprehension during reading. The following are a few strategies that are effective with struggling readers.

Using Mental Imagery.   *Mental imagery* is generally thought of as the formation of visual or spatial representations in one's mind, although all sensory modalities can be represented in imagery. It has been suggested that mental imagery can serve two metacognitive functions. First, mental imagery can be a means for activating background knowledge prior to reading (Johnson, 1987; Long, Winograd, & Bridge, 1989). Second, mental imagery can serve as a comprehension monitoring function during reading (Gambrell & Jawitz, 1993; Sadoski, 1985; Sadoski & Paivio, 2001; Schirmer, 1995). It is one of the comprehension strategies recommended by the National Reading Panel (2000).

Mental imagery instruction fits easily into any model that segments text reading. As with prediction, the strategy is taught before the students begin reading the passage. The teacher then returns to the strategy when they have finished reading the passage. Before reading, the students are told, "Make pictures in your mind to help you understand and remember." After reading, the students are asked, "Do you have any pictures or scenes in your mind that you remember from this part of the story?" When the strategy is first introduced, you should model your own mental images after reading so that they know what you mean by a mental image. Though modeling is important at the beginning, sharing images can be continued even when the students are comfortable with the strategy because through sharing images, you can guide them in attending to the most important aspects of the material.

Some authors refer to this type of modeling behavior as teacher think-alouds (e.g., Cunningham & Allington, 2007; McKenna, 2002) because the teacher expresses what he or she is thinking while carrying out the strategy. Davey (1983) noted, "The modeling process is founded on the belief that if teachers describe their own thoughts about a text (so that students can see a mind responding to a specific passage), the students will realize how and when to do the same" (p. 45).

Romeo (2002) suggested that using all senses in mental imagery is more powerful than using visual imagery alone, particularly for at-risk readers. In Romeo's *Sensory Imaging Strategy*, the teacher explains and models seeing, hearing, smelling, tasting, and feeling by stopping at points in the text that are particularly evocative of images.

Paraphrasing and Getting the Gist.   *Paraphrasing* narrowly refers to restating the meaning of something written. In order to paraphrase, the reader has to understand the meaning well enough to translate it into his or her own linguistic structures. The act of paraphrasing appears to improve comprehension because it forces the reader's attention to the main idea and supporting details (Manzo & Manzo, 2008). Instead of asking a comprehension question per se, you can ask the student to paraphrase a segment just read with a statement such as, "Tell me in your own words what that sentence/paragraph said."

143

CHAPTER 5

*During-Reading
Strategies:
Supporting
Strategic Reading*

Paraphrasing typically focuses on a relatively brief segment of text. The students can also be asked to express the gist of a somewhat longer segment of one or two pages. As with paraphrasing, the point is to restate the material in their own words and to use relatively brief statements in doing so. Again, this strategy can be used in place of a comprehension question aimed at helping the students identify key points in the material. The same prompt can be used as with paraphrasing, except they are asked to tell in their words what the page said rather than the sentence or paragraph.

As with mental imagery, teacher modeling of paraphrasing and stating the gist are important when introducing the strategy. For example, you might say, "If I put this in my own words, I would say, Stacy is looking for a picture of herself as a baby because she needs to bring one for the class bulletin board." Teacher think-aloud does not involve just modeling the paraphrase but, rather, expressing your thought process in arriving at this paraphrase. For example, you might say, "I was a little confused because I didn't know why Stacy was looking at baby pictures, then I read a little more and realized that she needs to bring a picture to school for the baby photo bulletin board so she is looking for a picture of herself as a baby."

Using Think-Pair-Share.   In *Think-Pair-Share*, students who are reading the same material work with partners. At stop points that are preset by the teacher, the students first pause to think about the passage and then discuss it with their partner. According to Rasinski and Padak (2004), older students can make brief notes while thinking to remind them of ideas they want to share.

This strategy fits particularly well within a Directed Reading Thinking Activity as an alternative to asking questions after each guided reading segment. With Think-Pair-Share, you can ask the students to focus on particular aspects of the material before they start reading or provide leeway in letting them decide with their partners what to discuss at each stop point. In another variation, *Character Sketches*, the students are asked to focus on character development and at each successive stop-point, they are expected to modify their ideas based on new insights gained through reading.

Playing Linguistic Roulette.   Another option to teacher questions during reading is *Linguistic Roulette*. After each passage is read, the students are asked to skim through the passage and choose a sentence that is special because it is interesting, important, confusing, unique, strange, or for some other reason. The students can write their sentences or mark their place with a bookmark.

144

CHAPTER 5

*During-Reading
Strategies:
Supporting
Strategic Reading*

As they take turns reading their sentences aloud, the students discuss their ideas and perspectives about each sentence, why it is special, and how it relates to the story line or character development.

Using Yellow Stickies.   Many authors suggest that students take notes or carry out other types of writing during reading. Although writing during reading may be very beneficial for improving comprehension, the struggling reader is likely to find the task of writing to be as daunting as the task of reading, and putting them together may add a burden to comprehension rather than facilitate understanding. Richek, Caldwell, Jennings, and Lerner (2002) described a strategy that may have the same benefits as writing during reading but with a simpler task. During reading, the students place *yellow stickies* (small note papers with one sticky edge) on the precise part of the text on which they wish to comment. They are taught to make one of three graphic messages: an exclamation point for something surprising, a smiley face for something enjoyable, or a question mark for something unclear. After the passage is read, discussion centers on the words, phrases, or sentences on which the students have placed yellow stickies, starting with the question marks and then moving to the surprising and enjoyable parts.

Using Vocabulary Knowledge and Learning Vocabulary in Context

During reading, the student will encounter vocabulary that was pretaught as well as new vocabulary. If concept-based approaches have been used before reading, attention can be drawn back to the Semantic Map, Semantic Feature Analysis, Concept Wheel, or other visual or graphic representation of a word's meaning. If the students cannot recall the word, the representation can be briefly reviewed. If they have remembered the word, new ideas can be added to the representation.

When the student encounters a new vocabulary word in text, *context-based approaches* can be used. Context-based approaches suffer from the tension between two realities. The first involves the probability that new words can be learned through context. Obviously, when context is explicit, it is more likely that the students will be able to derive the meaning of a new word. Nevertheless, even when context is not particularly supportive, it has been found that readers will acquire some aspects of a word's meaning but often not complete enough to write a definition or choose a synonym. With further exposures to the word in various contexts, more complete understanding of a word's meaning usually takes place (Jenkins, Stein, & Wysocki, 1984; Moore, 1987; Schatz & Baldwin, 1986). Based on their own study of eighth graders' ability to develop word knowledge from context as well as their review of the literature, Nagy, Herman, and Anderson (1985) concluded that "incidental learning from context accounts for a substantial proportion of the vocabulary growth that occurs during the school years" (p. 233). So context-based approaches may have limited benefit the first time a word is encountered in text but are increasingly successful when the reader has multiple encounters with a word in context.

The second reality involved in relying on context-based approaches is that you cannot explicitly teach all of the new words your students will encounter in every reading selection. By necessity, they will need to figure out the meanings of many words through context.

One approach for teaching vocabulary in context is to teach the students to follow a set of steps when encountering a new vocabulary word. Blachowicz and Fisher (2006) suggested that students be taught to:

- Look before, at, and after the word.
- Reason. Connect what they know to what the author has written.
- Predict a possible meaning.
- Resolve or redo. Decide if they know enough, should try again, or consult an expert or reference. (p. 30)

Another approach is *SCANR* (Jenkins, Matlock, & Slocum, 1989). The student is taught to *Substitute* a word or expression when encountering a word with an unknown meaning, *Check* the context to find clues that support or do not support the substitute word, *Ask* if the substitute word fits all of these context clues, determine if a new substitute word is *Needed*, and *Revise* and choose a new substitute word that better fits all context clues if necessary.

The *strategy lesson* format discussed earlier can also be used for teaching students how to figure out the meaning of new words from the context. At the point in the lesson at which you would typically ask a comprehension question, you can make sure that you ask a question that can be answered only if the students understand a target vocabulary word. Their answers will elicit whether they already knew the vocabulary word or were able to use context successfully. If not, you can conduct a brief strategy lesson in which you point out contextual clues and make hypotheses about the word's meaning. Indeed, you can do this as a think-aloud to model your own problem solving. Of course, you need to end the lesson by either confirming what the students thought the word meant or explaining the meaning as the author uses it in the current context.

Harmon (2002) developed the strategy of *facilitated peer dialogues* as an approach to support independent word-learning strategies of struggling readers. Students reading the same material are placed in a small group. They are taught to stop when encountering a confusing or unfamiliar word and to ask the rest of the group to stop as well. The student solicits assistance from the others in understanding the word's meaning. The teacher can facilitate the discussion if needed by providing explicit instruction of alternative strategies, reminding students of strategies, guiding problem-solving efforts, acknowledging student efforts, offering alternative strategies for figuring out the word's meaning, prompting, and ensuring that all students participate in the discussion.

The strategies discussed in this chapter are those that are taught during reading. Not all models provide opportunity for during-reading strategies. Some models, such as the Integrated Skills Method, provide intensive instruction before reading so that when the student actually encounters the material, the assumption is that he or she needs little further instruction to interact successfully with the text. Other models, such as Reciprocal Teaching, incorporate prereading and postreading instruction but the complete passage is read without the teacher's intervention. When a model offers during-reading instruction, it is because this is a crucial part of the scaffold needed by the reader to interact successfully with the material.

The next step is choosing strategies after reading. As with prereading and during-reading strategies, postreading strategies are essentially slotted into the steps of the reading model. In the next chapter, strategies that you can use after reading to support the student's strategic reading will be presented.

QUESTIONS FOR REFLECTION AND APPLICATION

1. After observing your reading instruction, the principal asks, "Why do you keep interrupting the students while they are reading?" How do you respond?

2. If a model does not provide opportunity for strategy instruction during reading, and your struggling readers need support with the material beyond what you could provide before reading, what should you do?

3. While you are working with a small group of students as they are reading, how can you provide meaningful reading instruction to the others in the class?

4. How will you know if the instruction you have provided during reading is helpful to the struggling readers?

SUGGESTED RESOURCES FOR ADDITIONAL READING

Beck, Isabel L., & McKeown, Margaret G. (2006). *Improving Comprehension with Questioning the Author.* New York: Scholastic.

McGregor, Tanny. (2007). *Comprehension Connections: Bridges to Strategic Reading.* Portsmouth, NH: Heinemann.

Raphael, Taffy E., Highfield, Kathy, & Au, Kathryn H. (2006). *QAR Now: A Powerful and Practical Framework That Develops Comprehension and Higher-Level Thinking in All Students.* New York: Scholastic.

Stebick, Divonna M., & Dain, Joy M. (2007). *Comprehension Strategies for Your K–6 Literacy Classroom: Thinking before, during, and after Reading.* New York: Corwin.

Valmont, William J. (2003). *Technology for Literacy Teaching and Learning.* Belmont, CA: Wadsworth.

After-Reading Strategies
Synthesizing and Extending

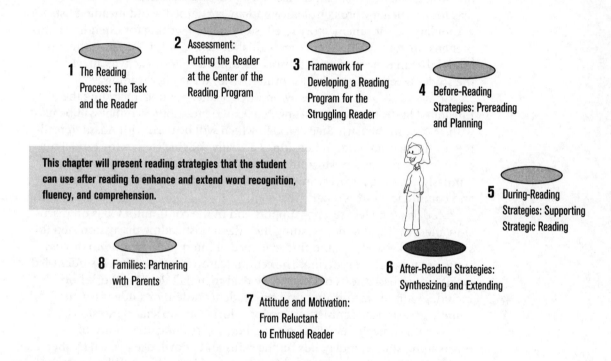

1 The Reading Process: The Task and the Reader

2 Assessment: Putting the Reader at the Center of the Reading Program

3 Framework for Developing a Reading Program for the Struggling Reader

4 Before-Reading Strategies: Prereading and Planning

This chapter will present reading strategies that the student can use after reading to enhance and extend word recognition, fluency, and comprehension.

5 During-Reading Strategies: Supporting Strategic Reading

8 Families: Partnering with Parents

6 After-Reading Strategies: Synthesizing and Extending

7 Attitude and Motivation: From Reluctant to Enthused Reader

Strategies that you employ after the students have read a story, novel, chapter, newspaper, magazine article, and other material provide opportunity for them to engage in activities that reinforce the skills you have taught before and during reading; synthesize what they have learned in order to move toward independence in applying these skills; and extend their ability to think critically and creatively about the ideas in the material.

Postreading strategies fit into any instructional model for teaching literacy regardless of whether the model specifically offers a postreading step. As you know from Chapter 3, several of the models offer suggestions for the kinds of activities that the teacher should carry out after reading.

148

CHAPTER 6

After-Reading
Strategies:
Synthesizing and
Extending

The Directed Reading Activity/Directed Reading Thinking Activity, which is the model that will be used with Maria, incorporates three postreading steps designed to extend comprehension and strengthen word recognition. The discussion step involves asking questions that stimulate discussion about the central story line and engaging the students in higher level and critical thinking. The skills development step incorporates activities that offer practice in a skill that the students needed in the passage they just read. And the enrichment step entails an activity designed to extend their comprehension.

Cooperative Integrated Reading and Composition, which may be used with Ellison, also incorporates multiple postreading activities including treasure hunt questions that emphasize story structure elements, word mastery lists for practicing words until automaticity is attained, word meaning lists for vocabulary development, story retell, story-related writing for extending comprehension, and spelling activities. Collaborative Strategic Reading, the other model that may be used with Ellison, includes a wrap-up activity in which the students self-question and summarize key ideas after reading.

Some models focus expressly on fluency after reading, including the Integrated Skills Method and Language Experience Approach that will be used with Marek. In the Early Steps Model, which will be used with Adani, rereading for fluency and comprehension is actually the first step in the model but essentially serves as a postreading strategy for the previous day's reading. Similarly, Reading Recovery involves rereading a familiar book for fluency and comprehension as a daily first step.

Models at the less-teacher-support end of the continuum focus on discussion after reading. Guided Reading includes a postreading discussion step for students to revisit the text to find evidence of interpretations and to discuss strategies for problem solving. The central feature of Book Club is student-led small-group discussions of commonly read material. Reading Workshop includes journal writing after reading, student-student or student-teacher conferences, and student-led discussions during group sharing sessions.

As with strategies taught before and during reading, the choice of postreading strategies depends on the skills and knowledge needed by the reader. The following strategies are summarized in Table 6.1. When comparing Tables 4.1, 5.1, and 6.1, you can see the commonalities and differences between strategies taught before, during, and after reading.

Word Recognition after Reading

After reading, strategies for word recognition are often referred to as skill-building activities because they tend to focus on systematically practicing the skills of phonic analysis, structural analysis, analogy, and automatic word recognition as well as applying strategies for figuring out complex sentence structures and figurative language.

TABLE 6.1 Instructional Strategies after Reading

Strategies	Reading Abilities		
	Word Recognition	*Fluency*	*Comprehension*
Phonemic awareness instruction			
Phonics, analogy, and structural analysis instruction	• Word study sorts, making words, using words you know, word building, word walls • Work sheets • Games		
Context strategy instruction			

Automatic word recognition instruction	• Word study sorts, making words, using words you know, word building, word walls
	• Work sheets
	• Games
		• Repeated readings
		  • Radio reading
		  • Tape-recorded readings
		• Paired reading
		• Choral reading
		• Oral recitation lesson	

Sentence structures and figurative language instruction			(See Key concept instruction)

Vocabulary instruction			• Definition-based approaches
			  • Puzzles
			  • Games
			  • Dictionaries
			  • Cubing
			• Concept-based approaches
			  • Semantic Mapping
			  • Semantic Feature Analysis
			  • Concept Attainment
			  • Concept Wheel

(continued)

TABLE 6.1 continued

Strategies	Reading Abilities		
	Word Recognition	*Fluency*	*Comprehension*

Key concept instruction			• Questioning
			• Scaffolded conversations
			• Discussion
			  • Grand conversations
			  • Reading conferences
			  • Reader's chair
			  • Literature circles
			• Journals
			• Retelling
			  • Verbal retelling
			  • Story maps
			  • Story frames
			  • Story pyramids
			  • Plot profiles
			  • Drama
			• Summarizing

Recalling Word Recognition Strategies

The word recognition strategies of phonics, structural analysis, analogy, and automatic word recognition are goals for Marek, Maria, and Adani. Having taught word recognition strategies before reading and having provided opportunity to apply these strategies during reading, their teachers can make use of postreading activities to offer further application, reinforcement, and successful practice to help these readers remember those strategies.

Many of the activities discussed in Chapter 4 for prereading are also appropriate as postreading activities to practice word recognition strategies. Examples include Word Study (also known as Word Sorts), Making Words, Using Words You Know, Word Building, and Word Walls.

Worksheets developed commercially or by teachers are also effective for isolated skill practice. The negative reputation of worksheets comes largely from overuse (too much time is devoted to completing short-answer questions in practice activities) and inappropriate use (worksheets take the place of strategy instruction and actual reading, and become an end in themselves rather than a means to strategic reading).

Games also can provide postreading practice in word recognition strategies, particularly sight word recognition. Examples include Concentration, Bingo, Scrabble, Hangman, and Wheel of Fortune. Somewhat more sophisticated games, such as Jeopardy (the teacher or student playing the "teacher" reads the answer and the students have to figure out the question) and Twenty Questions (the student can ask up to 20 questions with yes or no answers to figure out the identity of the mystery word, prefix, suffix, or letter sound), take greater teacher preparation but may be more engaging for older students.

Figuring Out Complex Sentence Structures and Figurative Language

Postreading strategies for figuring out complex sentence structures and figurative language are incorporated into postreading comprehension strategies discussed later in this chapter. During instruction involving the key concepts in the material, such as retelling and discussion, problems in understanding structures important to comprehending the text will emerge and you can focus instruction directly on the problematic structure, similar to the strategy lessons described in Chapter 5.

Fluency

Problems with fluency are common among struggling readers, though fluency issues often do not emerge in assessments because problems with phonemic awareness, phonics, and the other word recognition strategies are so much more obvious and urgent. Only Ellison and Marek demonstrated difficulties with fluency during their assessments. Mrs. Hong found that Ellison had relatively good word recognition skills but that he was a word-by-word reader, which resulted in a low reading rate and poor fluency. Mr. Rumrill found that Marek's fluency issues were a result of his difficulties with word recognition, particularly phonic analysis, analogy, and context for identifying words, but the teacher did not include fluency as a goal because he wanted to concentrate on Marek's word recognition difficulties first.

According to findings of the National Reading Panel (2000), two major approaches to fluency instruction have been investigated: *guided repeated oral reading procedures* and *independent silent reading*. The panel found that guided repeated oral reading procedures positively influence word recognition, fluency, and comprehension in readers across the grade levels and are effective with students experiencing reading difficulties as well as good readers. The panel further found that independent silent reading with minimal guidance or feedback is not directly related to fluency or general improvements in reading skills though better readers have been found to do more independent silent reading. The implications are that strategies incorporating guided repeated oral reading accompanied by ample opportunity to engage in independent silent reading would offer struggling readers the best combination of approaches to improve fluency.

152

CHAPTER 6

*After-Reading
Strategies:
Synthesizing and
Extending*

Teaching Fluency

Fluency strategies have the common denominator of involving the oral rereading of text. As the following strategies demonstrate, sometimes the text is relatively brief and reread several times in a row, and sometimes the text is lengthier and reread orally over time.

The text can be read silently prior to rereading, followed by teacher read-aloud of the same text, which Padak and Rasinski (2008) believe provides a model of voice, intonation, phrasing, rate, expression, and volume. Or the student can read the text silently and then orally reread it without the middle step of teacher read-aloud. Or each of the readings, including the first, can be done orally.

Several of the models incorporate steps for rereading text material to develop fluency. The students engage in partner reading after reading the text silently in the Cooperative Integrated Reading and Composition model; student-generated stories are reread initially with the teacher and then revisited over time in the Language Experience Approach; stories are reread in Early Steps and Reading Recovery; passages are reread with partners in the Guided Reading approach; and sentences and stories are reread until fluency is attained in the Integrated Skills Method.

Identifying Materials and Groupings for Fluency Instruction

When choosing material for fluency instruction, the major factor to consider is difficulty level. Although the zone of proximal development for word recognition and comprehension is found in instructional level material, the zone for fluency is found in instructional to independent level material because the students must be able to concentrate on phrasing, intonation, and expression. Another factor to consider in choosing material is text structure. Padak and Rasinski (2008) recommend using predictable or patterned text. A third factor involves the nature of the material. Therrien, Gormley, and Kubina (2006) suggest that the material contain a complete narrative and include themes commonly found in children's literature.

Given that a number of fluency-building strategies are conducted within paired readings, determining how to pair the students is a consideration. McKenna (2002) suggested four methods for choosing student partners:

- *Good reader–poor reader*: Pairing students so that one student is a more able reader and one student is a struggling reader.
- *Just friends*: Allowing students to choose their own partner.
- *Leveled pairs*: Pairing students who are reading at approximately the same reading level.
- *Clock partners*: Varying pairs by having students partner with a different peer during the day depending on whose name is written as the hour/minute hand on his or her personally stamped clock face.

Repeated Readings

153

CHAPTER 6
*After-Reading
Strategies:
Synthesizing and
Extending*

The procedure of *repeated readings* is a relatively simple activity involving the rereading of material until fluency is achieved. According to Therrien, Gormley et al. (2006), the passages should be short and contain a complete narrative. They suggest a passage length of 53–55 words for first-grade reading level, 89–111 words for second-grade reading level, 107–133 for third-grade reading level, and 123–153 for fourth-grade reading level. These ranges would enable most students to read the passage in 1–1.25 minutes.

The research on repeated readings indicates that the following essential components maximize the effectiveness of the approach to improving fluency (Dowhower, 1989; Samuels, 2002b; Therrien, 2004):

1. Students should read the passages aloud to a competent adult who can offer effective feedback.

2. The adult should provide corrective feedback on word errors.

3. Students should reread passages until reading with satisfactory speed, accuracy, and expression. The oral reading fluency norms first presented in Chapter 2 can be applied (53 correct words per minute for first, 89 cwpm for second, 107 cwpm for third, 123 cwpm for fourth, 139 cwpm for fifth, and 150 cwpm for sixth grades).

4. The teacher should select passages at a difficulty level that requires the students to reread between three and four times to achieve satisfactory fluency. Passages that can be read fluently in one or two readings are too easy and passages that cannot be read fluently in four readings are too hard.

Performance Readings

Fluency can also be built through activities involving the student in a kind of performance. For example, a struggling reader might read a story to a younger child, a poem to parents, or a script as part of a drama re-creation of the text. *Readers Theatre* (described later in the section on comprehension after reading) is also a motivating strategy for building reading fluency (Worthy & Prater, 2002) as is *radio reading* (Rhodes & Dudley-Marling, 1996; Searfoss, 1975). In radio reading, one student or a small group read a passage to an audience of peers after having practiced it several times. The audience members have not read the text and do not have a copy of it, so they listen to the performance as if they were listening to the radio. (The concept of listening to a story performed on the radio may seem antiquated, so you may want to rename the strategy "Podcast reading.") Readers Theatre has been found to be effective in improving oral reading fluency with low-ability readers as well as with average and high-ability readers (Keehn, 2003).

When practicing for a performance reading, Padak and Rasinski (2008) suggest *tape-recorder reading* as a fluency-building strategy. They found that struggling readers enjoy rereading texts into tape recorders, listening and

154

CHAPTER 6
*After-Reading
Strategies:
Synthesizing and
Extending*

critiquing their own readings, and determining ways to make subsequent readings more fluent. Needless to say, this approach is not workable for students who are deaf or hard of hearing.

Paired Reading

Paired reading is a term for an approach developed in the late 1960s called the *Neurological Impress Method* (Feazell, 2004; Heckelman, 1969; Hollingsworth, 1978). In paired reading, the struggling reader reads aloud with a partner who is a more skilled reader—usually a teacher or paraprofessional, but the partner can be a trained peer. The more skilled reader reads a bit louder or a bit ahead of the struggling reader until the struggling reader signals that he or she would like to take the lead or read alone. The text involves relatively short segments so that paired reading sessions take only 15 minutes or so.

> On sections of text that are difficult for the tutee, the pair read out loud to-gether. The tutor adjusts to the tutee's natural reading speed, and synchrony is established with practice. When the tutee makes an error, the tutor repeats the word correctly and requires the tutee to do likewise before proceeding . . . When an easier text has been selected that is more within the tutee's inde-pendent reading ability level, the tutee can choose to silence the tutor by a pre-arranged nonverbal signal, such as a knock, a nudge, or a squeeze. As the tutor becomes silent, the tutee continues to read aloud, receiving praise and participating in discussion about complex words, until there is a failure to read a word correctly within 5 seconds, at which point the tutor corrects the error and the pair resume reading together. (Topping, 1989, pp. 490–491)

A variation of this strategy is referred to as *echo reading*. The teacher or one of the students reads a sentence at a time and the other students serve as the echo. Cunningham and Allington (2007) suggest that the strategy is best used with very early material in which only one sentence appears per page.

Choral Reading

In *choral reading*, a group of students read a passage orally together. The Pledge of Allegiance is an example of choral reading that most students expe-rience almost every day during elementary school. Richek, Caldwell, Jennings, and Lerner (2002) observed that choral reading is particularly effective and enjoyable with material that contains rhythm and rhyme, such as the poetry of Shel Silverstein and Jack Prelutsky.

Choral reading is considered to be very valuable for struggling readers, notably those who are English language learners, because their performance is embedded into the performance of the group and so they do not experi-ence any embarrassment or awkwardness because of their own fluency diffi-culties (McCauley & McCauley, 1992; Strickland, Ganske, & Monroe, 2002).

Oral Recitation Lesson

155

CHAPTER 6

*After-Reading
Strategies:
Synthesizing and
Extending*

The *oral recitation lesson* is a postreading strategy that involves material not previously read by the students. As developed by Hoffman (1987), the oral recitation lesson includes the following steps:

1. The teacher reads a story aloud to the students.
2. The students discuss the story and develop a story map based on story structure components.
3. The students write a summary of the story using the story map to guide them.
4. The teacher reads aloud segments of the story and discusses what makes oral reading fluent and expressive.
5. The students read these same segments orally, individually and chorally, several times. During individual practice, the students read orally in a very soft voice.
6. Each student reads a chosen segment orally to a group or the class and solicits positive feedback.

Comprehension after Reading

Recalling Vocabulary

As discussed in Chapter 4, the three qualities of effective vocabulary instruction are integration, repetition, and meaningful use. Prereading strategies emphasize integration; during-reading and postreading strategies emphasize repetition and meaningful use. These postreading strategies are intended to reinforce students' recall of new vocabulary. Revisiting new vocabulary after reading is particularly important for students with language learning difficulties, deaf and hard of hearing students, and English language learners. The same two approaches for teaching vocabulary before reading are the same ones for postreading vocabulary instruction: definition-based and concept-based approaches.

Definition-Based Approaches

The most common way to revisit vocabulary after reading is with activities such as crossword puzzles, word find puzzles, word-definition matching games, adding illustrations and new sentences to personal dictionaries, and swapping dictionaries to practice words and definitions with peers.

Another approach is to return to an activity conducted before reading and add or modify what was developed. For example, the students could

156

CHAPTER 6

*After-Reading
Strategies:
Synthesizing and
Extending*

return to the sentences that they had developed before reading for the Possible Sentences activity (discussed in Chapter 4), decide whether the sentences could or could not be true based on what they have just read, and then modify the sentences to make them true.

Games provide another mode for practicing vocabulary after reading. Reutzel and Cooter (2007) described two such strategies that they noted are particularly effective for students learning English as a second language and those with language learning difficulties. *Cubing* involves writing six questions on the sides of a large foam or wooden cube: What does it look like? What is similar or different? What else does it make you think of? What is it made of? How is it used? Where can one be found? The cube is rolled and the students answer either orally or in writing. In *Vocabulary Bingo*, vocabulary words that were recently learned are written on bingo-like cards with several rows and columns, making sure that the order differs from card to card, and definitions are written on slips of paper. The slips of paper are placed in a bowl and the student or teacher, acting as the caller, selects one at a time and reads the definition. The students cover the correct word with a token or piece of cardboard. The rules of bingo are followed; the first student to cover a row, column, or diagonal is the winner and a new round of bingo can be played.

Blachowicz and Fisher (2006) described several variations of card games for vocabulary reinforcement. For each, the teacher prepares a deck of cards consisting of at least 40 word cards with pairs that are word synonyms or definitions. In *Fish*, all the cards are dealt and the students take turns picking a card from their partner's hand. In *Rummy*, seven cards are dealt to each player; each player chooses a card and then discards one, placing any pairs on the table. The first player to make all pairs is the winner. In *Old Teacher*, one card is made for the "old teacher." In turns, each student asks if the partner has a word/synonym/definition. Pairs are discarded until only the "old teacher" remains.

Richek et al. (2002) suggested putting small cards, which are made so that one end could be flipped up, on a vocabulary bulletin board. The new vocabulary words from a story, chapter, or book are divided among the students so that each student receives one or two new words. The students write their names on the front of their cards to establish that they are the "expert consultant" and on the inside, they write a definition and use the word in a sentence, which are approved by the teacher before posting on the bulletin board. The students can refer back to the bulletin board as needed and go to the "expert consultant" for clarification or help. The students can also work in pairs, taking turns as "expert" and "student" to practice the words.

Concept-Based Approaches

All of the concept-based approaches provide opportunity after reading to revisit and expand on definitions developed before reading. For the "sports' Semantic Map discussed in Chapter 4, additional "benefits," "kinds," and "related concepts" can be added and ideas proposed prior to reading can be revised based on what the students have read. If the teacher used a word map, the students can generate further information to answer the questions: What is it? What is it like? What are some examples? Similarly, if the teacher used Semantic Feature Analysis, the students can add words related to the topic word and features of the concept, and if the teacher used the Concept Attainment activity, the students can add attributes of the word along with related terms gleaned from reading the text.

Extending Understanding of Key Concepts

The individual assessments of the case study children indicated that all would benefit from postreading strategies designed to extend their understanding and develop self-monitoring strategies they could ultimately use independently to improve comprehension (see Figure 6.1). Adani's assessment showed that she could predict and retell but that she was highly reliant on details and had difficulty making inferences and synthesizing ideas. She understood that stories are made up of characters, problems, and solutions; however, she had difficulty identifying story setting. Maria's assessment indicated that she thought reading meant correctly identifying words; she did not fully realize that reading is a meaning-making endeavor. Ellison showed difficulty identifying main idea and determining sequence of events in his assessment. Marek's weak phonemic awareness skills made it less pressing to assess his cognitive strategies for comprehension during the assessment; however, his ability to provide contextually appropriate words in a cloze activity indicated that he has a fundamental awareness of the link between written words and text meaning.

Teacher questions, discussion, and writing are the most common strategies for text comprehension after reading. The following examples offer ways for you to vary the strategies you use with your struggling readers from lesson to lesson.

Questioning

During reading, questioning typically takes the form of relatively brief answers related to detail-oriented information in the text. After reading, questions can push the students to delve more deeply into the material, synthesize ideas into a coherent whole, and think analytically, critically, and creatively.

Two areas of questioning are particularly effective with struggling readers after reading. The first involves asking questions beyond the literal. Depending on the taxonomy, these would be questions requiring analysis, synthesis, and evaluation according to Bloom's taxonomy; evaluation and appreciation according to Barrett's taxonomy; and Think and Search/Putting It Together and In My Head questions according to Question-Answer Relationships. Regardless of the taxonomy used, such questions have been found to promote higher order thinking in skilled and less skilled readers (Hansen & Pearson, 1983; Schirmer & Woolsey, 1997).

FIGURE 6.1 Before-, During-, and After-Reading Strategies with Case Study Children

	Before	During	After
Adani (Early Steps)	Word study of letter sound and spelling patterns; Reread for automaticity and fluency	Self-correction for word recognition; Application of comprehension strategies; Sentence strips and PQR for syntax; Predicting	Reread for fluency; Choral reading; Readers Theatre
Maria (DRTA)	Sight word flash cards + phonic, analogy, and structural features + discussing new meanings; Reconciled Reading Lesson to build background knowledge	Comprehension questions; Strategy lessons targeted at word recognition and comprehension; Predicting	Games for sight word practice; Personal dictionary and games for vocabulary; Story maps
Ellison (CIRC/CSR)	Semantic mapping for new vocabulary; Predicting	Partner reading; Monitor comprehension and apply fix-up strategies; Predicting; Question generation; Look-Reason-Predict-Resolve for vocabulary	Word mastery for automaticity; Summarizing; Retelling; Story structure questions; Story related writing; Repeated reading
Marek (ISM/LEA)	Phonemic awareness activities; Letter-sound and pattern decoding activities; Sight word flash cards; Sentence rereading until automaticity	Read together for meaning, pointing out punctuation; Think-aloud for word recognition	Word walls for sight word practice; Reread for fluency; Story frames

Selection of New Strategies

Ongoing Assessment

The second area of questioning involves asking questions that highlight story structure. For students who have some difficulty with text structure, such as Adani (identifying setting) and Ellison (sequencing), questions that highlight text structure have been found to be effective in improving comprehension. Indeed, using *story structure questions* has been found to be more effective than explicitly teaching readers to pinpoint and define story structure components as a method for increasing comprehension (Johnson & Bliesmer, 1983; Schmitt & O'Brien, 1986). Instead of teaching students the labels for text components, it has been suggested that teachers use questions to bring significant text components and the causal relationships between components to the reader's attention. Through questions that highlight the information reflecting the basic structure of narrative or expository text, the teacher in essence can "show" readers what it means to understand written discourse. Ultimately, such questions over time help students—particularly struggling readers who may not discern structures intuitively through multiple encounters with text—to internalize text structure into their schema (Carnine & Kinder, 1985; Schirmer & Bond, 1990).

You can create questions that emphasize text structure by first analyzing the structure of the material and then creating questions based on key components. The following are examples of story structure questions for *Goldilocks and the Three Bears:*

Where did the three bears live? (Setting)

Why did the three bears go for a walk? (Initiating Event/Reaction)

Who showed up at the Bears' home? (Action)

What did Goldilocks do when she entered the house? (Consequence)

What happened when Goldilocks tasted the porridge, sat in the chairs, and walked upstairs? (Reaction/Action)

What happened when the three bears came home? (Consequence)

What did Goldilocks do when she woke up? (Ending)

Scaffolded Conversations

School discourse is different from home discourse, and home discourses vary by culture. One of the common types of classroom exchanges that students never see at home is question-answer-evaluate, sometimes called question-answer routines. For example, the teacher asks, "What is the capital of Oregon?" One student answers, "Salem." The teacher responds, "That's right" and then asks, "Where is the Columbia River?" The exchange between the teacher and students is characterized by teacher control of the dialogue, brief answers by the students, and lack of logical connection between the student's answer and the teacher's next question (Nippold, 2007). School discourse is also marked by a high proportion of teacher language and a relatively small proportion of individual student language; teachers generally take longer

160
....

CHAPTER 6

*After-Reading
Strategies:
Synthesizing and
Extending*

turns, they monitor who takes turns and how long their turns are, and they determine when the topic should be changed or terminated (Cazden, 2001; Wells, 1986). When students expect communication to be conversational in nature, typical school discourse can be baffling.

An approach that can be more effective than question-answer routines with struggling readers has been termed *scaffolded conversations.* The intent of scaffolded conversations is for the teacher to provide a support structure for ways to think about the text within the context of the give-and-take character-istic of real conversations. The term *scaffolding* applies the metaphor of the scaffold, which in construction parlance is a temporary platform for support-ing workers building an edifice. In current learning theory, a scaffold is a tem-porary supportive structure that enables learners to complete a task they would not be able to complete without support. These supports are removed or faded in stages until the learner is able to complete the task independently.

In the scaffolded conversations model, the teacher engages the students in dialogue about the material, which can be a paragraph, page, chapter, or complete text. Within this dialogue, you contribute your ideas in ways that act as a scaffold for the students to think about and respond to the material (Aukerman, 2007; Echevarria, 1995; Goldenberg, 1993). For example, in the Diagnostic Teaching Lesson in Chapter 2, Ms. Tankersley asked many compre-hension questions. If she conducted this same DRTA lesson with a small group of students using a scaffolded conversation, instead of asking, "What was Stacy doing at the beginning of the story?" and "She and her sister, Emily, were looking at baby pictures. They were where?" she might say, "I was con-fused at the beginning of the story. It was hard to figure out what Stacy and Emily were doing." Ms. Tankersley would then wait for the students to con-tribute their thoughts, when she might say, "I can see that Stacy is excited to bring a baby picture to school. I hope she is careful with it" instead of asking, "How did she bring the picture to school?"

Discussion

Postreading *discussion* enables the students to express their thoughts and impressions with the teacher and peers, who can provide other perspectives, share information, help solve problems, explore ideas, provide immediate feedback, and clarify thinking.

Suggestions for what not to do in leading a discussion tend to outweigh what is known about how to lead effective classroom discussions after read-ing. Wilen (1990) observed that while discussion should be an educative, reflective, and structured group conversation with students, in actuality, teach-ers generally dominate discussions with the presentation or review of basic information. Sparks-Langer, Starko, and their colleagues (Sparks-Langer et al., 2004; Starko et al., 2002) pointed out that when the dialogue travels from teacher to student and student to teacher like a many-armed spider, the pattern represents questioning and not discussion. If communication travels variously between students as well as teacher to student and student to teacher, the pattern represents discussion. According to Orlich, Harder, Callahan, Trevison, and Brown (2007), true discussions are characterized by verbal interaction, both objective and emotional, in the exchange and evaluation of information and ideas.

Tompkins (2006) referred to true discussions as *grand conversations*. She noted that in grand conversations, students sit in a circle so that they can see each other, the teacher's role is to be a facilitator, and the students share their interpretations and reflections on the text they have read. If the dialogue bogs down, Tompkins suggested that the teacher use open-ended questions that encourage the students to attend to something that no one has yet mentioned, personal connections to the story line, illustrations, author, language, or literary characteristics.

Depending on how you group your students for reading, students who are less proficient with English may be more likely to be quiet and less participatory. To engage English language learners more fully in discussions, Mohr and Mohr (2007) developed the *response protocol* strategy. The protocol offers ways for the teacher to reply to responses that are correct to encourage collaboration (e.g., "Great answer. Tell me more."), responses that are partially correct (e.g., "Those are good ideas but not quite complete. What else could you add?"), responses in a language other than English (e.g., "Can you say that using any English words?"), responses that are questions (e.g., "That's a great question. Does anyone know the answer?"), responses that are inappropriate or wrong (e.g., "I don't quite understand what you're telling us. Do you mean . . . ?"), and silent responses (e.g., "Let me give you an example of what I mean.").

Many educators believe that peer-led discussions are richer and more complex than teacher-led discussions (Almasi, 1995; Koskinen & O'Flahavan, 1995; Leal, 1993). On the other hand, less able readers have been found to experience greater difficulty participating in literature discussions, displaying their knowledge, and constructing meaning collaboratively (Wollman-Bonilla, 1994). Finn (2009) noted that children from working-class backgrounds may not experience habits of communication and ways of using language that are compatible with student-to-student discussions and that in order to create this type of literacy environment, their teachers must be aware of the attitudes, beliefs, values, and behaviors in their cultural communities and develop a bridge between home and school discourse.

Teacher-led discussions typically occur within a group setting in which all the students have read the same material. Another format for discussions is called *reading conferences*. Reading conferences are a hallmark of the Reading Workshop model. These conferences typically last between 5 and 15 minutes and, as with scaffolded conversations, look very different from typical school discourse. Unlike question-answer routines, reading conferences involve open-ended questions with no "known" answers and discussion about mutually interesting stories and characters (Hansen, 2001; Strickland, Dillon,

162

CHAPTER 6

*After-Reading
Strategies:
Synthesizing and
Extending*

Funkhouser, Glick, & Rogers, 1989). Once students have been involved in many one-to-one conferences with the teacher and have learned how to be an interested listener, peer conferences are recommended to proportionally increase their opportunities to engage in literature discussion.

Reader's Chair and *literature circles* are two other formats for discussion. During Reader's Chair, one student shares what he or she has read or is currently reading with a group of fellow students and then "chairs" the subsequent discussion. In their study involving elementary level students, Strickland and her associates (1989) found that student-led literature discussion groups were a valuable resource for learning language, learning through language, and learning about language. They observed the following:

> One of the most significant features of these discussion groups is that it puts the student in the role of expert or resource. The presenter makes the decisions about what is important to reveal about the book and what is to be read aloud. Not only do students have a greater sense of control over the talk, they have more opportunities to talk in an interactional pattern that is likely to criss-cross among the group members rather than remain dyadic. (p. 199)

Literature circles are small, student-led discussion groups about a book that all the students in the group have read. The purpose and function of this type of literature response group is similar to book clubs for adults. In an adult book club, a small group of enthusiastic readers decide on a book they are all interested in reading and then get together for a discussion after the members have had time to read the book. The same is true for literature circles. A small group of students read the same book and then get together to discuss it. Literature circles have been found to be an effective approach with middle school English language learners (Farris, Nelson, & L'Allier, 2007) as well as a valuable venue for bringing multicultural literature to all students (Wang & Aldridge, 2007).

The following are recommended guidelines for setting up literature circles (Clarke & Holwadel, 2007; Daniels, 2002):

- Reading material is self-selected by the students.
- Groups are formed based on commonly selected material. When new material is chosen, new groups are formed. Thus, at any one time, different groups are reading different material.
- Groups meet regularly for discussion.
- The students lead their own discussions, using notes they have taken during reading. The teacher's role is to be a facilitator.
- Students are coached to be respectful of each other's ideas, take turns, and give compliments.

- Discussions are characterized by conversational give-and-take, personal connection to the material, and open-ended questions.

A key component of the Book Club model is the literature circle. One of the students in the Book Club Program wrote the following:

When we talk with our peers, we find out about other people's ideas, have a chance to say something really important, get to tell what the author should do better or different, ask questions about the book, and express our feelings and ideas. Also, sometimes books were hard for me to understand. In Book club, other students, or the teacher, helped one another to understand the story. So, a big advantage of Book club was talking with friends. (McMahon & Raphael, 1997, p. 24)

Journals

Response journals are another venue for providing students with ways to respond actively to what they are reading. Harste, Short, and Burke (1988) called this kind of journal a *literature log*. They considered it to be one type of a learning log. In a learning log, students are asked to write about their reactions to something new they learned that day or their response to how they went about learning it. In a literature log, students are asked to write their response and reactions to what they are reading. Saunders and Goldenberg (1999) found literature logs to be more effective for English language learners, particularly when combined with scaffolded conversations, than for students who are English proficient.

Reading logs are a component of the Book Club model. Raphael and her associates (Goatley et al., 1995; McMahon & Raphael, 1997; Raphael et al., 2002) found that it was helpful to provide the students with think sheets as a scaffold for writing in logs. For example, think sheets might include spaces for the students to write unusual vocabulary, questions for the author, a comparison of a current and previous book, and the quality of book club discussions.

Berger (1996) suggested that students be given a guide for writing a response journal through questions such as the following: What do you notice? What do you question? What do you feel? What do you relate to?

Hancock (1993b) suggested that students be given the following guidelines:

- Feel free to write your innermost feelings, opinions, thoughts, likes, and dislikes.
- Take time to write down anything that you are thinking while you read.
- Don't worry about the accuracy of spelling and mechanics in the journal.

- Record the page number on which you were reading when you write your response.
- Relate the book to your own experiences and share similar moments from your life or from books you have read in the past.
- Ask questions while reading to help you make sense of the characters and the unraveling plot.
- Make predictions about what you think will happen as the plot unfolds.
- Talk to the characters as you begin to know them.
- Praise or criticize the book, the author, or the literary style.
- There is no limit to the types of responses you may write. (p. 472)

One type of focused response journal is a character journal, which is a diary written by the student as if she or he were a character in the story. The student writes in the first person and responds to the events occurring in the character's life. When Hancock (1993a) used character journals with her eighth graders, she found that they preferred to write two types of entries, one as the character and the other as a spectator, so that they could respond as themselves and share their own thoughts.

Reading logs clearly involve a level of independence that may be not be realistic for struggling readers, such as Marek, Maria, Ellison, and Adani, with instructional level material. However, if the teacher provides guidelines for writing journal entries and offers feedback through frequent responses, journal writing can be used effectively with independent level material that supplements the instructional reading program.

Retelling

Retelling after reading provides readers with the chance to make sense of the text as a whole and how the major text structure components fit together. Typically conducted with narrative text, retellings can be viewed as reconstructions of text that help you assess the students' comprehension of the central story line, awareness of supporting details, and identification of key story structure elements. As a postreading strategy, retellings can serve as constructions that enhance comprehension.

Verbal retelling has been found to significantly improve reading comprehension and recall (Gambrell, Pfeiffer, & Wilson, 1985; Koskinen, Gambrell, Kapinus, & Heathington, 1988). Gambrell and her associates observed that "practice in verbal rehearsal of what has been read results in significant learning with respect to the comprehension and recall of discourse, and that what has been learned, as a result of practice in retelling, transfers to the reading of subsequent text" (Gambrell et al., 1985, p. 220). Research has shown that practice in retelling improves both the richness of retellings as well as reading comprehension (Kapinus, Gambrell, & Koskinen, 1987; Morrow, 1985). Story retelling has also been found to help develop students' story schema and help them recognize which components of a story carry the most meaning (French, 1988; Morrow, 1985).

Guidelines for verbal retelling include the following (Koskinen et al., 1988):

- Provide a model of retelling for students with limited retelling experience.
- Guide their retellings through open-ended questions and prompts.
- Provide frequent opportunity for retelling through partner retelling.
- Teach students how to give constructive feedback when someone else retells a story or text segment.

Another retelling technique that has been found to be effective is *story maps* and *story frames* (Idol, 1987). Story maps are a type of semantic map in which the key elements of a story and the relationship between elements are displayed graphically. Story maps are typically created through discussion after a group of students have read a complete story, chapter, or book (Davis & McPherson, 1989; Keeler, 1993).

The most common type of story map is the main idea–sequential detail map (Reutzel, 1985b). The students identify the main idea and place it in the center of the map. Salient details are placed in circles and connected in sequence around the main idea. This is particularly valuable for readers who have difficulty distinguishing between important and unimportant details. If the difficulty is with sequencing, the main idea–sequential map can be used or the teacher might substitute key events for salient details. Other types of story maps are character perspective–comparison maps, inferential maps, cause-effect maps, compare-contrast maps, drawing conclusion maps, and story structure maps (Davis & McPherson, 1989; Dymock, 2007; Emery, 1996; Reutzel, 1985b; Richards & Gipe, 1993). Story mapping has been found to be effective with students identified as poor readers and those with learning disabilities (e.g., Boulineau, Fore, Hagan-Burke, & Burke, 2004; Davis, 1994; Gardill & Jitendra, 1999).

Story frames are summaries with information left out for the students to fill in. Some authors view them as story-level cloze (Cairney, 1987; Cudd & Roberts, 1987). Story frames are usually based on story-structure components. You can include a great deal of information and leave just a word or phrase for the students to complete or you can provide minimum guidance by including sentence openers and leaving a line or more for them to

166

CHAPTER 6

*After-Reading
Strategies:
Synthesizing and
Extending*

complete. An open-ended story map might include the following sentence openers:

This story takes place _____.

In this story, the problem starts when _____.

After that, _____.

Next, _____.

Then, _____.

Finally, _____.

The problem is solved when _____.

The story ends when _____.

Story frames can also focus on one aspect of story structure, such as setting, or the frames can focus on character analysis. Unlike verbal retellings, in which there is a tendency for all ideas to be seen as equally important by the student, you can structure story frames to help the students clearly differentiate between central story ideas and supporting details.

Richek et al. (2002) suggest a strategy they coined, *story pyramids*, for students with reading problems. The format follows the design of a pyramid with one word at the top followed in the next line by two words and so on through eight words at the bottom using the following rules:

- One word naming the main character
- Two words describing the main character (for students in grades 3 and above, encourage the use of adjectives)
- Three words describing the setting (time and place)
- Four words describing the problem (for students in primary grades who have difficulty with problem identification, ask them for four words describing the first thing that happened)
- Five words describing important events
- Six words describing more important events
- Seven words describing more important events
- Eight words describing the end (pp. 207–208)

Plot profiles are yet another retelling strategy. According to Tompkins (2006), the students use a graph to plot how tense or exciting the story line is; intervals for plotting are usually at chapter endings. Tompkins noted, "Students learn that plot is the sequence of events involving characters in conflict situations and that a story's plot is based on the goals of one or more characters and how they go about attaining these goals. Chapter by chapter, as they read and mark a plot profile, students talk about plot development and the conflict situations in which characters are involved. They also learn that conflict is the tension between the forces in the plot and that it is what interests readers enough to continue reading the story" (p. 73).

Drama provides an experiential mode for retelling. It has been suggested that children in preschool and kindergarten be provided with structured and free-play opportunities to re-create stories that are read aloud to them (Christie, 1990; Pellegrini & Galda, 1982). At the elementary and middle school levels, drama can be improvisational or students can write a script based on the material they have read, which is a technique sometimes referred to as *Readers Theatre*. Students can read the parts in the traditional manner with each student reading one part or the students can take turns reading all the parts, alternate reading the same part, or read the parts together chorally (Flynn, 2004/2005; Kinniburgh & Shaw, 2007; Wolf, 1994). Yet another alternative to drama is the *tableaux strategy* in which the students form a set of still-life poses that captures the essence of the story (Richek et al., 2002).

167

CHAPTER 6

*After-Reading
Strategies:
Synthesizing and
Extending*

Summarizing

Summarizing involves bringing the important ideas together to make a coherent yet shorter version of the original text. It involves drafting and revising until the written summary represents an accurate abstract of the text.

Summarizing has been found to improve comprehension, enhance recall, and encourage higher order thinking (Casazza, 1993; Rinehart, Stahl, & Erickson, 1986) and is one of the text comprehension strategies recommended by the National Reading Panel (2000). It has been observed that the ability to summarize improves with age, that able readers write better summaries than less able readers, and that even good readers may need explicit instruction in the rules of summary writing (Englert, Raphael, Anderson, Anthony, & Stevens, 1991; Wood, Winne, & Carney, 1995).

When teaching summarization to struggling readers, you should keep the rules relatively brief and simple. Noyce and Christie (1989) suggested the following:

- Identify a topic sentence that captures the theme.
- Leave out unnecessary detail such as repetitious information and unimportant ideas, even if it is interesting.
- State each point once only.
- Substitute a general term for a list of specific items or set of actions.

168

CHAPTER 6

*After-Reading
Strategies:
Synthesizing and
Extending*

Next Step

The strategies presented in this chapter and in the previous two chapters encompass before, during, and after reading. They are essentially slotted into the before, during, and after steps of the reading model that you chose as the one that best matched areas of reading difficulty identified in the student's assessment. If reading only involved obtaining the knowledge and skills involved in word recognition, fluency, and comprehension, then your job would be done once such learning successfully emanated from your instruction. However, the student's own motivation and interest and the family's involvement are crucial aspects to the struggling reader's literacy development.

The next step involves examining the reasons that students who are struggling readers often become reluctant readers and what teachers can do to help them become enthused about reading.

QUESTIONS FOR REFLECTION AND APPLICATION

1. In what ways are the strategies taught after reading significantly different from or similar to the strategies taught before and during reading?

2. If you had only enough time after reading to devote to two strategies, which would they be?

3. What is the ideal balance between time spent reading and time devoted to strategy instruction?

4. How will you know if the strategy instruction you have provided after reading is helpful to the struggling reader?

SUGGESTED RESOURCES FOR ADDITIONAL READING

Daniels, Harvey. (2001). *Literature Circles: Voice and Choice in Book Clubs and Reading Groups* (2nd ed.). Portland, ME: Stenhouse.

Ganske, Kathy. (2006). *Word Sorts and More*. New York: Teachers College.

Harvey, Stephanie, & Goudvis, Anne. (2007). *Strategies That Work: Teaching Comprehension for Understanding and Engagement*. Portland, ME: Stenhouse.

Hoyt, Linda. (2008). *Revisit, Reflect, Retell*. Portsmouth, NH: Heinemann.

Kissner, Emily. (2006). *Summarizing, Paraphrasing, and Retelling*. Amsterdam: Reed Elsevier.

Kuhn, Melanie R. (2009). *The Hows and Whys of Fluency Instruction*. Columbus, OH: Allyn & Bacon/Merrill.

Rasinski, Timothy V., & Padak, Nancy D. (2008). *From Phonics to Fluency* (2nd ed.). Columbus, OH: Allyn & Bacon/Merrill.

Attitude and Motivation

From Reluctant to Enthused Reader

1 The Reading Process: The Task and the Reader

2 Assessment: Putting the Reader at the Center of the Reading Program

3 Framework for Developing a Reading Program for the Struggling Reader

4 Before-Reading Strategies: Prereading and Planning

This chapter will discuss the reasons that students who are struggling readers often become reluctant readers and what teachers can do to help them become enthused about reading.

5 During-Reading Strategies: Supporting Strategic Reading

8 Families: Partnering with Parents

6 After-Reading Strategies: Synthesizing and Extending

7 Attitude and Motivation: From Reluctant to Enthused Reader

*W*hen students struggle with reading, the likelihood that they will become reluctant readers is great. And once they are reluctant readers, they are less likely to become skilled readers because much of what students learn about reading happens while they are reading, which is why motivation is related to reading achievement (Guthrie, Wigfield, Metsala, & Cox, 1999). The challenge for teachers is to help the struggling reader maintain a positive attitude toward reading in the face of much difficulty.

The motivation to read involves multiple factors. As defined by Guthrie and Wigfield (2000), "Reading motivation is the individual's personal goals, values, and beliefs with regard to the topics, processes, and outcomes of reading" (p. 405). Although virtually all very young children are

170

CHAPTER 7

*Attitude and
Motivation:
From Reluctant to
Enthused Reader*

intrinsically motivated to learn and to improve their abilities, intrinsic motivation declines in many students as they are confronted with the slow pace involved in learning to read and the inevitable multiple mistakes they make day after day (Pressley, 2006). Researchers have identified a number of factors related to motivation to read.

Factors Impacting Motivation

Motivation is often described in terms of intrinsic and extrinsic factors, with *intrinsic motivation* for reading involving curiosity, engagement, and self-efficacy and *extrinsic motivation* involving recognition, incentives, and rewards.

Intrinsic Motivation

Although all children seem cognitively endowed to be intrinsically motivated to learn to read, several factors seem to negatively influence this motivation during the elementary and middle school years (Chapman, Tunmer, & Prochnow, 2000; Rasinski & Padak, 2004).

1. *Frustration.* When reading experiences are always difficult, students are likely to become frustrated and weary from repeatedly failing. Alternatively, when readers experience regular success, even if such success does not happen every day, they are more likely to feel confident in their ability to learn to read and essentially shrug off the difficulties and periodic failures.

2. *Fear of Failure.* Struggling readers may see reading as such a high-risk endeavor that they avoid the risk by being uncooperative or disinterested. However, if readers have reason to believe that they will be successful, their fear of failure will be minimized to the point that they are willing to tackle the material.

3. *Learned Helplessness.* According to attribution theory, individuals attribute successes and failures to ability, effort, and luck. Students who are skilled readers tend to attribute their success to ability and any difficulties to lack of effort. Students who are struggling readers tend to attribute their difficulties to ability (or more accurately, lack of ability) and any success to luck. Over time, they may develop a sense of learned helplessness and believe that no amount of effort will bring about positive change. The result is an avoidance of reading. By engaging in reading tasks that are challenging but attainable, students can come to realize that if they put forth the effort, they can be successful because they do, indeed, have the ability.

4. *Self-Esteem*. It is self-evident to all students how important reading is to school success and, ultimately, life success, so when they are not successful, their self-esteem may be adversely affected. Poor self-esteem can manifest as withdrawal and hostility toward reading. When engaging in literacy tasks with which they can be successful, their self-concept can improve and willingness to engage in reading can increase.

5. *Perfectionism*. Many students, including those who are struggling readers, are very high achieving and have great difficulty making any mistakes at all. They may be unwilling to respond unless they are certain they have the answer the teacher is seeking and, thus, may resist reading if the teacher will require them to make inferences, draw conclusions, suggest alternatives, evaluate, or provide any other open-ended response. If their responses are met with positive feedback, though not platitudes and false praise, they may feel encouraged to take risks in their reading.

Extrinsic Motivation

Guthrie and Wigfield (2000) identified nine classroom factors that impact the motivation of readers.

1. *Learning and knowledge goals*. If the instructional goals developed by the teacher are achievable by the students, and they believe these goals are achievable, struggling readers will be more likely to engage in reading.

2. *Real-world interactions*. If learning activities are connected to the students' personal experiences, these activities are more likely to evoke interest and engagement.

3. *Autonomy support*. If students are offered choice in reading materials and activities involved in using these materials, a sense of autonomy is encouraged.

4. *Interesting texts for instruction*. Materials that have high interest to students are more likely to be motivating.

5. *Strategy instruction*. Explicit and systematic instruction in reading strategies that the students can readily perceive as assisting them in reading provides them with confidence about the reading task.

6. *Collaboration*. Opportunity to interact with peers about reading material provides social support for reading.

7. *Praise and rewards*. Positive response to effort and performance is very effective in encouraging students to persist in challenging reading tasks when this feedback is frequent, precise, and sincere.

172

CHAPTER 7

Attitude and
Motivation:
From Reluctant to
Enthused Reader

8. *Evaluation.* If evaluation of performance is viewed by students as both fair and helpful in identifying areas on which to focus efforts, they will be more likely to see evaluation as feedback designed to improve reading skills rather than an indication of reading weaknesses and failure.

9. *Teacher involvement.* The more knowledgeable the teacher is about each student's needs, the more confident the student will be that the teacher can provide support with difficult reading tasks.

Improving Attitude and Increasing Motivation

Strategies for improving attitude and increasing motivation can be seen as falling into the two categories of intrinsic motivation and extrinsic motivation. Strategies aimed at intrinsic motivation are intended to increase students' ability to understand their own performance, develop confidence in their potential for success, and promote willingness to engage in challenging reading tasks. Strategies aimed at extrinsic motivation are intended to establish an instructional environment that encourages struggling readers to view reading as a positive experience through praise and activities that offer tangible reinforcers.

Adani, who is 7 years old, showed a positive attitude toward reading during the assessment and was able to share her favorite book with her teacher, Ms. Edberg. Just two years older than Adani, Marek had already differentiated between home and school reading. Mr. Rumrill found that although Marek enjoyed reading for pleasure, he did not particularly enjoy school reading and simply thought reading to be too hard. Maria is 11 years old and quite aware that reading is a struggle for her. During the assessment, she told Mr. Ginnetti that she doesn't enjoy reading and rarely reads at home. As an eighth grader and 14-year-old, Ellison displayed an openly negative attitude toward reading. His mother reported that he seldom reads at home and expresses that he doesn't like to read. He told Mrs. Hong during the assessment that he does not like to visit the library, go to a bookstore, or read at home. The increased negativity toward reading shown by the case study children from the youngest at 7 to the oldest at 14 is reflective of how attitudes decline among struggling readers from elementary through middle and high school.

Mrs. Hong made an observation about Ellison that serves to underlie all of the strategies described in the next sections for improving attitude and increasing motivation. She realized that success with reading would improve Ellison's attitude and if his attitude improved, he might be more willing to do independent reading, which in turn might further improve his reading ability.

Focusing on the Reader

Attribution Retraining

Underlying *attribution retraining* is the recognition that once students have come to attribute their failures to ability and successes to luck, direct intervention is needed. Two features characterize attribution retraining: (a) teaching students to use strategies for word recognition, fluency, and comprehension and (b) emphasizing that their ability to recognize words and comprehend text is a direct result of applying these strategies rather than any inherent word recognition and comprehension abilities (Borkowski, Weyhing, & Carr, 1988; Carr & Borkowski, 1989; Pressley, 2006). In attribution retraining, the key is reinforcing the student's efforts and capability to learn effective reading strategies.

Certainly the first step is included in the selection of models and strategies discussed in the previous chapters. If you have assessed the students well; selected a reading model that allows you to focus instruction on needs identified in the assessment; and chosen strategies to slot into the model before, during, and after reading, then your struggling readers will become increasingly proficient readers. The second step of attribution training involves making sure that the students attribute their increasing proficiency to their own ability to apply the strategies you have taught.

Concept-Oriented Reading Instruction

Concept-Oriented Reading Instruction (CORI) is a reading instructional program designed to integrate reading strategy instruction and content area inquiry activities for motivation and learning (Guthrie & McCann, 1997; Guthrie, McRae, & Klauda, 2007; Guthrie, Wigfield, & VonSecker, 2000; Swan, 2003). The goal is to increase reading comprehension, reading motivation, and subject matter knowledge through integrated instruction of reading and content.

In Concept-Oriented Reading Instruction, the teacher creates instructional units that typically encompass a 12- to 18-week period. The first step is choosing a conceptual theme that is broad enough to serve as an overarching concept for several topics during the 3- to 4-month unit. Such themes are typically taken from district and statewide curriculum such as life cycles, nature of matter, and civil rights. The second step is to integrate four phases of activities into the unit so that each week, one of the phases of instruction is

174

CHAPTER 7

Attitude and
Motivation:
From Reluctant to
Enthused Reader

emphasized. The first is the *Observe and Personalize* phase, in which the students observe phenomena and pose their own questions. The second is the *Search and Retrieve* phase, in which the students locate information from a variety of sources to answer their questions. The third is the *Comprehend and Integrate* phase, in which the teacher provides explicit instruction in reading strategies to help the students read different types of materials and integrate the information they are learning. The fourth is the *Communicate to Others* phase, in which the students share what they have learned through discussion and writing. Within each of these phases, the nine classroom factors that impact motivation presented earlier (i.e., learning and knowledge goals, real-world interactions, autonomy support, interesting texts for instruction, strategy instruction, collaboration, praise and rewards, evaluation, and teacher involvement) are incorporated.

Wigfield and his colleagues (2008) found that Concept-Oriented Reading Instruction showed better comprehension outcomes than strategy instruction aimed at comprehension alone because CORI encouraged a higher level of reading engagement during classroom instruction. They concluded that instruction will improve reading comprehension only to the extent that students are engaged in the reading process.

Using Literature to Improve Self-Concept

Modeled on bibliotherapy, which is the use of reading material to help individuals solve problems, *biblio-support* is the use of reading material to help students deal with their problems (Manzo & Manzo, 2008). For the struggling reader whose self-esteem is weak, biblio-support can both motivate reading and help the student deal with feelings of worth and accomplishment. The teacher identifies material on personal or emotional themes that are similar to issues in the student's life, which enables the reader to see how characters cope with these issues and solve their personal problems. If the themes are personally relevant, then the material may be motivating. The insight gained from these stories, along with success in reading these materials, can have a positive influence on the student's self-esteem, which in turn can increase motivation to read.

Miller (1993) used biblio-support with a group of adolescent females who were at risk for academic failure. Calling it the Literature Project, Miller identified novels with themes and characters that would produce a vicarious experience in the reader, a story that was relevant to these adolescents, and characters with whom they could identify in order to enhance their self-concept and aspirations. After 15 weeks of instruction, Miller concluded, "A well planned program of literature-based instruction that addresses a variety of contemporary issues through new and old literary classics is a powerful tool in changing the self-concept of at-risk adolescent females" (p. 447).

Focusing on the Classroom

Interesting Materials

The most effective way to identify materials that are interesting to students is to allow them to choose their own. Materials for independent reading can always be self-selected, though some struggling readers need help figuring out which materials they can read independently.

For many of the reading models, and certainly for the models most appropriate for struggling readers, materials for instructional reading are selected by the teacher, so it is up to you to consider factors that make materials interesting to a particular student or reading group. By paying attention to what was learned about the student's interests during the assessment, you can identify material likely to be appealing and adjust as the student does or does not show interest. For example, although Ellison's attitude toward reading was negative, he expressed interest in reading about flowers, plants, gardening, and animals during the assessment. The two reading models that may be used with Ellison provide some choice of materials by the teacher. The Cooperative Integrated Reading and Composition model utilizes a basal reading series. Within the anthology he is reading, there may be a number of stories that are not of interest to Ellison. However, if Mrs. Hong recognizes that she can choose to leave out some stories rather than feel compelled to have him read each one in sequence, there is a greater likelihood that Ellison will find most of the material interesting. The other model that might be used with Ellison, Collaborative Strategic Reading, provides a great deal more choice for the teacher and, indeed, Mrs. Hong might even allow Ellison and the other students in his reading group to choose their material from among a group of stories or novels that she has identified to be at their instructional reading level.

Another way to identify material likely to be of interest is to choose from books that you have previously read aloud to the class, books based on television programs or movies that the students have watched, books written by authors they have previously read and enjoyed, series books that you know are commonly enjoyed by students, and books that other students have discussed during activities such as Reader's Chair.

Worthy and her colleagues found three categories of texts to be interesting for struggling and reluctant readers: (a) repetitive texts such as pattern books, poetry and verse, and jump-rope and street rhymes; (b) performance texts such as books, stories, and poems for Readers Theatre and speeches; and (c) popular texts such as comic books, cartoon collections, series books, mysteries or books with scary themes, funny books, magazines about popular culture, books about animals, sophisticated picture books, and books and magazines about sports, cars, and trucks (Worthy, 1996, 2002; Worthy, Moorman, & Turner, 1999).

176

CHAPTER 7

*Attitude and
Motivation:
From Reluctant to
Enthused Reader*

Challenging Materials and Tasks

As discussed in Chapter 3, materials for learning should be at the student's instructional reading level because reading abilities develop as a result of being supported in successfully reading text that the student could not read independently. These materials are aimed at the student's zone of proximal development. When materials and tasks are appropriately challenging, the teacher is implicitly communicating the message to students that they are capable of reading. Challenging materials and tasks strengthen confidence; on the other hand, easy or frustration materials and tasks, when used exclusively, undermine confidence (Lutz, Guthrie, & Davis, 2006; Miller & Meece, 1999; Pressley, 2006). Meece and Miller (1999) found that instructional practices in which "teachers provided many opportunities for student input and choice, linked instructional activities to students' interests, promoted interactions among students of different achievement levels, and gave students multiple opportunities to complete challenging academic tasks" have the "strongest influence on performance goals and the avoidance orientations of lower ability students" (p. 225).

These factors may not be sufficient, however, for students whose classroom experiences have not been rich in what Finn (2009) terms "powerful literacy," which is using literacy for critical thinking, creative thinking, and problem solving. He described four mechanisms that serve to maintain domesticating education and functional literacy for working-class and, to some degree, middle-class children rather than the empowering education and powerful literacy that wealthy children receive.

- Some minorities feel that they have been wronged by mainstream Americans and that "acting white" is a betrayal of their people. They develop what sociologists call "oppositional identity." Oppositional identity appears among working-class whites to some extent as well. Talking and acting like a schoolteacher and valuing things schoolteachers value doesn't win you a lot of friends in working-class communities.

- Working-class children with varying degrees of oppositional identity resist school through means reminiscent of the factory shop floor—slowdowns, strikes, sabotage, and occasionally open confrontation. The result is the "pretend-school model." Teachers ask little of students in return for enough cooperation to maintain the appearance of conducting school.

- The discourse (ways of communication and the beliefs, attitudes, values, habits, and behaviors that underlie them—especially attitudes related to authority, conformity, and power) of working-class communities is at odds with the discourse of the schools. This makes acquisition of school discourse and powerful literacy difficult for working-class children.

- Progressive methods, empowering education, and powerful literacy tend to go together. Traditional methods, domesticating education, and functional literacy tend to go together. Progressive methods are nearly impossible unless children want school knowledge and cooperate. (Finn, 2009, pp. xvi–xvii)

177

CHAPTER 7

*Attitude and
Motivation:
From Reluctant to
Enthused Reader*

Finn noted that for these mechanisms to change, teachers must connect literacy and school knowledge to the real lives of children.

Interacting with Peers

Sometimes referred to as social interactions involving books, opportunity to interact with peers appears to be highly motivating for reading (Antonio & Guthrie, 2009; Worthy, Patterson, & Salas, 2002). At the heart of social interaction is the implicit message that reading has a larger purpose than answering the teacher's questions correctly, writing a book report that only the teacher will read, or other such teacher-focused activity. When interacting with peers about reading, the many purposes of literacy are experienced firsthand, such as sharing ideas, providing information, and recognizing different perspectives.

Incentive Programs

A common approach to encouraging students to engage in reading is through incentive programs. *Bulletin board charts* provide a prominent classroom location for students to record the books they have read. *Awards* can be given for reading a target number of books.

Some of these programs have corporate sponsors. For example, *Book It!*, sponsored by Pizza Hut, offers coupons for small pizzas that students receive when they read a certain number of books or minutes that are set by their teacher. Goals may also include parents reading to or with their child. Another example is the *All-American Reading Challenge* sponsored by McDonald's with the American Library Association and Scholastic, Inc. Students are given a free meal coupon for every 10 books they read. These programs are highly commercial in nature.

Although incentive programs may be motivational, they tend to foster competition among students. A few programs are designed to encourage cooperation among students. One is *Reading Millionaires* (Baumann, 1995; O'Masta & Wolf, 1991), which involves aggregating the number of minutes read by all of the students. When a preset goal is met (i.e., 1 million minutes over a specified amount of time), all students receive a memento or the school holds a special celebration. Another collaborative activity is *Read-In* (Pressley, 2006), which is patterned after sleepovers because the activity takes place overnight. In read-ins, children, parents, and teachers spend the evening reading silently and aloud, performing stories or parts of stories, and talking about what they are reading.

178
....

CHAPTER 7

Attitude and
Motivation:
From Reluctant to
Enthused Reader

Another consideration with incentive programs is the conditions under which they are effective and not effective. Marinak and Gambrell (2008) found that students who received a book as a reward and students who received no reward at all were more motivated to engage in subsequent reading than students who received some type of token as a reward. In other words, tokens were not effective in inspiring intrinsic motivation to read. They suggested that teachers use literacy-related rewards, such as books, increased time for self-selected sustained silent reading, and added visits to the library or greater library time. They note, "It may be that providing reading-related rewards sends a message about the value of reading and sustained engagement with text" (p. 23).

Guidelines for Generating Enthusiastic Readers

As students advance in school, attitude toward reading and motivation to engage in literacy tasks often declines (McKenna, Ellsworth, & Kear, 1995; Unrau & Schlackman, 2006; Wigfield et al., 1997). To diminish reluctance and generate enthusiasm in all students, but particularly struggling readers, the following guidelines are suggested (Pressley, 2006):

- Ensure student success by making tasks appropriately challenging and providing the support they need.
- Scaffold learning by monitoring student difficulties and providing needed support.
- Encourage students to attribute their successes to the effort they expended and their failures to employing an ineffective strategy or not putting forth effort.
- Encourage students to recognize that intelligence is not a quality a person has or does not have but that intelligence grows with learning new concepts.
- Promote awareness that failure is a natural part of the learning process.
- Reassess instructional strategies and materials when the student is persistently failing and make adjustments so that every student experiences many successes on a daily basis.
- Encourage cooperation and discourage competition among students.
- Provide frequent opportunity for students to interact over literacy tasks.

- Use evaluation strategies that emphasize effort and learning and deemphasize grades per se.

- Provide access to a wide assortment of reading material.

- Embed ample opportunity for students to choose their own reading material.

- Connect literacy instruction with content area instruction so that students read expository material in their content subjects and they read about content area topics during literacy instruction.

- Choose motivating topics that are covered in depth during the school year.

Ivey and Broaddus (2001) found that reading and language arts classrooms that motivated students to read were characterized by ample time to read, time to listen to the teacher read, and access to personally interesting reading materials. As researchers, they were interested in what inspires students to read in school. What they found surprised them because "students seemed more concerned about the conditions that would help them learn and grow from their reading rather than about motivation to read in general" (p. 370). Ivey and Broaddus suggested that teachers should ask themselves how they can use reading and reading instruction to motivate students to learn rather than how they can motivate students to read per se.

The best measure of attitude and motivation toward reading is whether students voluntarily read out of school. In examining the factors that influence out-of-school reading habits, McKool (2007) found that out-of-school reading competed unsatisfactorily with organized activities, homework demands, chores, taking care of younger siblings, computer games, and watching television. She observed that students who made time for recreational reading were those with higher self-concepts and whose parents placed obvious value on reading. She further found that classrooms that supported reading for pleasure had a positive impact on voluntary reading at home.

Next Step

Each of the chapters has contributed to a unifying schema for developing a reading program for students who are struggling with reading. At this point, you have assessed the students, chosen a reading model, and selected strategies to teach before, during, and after reading. You have also implemented strategies to improve attitude and increase motivation. If the model and

180

CHAPTER 7

*Attitude and
Motivation:
From Reluctant to
Enthused Reader*

strategies have been chosen wisely and implemented effectively, the school learning environment is as supportive as possible to enable each student to become a proficient reader. Yet you have something more to consider—the student's family.

The next step involves discussing the salient role of parents in their children's literacy development and how teachers and parents can become partners in helping struggling readers.

QUESTIONS FOR REFLECTION AND APPLICATION

1. Are there reasons to believe that struggling readers are more likely to become reluctant readers than students with other issues and difficulties?

2. What are the challenges in turning around the attitude of students who do not like to read and resist carrying out work that requires reading?

3. Which is more important, intrinsic motivation or extrinsic motivation?

4. If you had to select one strategy for improving attitude and increasing motivation, which would it be?

SUGGESTED RESOURCES FOR ADDITIONAL READING

Fink, Rosalie, & Samuels, S. Jay. (2007). *Inspiring Reading Success: Interest and Motivation in an Age of High Stakes Testing*. Newark, DE: International Reading Association.

Jones, Patrick, Hartman, Maureen L., & Taylor, Patricia P. (2006). *Connecting with Reluctant Teen Readers*. New York: Neal-Schuman.

Reeves, Anne. (2004). *Adolescents Talk about Reading: Exploring Resistance to and Engagement with Text*. Newark, DE: International Reading Association.

Reynolds, Marilyn. (2004). *I Won't Read and You Can't Make Me: Reaching Reluctant Teen Readers*. Portsmouth, NH: Heinemann.

Wilhelm, Jeffrey D. (2007). *"You Gotta BE the Book": Teaching Engaged and Reflective Reading with Adolescents*. New York: Teachers College.

CHAPTER 8

Families

Partnering with Parents

1 The Reading Process: The Task and the Reader

2 Assessment: Putting the Reader at the Center of the Reading Program

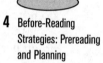

3 Framework for Developing a Reading Program for the Struggling Reader

4 Before-Reading Strategies: Prereading and Planning

This chapter will discuss the salient role of parents in their children's literacy development and how teachers and parents can become partners in helping struggling readers.

5 During-Reading Strategies: Supporting Strategic Reading

8 Families: Partnering with Parents

6 After-Reading Strategies: Synthesizing and Extending

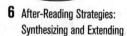

7 Attitude and Motivation: From Reluctant to Enthused Reader

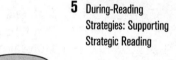

*T*hroughout this book, models and strategies for supporting the struggling reader have been directed to classroom teachers of students from preschool through high school. Yet, although the classroom is certainly an important place for literacy learning to happen, this final chapter will acknowledge the place and the individuals that are as important, if not more important, to the student's literacy development. This place is, obviously, the home and the individuals are, of course, the child's parents.

Perspectives on
Family-School Partnerships

Partnerships do not always work smoothly. The mutual respect, goodwill, and shared interests that bring partners together are difficult to sustain when there is disagreement about goals, priorities, and specific actions. It is an understatement to say that parents and professionals do not necessarily work in harmony with one another.

The families of all the case study children want their children to succeed in school. Each family is different. In Adani's home, English is not the primary language. Ms. Edberg may need to use an interpreter in order to communicate effectively and clearly with Adani's parents in person. Further, she may need to figure out how to send written material home if Adani's parents do not read and write in English.

Mr. Ginnetti met with Maria's parents and they expressed their concern about her academic progress. Maria told Mr. Ginnetti that a good reader sounds out words and asks the teacher or parent for help when sounding out doesn't work, so Mr. Ginnetti knows that Maria's parents spend time reading with her.

Ellison's mother expressed her concern about his reading when she met with Mrs. Hong at the fall parent-teacher conference. She also told Mrs. Hong that Ellison seldom reads at home and expresses his dislike of reading. Mrs. Hong also learned from Ellison's mother that she likes to read the newspaper and sometimes shares information from something she has read with Ellison, particularly if it's about agriculture because Ellison wants to go into farming. Thus, Ellison's mother is obviously very aware of her son's attitudes about reading as well as ways to hook him to read through his own interest in agriculture.

All that Mr. Rumrill learned about Marek's family is that they recently moved into the area. However, given that Marek's delayed language was caused by lead poisoning when he was 5 years old, Mr. Rumrill might assume that Marek's family is from a low socioeconomic background because children from low-income families are significantly more likely to be poisoned than those from higher income families (Alliance for Healthy Homes, 2008; Connor, Son, & Hindman, 2005). However, Mr. Rumrill also knows that lead poisoning crosses all socioeconomic, geographic, and racial boundaries and would withhold any assumptions about Marek's background until he can meet with his parents.

For partnerships to be more than a catchword, parents like those of Adani, Maria, Ellison, and Marek—and professionals like Ms. Edberg,

Mr. Ginnetti, Mrs. Hong, and Mr. Rumrill—must be able to follow a common set of principles guiding their interactions. The following principles represent a point for beginning a partnership and avoiding the kind of blaming that all too often characterizes the relationship between home and school.

Principle 1: The Child Is Part of a Family System.

When teachers intervene with the child, they impact on every other member of the child's family. In family systems theory, the family is viewed as a whole, and each member understood by looking at the interactions and relationships among all the family members (Bailey & Simeonsson, 1998; Dunst, Trivette, & Deal, 1988; Turnbull, Turnbull, Erwin, & Soodak, 2005).

Viewing the student as an interdependent member of a family system is important for two reasons. First, it helps you realize that anything they do educationally for your student will influence the interactions and relationships *between* the child and the child's family member and *among* the mother, father, siblings, as well as perhaps the grandparents and others in the extended family.

Second, viewing your student within the family context compels you to recognize and be sensitive to the many demands on families. It has been observed that when the family unit is supported, each member is strengthened. When the family unit is ignored, the result is often a weakening of every member and a lack of cooperation with the educational system that is purporting to help the child (Turnbull et al., 2005; Winton, 1986).

As you seek to understand each student's unique family structure, it is important to remember that traditional definitions of family structures have changed in response to social, political, and economic pressures. As you know, the students you teach come from families with one parent, foster families, families with two adults of the same gender, homeless families, families that migrate frequently for work, blended families, extended families, families with multiple ethnicities, and families with two biological parents.

Awareness and sensitivity to the values, attitudes, beliefs, and customs of each child's family is part of what is called *culturally responsive teaching*. Culturally responsive teaching is characterized by pedagogy that affirms the cultures of students, considers their cultures and experiences to be strengths, and incorporates their cultural experiences within the teaching process (Gollnick & Chinn, 2009). To be a culturally responsive teacher, you need to:

1. Place the student at the center of the teaching and learning process.
2. Promote human rights and respect for cultural differences.
3. Believe that all students can learn.
4. Acknowledge and build on the life histories and experiences of student's microcultural memberships.

5. Critically analyze oppression and power relationships to understand racism, sexism, classism, and discrimination against the disabled, gay, lesbian, young, and elderly.

6. Critique society in the interest of social justice and equality.

7. Participate in collective social action to ensure a democratic society. (Gollnick & Chinn, 2009, p. 321)

Principle 2: Parents Need to Be Encouraged to Develop the Skills and Knowledge That Will Enable Them to Become Competent and Capable. The traditional relationship between parents and professionals has been paternalistic. Professionals have taken responsibility for the educational needs of the child without expecting much more than cooperation from the parents. Instead of a paternalistic relationship, this principle suggests that the child benefits when parents are confident of their knowledge and skills and respected for their contributions to educational decision making.

The implication is that educators need to help parents identify and build on their strengths and capabilities and not focus on identifying and attempting to correct family weaknesses and deficiencies.

Principle 3: Families Experience a Life Cycle in Much the Same Way That Individuals Do, and the Changes Inherent in Major Family Events Need to Be Understood by Individuals Working with Any Family Member. The shifts experienced by families during transition times, such as when a parent changes jobs or a grandparent dies, disrupt the interactions and relationships among family members. Just as individuals experience anxiety and stress when they pass from one stage to another, so does the whole family experience anxiety and stress when the family passes from one stage to another.

Complicating this picture is that while the family undergoes passages through development phases, family members undergo their own individual life passages such as a child passing from childhood to puberty. Furthermore, mothers and fathers undergo change as they develop their parental abilities.

Recognizing the changes in a family's life can help you understand the relationship between home issues and school performance.

Principle 4: Educational Decisions Should Be Made Collaboratively between Parents and Professionals. There is a great difference between soliciting parent input for the purposes of making educational decisions and jointly making educational decisions. Collaboration is crucial to any partnership. It recognizes that both partners have essential insights to contribute. When decisions are made collaboratively, both partners are vested in the implementation and results.

Ultimately, there are three arguments in favor of family-school partnerships. One is that it is the rightful role of parents to decide what is best for their child. The second is that decisions made as a result of an equal sharing of ideas will be fully supported by the parents and, therefore, are more likely to result in positive outcomes for your student. And the third is the extensive body of research showing that parent involvement in their children's schooling is highly beneficial to the children's educational achievement (e.g., Jeynes, 2005; Pomerantz, Moorman, & Litwack, 2007).

Family Literacy

Family literacy is an approach to developing partnerships between families and schools for the purpose of improving the literacy of children through their families. In 1989, then First Lady Barbara Bush established the Barbara Bush Foundation for Family Literacy to promote family literacy initiatives. Since it was launched, the foundation has awarded over $30 million to almost 700 family literacy programs in every state and the District of Columbia. The mission has remained constant:

> To establish literacy as a value in every family in America, by helping every family in the nation understand that the home is the child's first school, that the parent is the child's first teacher, and that reading is the child's first subject; and to break the intergenerational cycle of illiteracy, by supporting the development of family literacy programs where parents and children can learn and read together. (Barbara Bush Foundation for Family Literacy, 2008)

In 1998, family literacy services were defined under the Adult Education and Family Literacy Act, Title II of the Workforce Investment Act of 1998 to mean "services that are of sufficient intensity in terms of hours, and of sufficient duration, to make sustainable changes in a family, and that integrate all of the following activities: (1) interactive literacy activities between parents and their children; (2) training for parents regarding how to be the primary teacher for their children and full partners in the education of their children; (3) parent literacy training that leads to economic self-sufficiency; and (4) an age-appropriate education to prepare children for success in school and life experiences."

Family literacy initiatives, therefore, have focused on four components: adult literacy, early childhood literacy, parent education, and intergenerational literacy activities (Dyer, 2001; Paratore, 2002). Each component has its own goals. The goal of the adult literacy component is to increase literacy skills, which will lead to increased employability and ability to support and advocate for one's children. The aim of the early childhood component is to promote the development of preliteracy skills and literacy skills of children from birth through age 8. The parent education component is intended to provide parents with information and support so that parents can engage in positive parenting styles, promote literacy learning in the home, advocate effectively for their child, and be able to partner in their child's education. The intergenerational component is considered the heart of family literacy programs and targets the development of a positive, literacy-rich home environment.

Since the inception of family literacy programs, much has been learned about what works and what does not. One body of research has involved examining the uses of literacy within families. Researchers have observed the literacy experiences of children from low socioeconomic backgrounds and found that their families engaged in a number of print-embedded family activities involving daily living routines, entertainment, school-related activities, interpersonal communication, literacy for the sake of teaching or learning literacy, storybook reading, religion, participation in information networks, and work (McTavish, 2007; Purcell-Gates, L'Allier, & Smith, 1995).

Studies such as these suggest that teachers should, first, recognize that almost all families use literacy in their homes, though some of these ways may be different from how literacy is used and promoted in school, and second, use these home literacies as a foundation for classroom literacy. For example, in some cultures, storytelling is more central than reading and writing for passing on traditions. Not typically a part of classroom literacy programs, by including storytelling in the classroom, the teacher can connect directly to the child's home literacy. The bonus to finding ways to connect school and home literacy is that a home literacy activity such as storytelling may be valuable for all children. For example, it has been found that children who observe storytelling are often highly motivated to read the same story, to write the story or a similar story, to write their reactions in a journal, and to pay attention to stories in their reading that would be appropriate ones for their own storytelling. And storytelling has been found to promote reading comprehension, writing development, and expressive language (Schirmer, 2000).

A number of school activities have been found to contribute positively to family literacy outcomes. These activities are designed to inform parents about school literacy activities and inform teachers about home literacy activities. Examples include parent read-aloud or storytelling at school, dialogue journal writing between parents and teachers, establishing a classroom lending library for parents, instituting a school resource center of information and items that can assist parents in improving their own literacy abilities and supporting their child's reading and writing development, providing frequent newsletters that highlight classroom activities through pictures as well as text, and creating homework packets that provide easy-to-follow directions for parents to help their children (Collins & Matthey, 2001; Crawford & Zygouris-Coe, 2006; Cunningham & Allington, 2007; Kelly-Vance & Schreck, 2002; Morningstar, 1999; Richardson, Miller, Richardson, & Sacks, 2008; Zygouris-Coe, 2007).

Evaluation of family literacy programs has shown important positive outcomes for children. For example, Dearing, Kreider, and Simpkins (2006) examined the relationship between family involvement in school and their children's literacy performance in ethnically diverse, low-income families of children in kindergarten through grade 5 and found that that increased school involvement predicted improved child literacy. In a study conducted by Anderson and Morrison (2007), parents and caregivers reported that their ability to support their children's literacy learning was enhanced through participation in a family literacy program that involved them in classroom literacy activities.

Two factors have been found to impede effectiveness—lack of full participation by families and lack of efficacy for curriculum content and instruction (St. Pierre, Ricciuti, & Riihdzius, 2005). As with all educational programs, evaluation serves an important role in identifying problems and shifting to strategies that are more effective. The Barbara Bush Foundation for Early Literacy (2008) notes, "A good evaluation plan that includes regular assessments of progress benefits learners, whose confidence is strengthened by recognition of success, as well as the quality of the overall program."

Final Comments

As part of the final assessment for the professional development course in reading that Ms. Edberg, Mrs. Hong, Mr. Ginnetti, and Mr. Rumrill took online, the professor asked the students to look back at the essay they had written at the outset and to revise or affirm what they had written as the lesson learned as a teacher from their most memorable teacher. They were asked, again, to post their answer on the course online bulletin board. Ms. Edberg's response affirmed the lesson she had learned from Linda Fields, her tenth-grade social studies teacher.

> Due to some strange conjoining of fates, I ran into Linda Fields when I was a senior in college, far from where I went to high school. I was a student teacher and I was told that a woman was coming to interview for a part-time position. Imagine my amazement, let alone my excitement, when it turned out to be Miss Fields, who was not "Miss Fields" anymore but married with a name that never registered with me because, of course, she was my Miss Fields. She taught a lesson that I watched with intense interest. Here I was a student teacher with the opportunity to watch her teach my students. I can't say I remember much except the machete that she brought as a prop for the lesson on Indonesia, where she had lived. I do remember that I was the most engaged student that day.
>
> I only had a few minutes to talk with her during lunch. I wanted to tell her how much I appreciated the kind of teacher she was, how I had thought about her during my own preparation as a teacher, and how much I wanted to be the kind of influence on my students that she had

been for me. I know I didn't tell her any of that. I guess I was just too shy. I hope she saw that I admired and emulated her, but I know I didn't tell her that either. I just told her about my life, that I was going to graduate school to pursue a master's degree in special education and then I would be getting married.

A few years later, I realized that the best way to say thanks is to say it forward (and, indeed, someone made a movie on the concept but I like to take personal credit for the idea). I always strive to take the lesson and apply it every day to each child I teach. It is the power of one teacher to influence one child, particularly the one who is struggling.

This book began with two assumptions about you, the reader. The first is that teachers are aware of many components of the reading process and strategies common in teaching children to read. The second is that teachers do not have a unifying schema for putting the pieces together into a coherent reading program that will enable struggling readers to become proficient readers. From understanding the reader to understanding his or her family, from choosing a reading model to selecting strategies before, during, and after reading, the intent has been to provide you with the knowledge and skills to deliver a coherent and differentiated instructional program for students who struggle with reading.

Questions for Reflection and Application

1. Why do parents and professionals sometimes have conflicting views of what is best for the child?

2. What kinds of everyday literacy activities would you expect to find in the homes of the students where you teach or live?

3. Can parents ensure that their children will become skilled readers by doing certain things?

4. What can you do to develop a partnership with the parents of struggling readers?

Suggested Resources for Additional Reading

Allen, JoBeth. (2007). *Creating Welcoming Schools: A Practical Guide to Home-School Partnerships with Diverse Families*. New York: Teachers College.

Feller, Anthony, Andrews, Jane, Greenhough, Pamela, Hughes, Martin, Johnson, David, Scanlan, Mary, & Yee, Wan Ching. (2007). *Improving Primary Literacy: Linking Home and School*. New York: Routledge.

Gaitan, Concha D. (2004). *Involving Latino Families in Schools*. Thousand Oaks, CA: Corwin.

Rowsell, Jennifer. (2006). *Family Literacy Experiences: Creating Reading and Writing Opportunities That Support Classroom Learning*. Portland, ME: Stenhouse.

Wasik, Barbara H. (Ed.). (2004). *Handbook of Family Literacy*. New York: Routledge.

References

Adams, G. L., & Engelmann, S. (1996). *Research on Direct Instruction: 25 years beyond DISTAR*. Seattle, WA: Educational Achievement Systems.

Adams, M. J., Foorman, B. R., Lundberg, I., & Beeler, T. (1998). *Phonemic awareness in young children: A classroom curriculum*. Baltimore: Paul H. Brookes.

Adult Education and Family Literacy Act of 1998, §202, 20 USC § 9201 (1998).

Alliance for Healthy Homes. (2008). *Children at risk*. Retrieved July 19, 2008, from www.afhh.org.

Allor, J. H. (2002). The relationships of phonemic awareness and rapid naming to reading development. *Learning Disabilities Quarterly, 25*, 47–57.

Almasi, J. F. (1995). The nature of fourth graders' sociocognitive conflicts in peer-led and teacher-led discussions of literature. *Reading Research Quarterly, 30*, 314–351.

Almasi, J. F. (2003). *Teaching strategic processes in reading*. New York: Guilford.

Alvarez, M. C. (1983). Using a thematic pre-organizer and guided instruction as aids to concept learning. *Reading Horizons, 24*, 51–58.

American Psychiatric Association. (2000). *Diagnostic and statistical manual of mental disorders* (4th ed., Text Revision). Washington, DC: Author.

Anderson, J., & Morrison, F. (2007). "A great program . . . for me as a gramma": Caregivers evaluate a family literacy initiative. *Canadian Journal of Education, 30*(1), 68–89.

Anderson, L. W., Krathwohl, D. R., Airasian, P. W., Cruikshank, K. A., Mayer, R. E., Pintrich, P. R., Raths, J., & Wittrock, M. C. (2001). *A taxonomy for learning, teaching, and assessing: A revision of Bloom's Taxonomy of Educational Objectives* (Abridged ed.). Boston: Allyn and Bacon.

Anderson, R. C., & Freebody, P. (1981). Vocabulary knowledge. In J. T. Guthrie (Ed.), *Comprehension and teaching: Research reviews* (pp. 77–117). Newark, DE: International Reading Association.

Anderson, R. C., Pichert, J. W., & Shirey, L. L. (1983). Effects of the reader's schema at different points in time. *Journal of Educational Psychology, 75*, 271–279.

Anderson, R. C., Spiro, R. J., & Anderson, M. C. (1978). Schemata as scaffolding for the representation of information in connected discourse. *American Educational Research Journal, 15*, 433–440.

Antonio, D., & Guthrie, J. T. (2009). Reading is social: Bringing peer interaction to the text. In J. T. Guthrie (Ed.), *Engaging adolescents in reading* (pp. 49–50). Thousand Oaks, CA: Sage.

Atwell, N. (1998). *In the middle: New understandings about writing, reading, and learning*. Portsmouth, NH: Boynton/Cook/Heinemann.

Au, K. H. (2000). A multicultural perspective on policies for improving literacy achievement: Equity and excellence. In M. L. Kamil, P. B. Mosenthal, P. D. Pearson, & R. Barr (Eds.), *Handbook of reading research, Volume III* (pp. 835–851). Mahwah, NJ: Erlbaum.

Aukerman, M. S. (2007). When reading it wrong is getting it right: Shared evaluation pedagogy among fifth grade readers. *Research in the Teaching of English, 42*, 56–103.

Ausubel, D. P. (1960). The use of advance organizers in the learning and retention of meaningful material. *Journal of Educational Psychology, 51*, 267–272.

Avalos, M. A., Plasencia, A., Chavez, C., & Rascón, J. (2007). Modified Guided Reading: Gateway to English as a second language and literacy learning. *The Reading Teacher, 61*, 318–329.

Bailey, D. B., & Simeonsson, R. J. (1998). *Family assessment in early intervention*. Upper Saddle River, NJ: Pearson Education.

Baker, S. K., Simmons, D. C., & Kame'enui, E. J. (1998). Vocabulary acquisition: Instructional and curricular basics and implications. In D. C. Simmons & E. J. Kame'enui (Eds.), *What reading research tells us about children with diverse learning needs: Bases and basics* (pp. 219–238). Mahwah, NJ: Lawrence Erlbaum.

Barbara Bush Foundation for Family Literacy. (2008). Retrieved July 19, 2008 from www.barbarabushfoundation.com.

Barrera, I. (1995). To refer or not to refer: Untangling the web of diversity, "deficit," and disability. *New York State Association for Bilingual Education Journal, 10*, 54–66.

Barrett, T. C. (1976). Taxonomy of reading comprehension. In R. Smith & T. C. Barrett (Eds.), *Teaching reading in the middle grades* (pp. 51–58). Reading, MA: Addison-Wesley.

Barron, R. F. (1969). The use of vocabulary as an advance organizer. In H. I. Herber & P. L. Sanders (Eds.), *Research in reading in the content areas: First year report* (pp. 29–39). Syracuse, NY: Syracuse University, Reading and Language Arts Center.

Baumann, J. F. (2005). Vocabulary-comprehension relationships. In B. Maloch, J. V. Hoffman, S. L. Schallert, C. M. Fairbanks, & J. Worthy (Eds.), *54th yearbook of the National Reading Conference* (pp. 117–131). Oak Creek, WI: National Reading Conference.

Baumann, J. F., Edwards, E. C., Font, G., Tereshinski, C. A., Kame'enui, E. J., & Olejnik, S. (2002). Teaching morphemic and contextual analysis to fifth-grade students. *Reading Research Quarterly, 37*, 150–176.

Baumann, N. L. (1995). Reading millionaires—it works! *The Reading Teacher, 48*, 730.

Bean, T. W., Readence, J. E., & Baldwin, R. S. (2008). *Content area literacy: An integrated approach* (9th ed.). Dubuque, IA: Kendall/Hunt.

Bear, D. R., Helman, L., Templeton, S., Invernizzi, M., & Johnston, F. (2007). *Words their way with English learners: Word study for phonics, vocabulary, and spelling instruction.* Upper Saddle River, NJ: Merrill/Prentice Hall.

Bear, D. R., Invernizzi, M., Templeton, S. R., & Johnston, F. (2008). *Words their way: Word study for phonics, vocabulary, and spelling instruction* (4th ed.). Columbus, OH: Allyn and Bacon/Merrill.

Beck, I. L., & McKeown, M. G. (2007). *Improving comprehension with Questioning the Author.* New York: Scholastic.

Bender, W. N., & Larkin, M. J. (2003). *Reading strategies for elementary students with learning difficulties.* Thousand Oaks, CA: Corwin.

Berger, L. R. (1996). Reader response journals: You make the meaning . . . and how. *Journal of Adolescent and Adult Literacy, 39,* 380–385.

Bergman, J. L. (1992). SAIL—A way to success and independence for low-achieving readers. *The Reading Teacher, 45,* 598–602.

Betts, E. A. (1946). *Foundations of reading instruction.* New York: American Book.

Blachowicz, C., & Fisher, P. (2009). *Teaching vocabulary in all classrooms* (4th ed.). Upper Columbus, OH: Allyn & Bacon/Merrill.

Blachowicz, C. L. Z., Fisher, P. J. L., Ogle, D., & Watts-Taffe, S. (2006). Vocabulary: Questions from the classroom. *Reading Research Quarterly, 41,* 524–539.

Blanton, W. E., Wood, K. D., & Moorman, G. B. (1990). The role of purpose in reading instruction. *The Reading Teacher, 43,* 486–493.

Bloom, B. S., Engelhart, M. D., Furst, E. J., Hill, W. H., & Krathwohl, D. R. (1956). *Taxonomy of educational objectives: The classification of educational goals. Handbook I: Cognitive domain.* New York: David McKay.

Borkowski, J. G., Weyhing, R. S., & Carr, M. (1988). Effects of attributional retraining on strategy-based reading comprehension in learning-disabled students. *Journal of Educational Psychology, 80,* 46–53.

Borman, G. D., Slavin, R. E., Cheung, A. C. K., Chamberlain, A. M., Madden, N. A., & Chambers, B. (2007). Final reading outcomes of the national randomized field trial of Success for All. *American Educational Research Journal, 44,* 701–731.

Bos, C. S., & Anders, P. L. (1992). Using interactive teaching and learning strategies to promote text comprehension and content learning for students with learning disabilities. *International Journal of Disability, Development and Education, 39,* 225–238.

Bosman, A. M. T., Gompel, M., Vervloed, M. P. J., & von Bon, W. H. J. (2006). Low vision affects the reading process quantitatively but no qualitatively. *The Journal of Special Education, 39,* 208–219.

Boulineau, T., Fore, C. III, Hagan-Burke, S. & Burke, M. D. (2004). Use of story-mapping to increase the story-grammar text comprehension of elementary students with learning disabilities. *Learning Disability Quarterly, 27,* 105–121.

Boulware, B. J., & Crowe, M. L. (2008). Using the concept attainment strategy to enhance reading comprehension. *The Reading Teacher, 61,* 491–495.

Boyd-Batstone, P. (2004). Focused anecdotal records assessment: A tool for standards-based, authentic assessment. *The Reading Teacher, 58,* 230–239.

Brown, A. L. (1980). Metacognitive development and reading. In R. J. Spiro, B. C. Bruce, & W. F. Brewer (Eds.), *Theoretical issues in reading comprehension* (pp. 453–481). Hillsdale, NJ: Lawrence Erlbaum.

Bryant, D. P., Vaughn, S., Linan-Thompson, S., Ugel, N., & Hamff, A. (2000). Reading outcomes for students with and without learning disabilities in general education middle school content area classes. *Learning Disability Quarterly, 23,* 24–38.

Burns, M. K., MacQuarrie, L. L., & Campbell, D. T. (1999). The difference between curriculum-based assessment and curriculum-based measurement: A focus on purpose and result. *NASP Communique, 27*(6), 18.

Cairney, T. H. (1987). Story frames—story cloze. *The Reading Teacher, 41,* 239–241.

Carnine, D., & Kinder, D. (1985). Teaching low-performing students to apply generative and schema strategies to narrative and expository material. *Remedial and Special Education, 6,* 20–30.

Carnine, D. W., Silbert, J., Kame'enui, E. J., & Tarver, W. (2004). *Direct Instruction reading* (4th ed.). Upper Saddle River, NJ: Merrill/Prentice Hall.

Carnine, D. W., Silbert, J., Kame'enui, E. J., Tarver, S. G., & Jungjohann, K. (2006). *Teaching struggling and at-risk readers: A Direct Instruction approach.* Upper Saddle River, NJ: Merrill/Prentice Hall.

Carr, M., & Borkowski, J. G. (1989). Attributional training and the generalization of reading strategies with underachieving children. *Learning and Individual Differences, 1,* 327–341.

Cartledge, G., & Kourea, L. (2008). Culturally responsive classrooms for culturally diverse students with and at risk for disabilities. *Exceptional Children, 74,* 351–371.

Casazza, M. W. (1993). Using a model of direct instruction to teach summary writing in a college reading class. *Journal of Reading, 37,* 202–208.

Catts, H. W., & Kamhi, A. G. (2005). *Language and reading disabilities* (2nd ed.). Upper Saddle River, NJ: Pearson Education.

Cazden, C. B. (2001). *Classroom discourse: The language of teaching and learning* (2nd ed.). Portsmouth, NH: Heinemann.

Chall, J. (1967). *Learning to read: The great debate.* New York: McGraw-Hill.

Chall, J. S., Bissex, G. L., Conard, S. S., & Harris-Sharples, S. (1996). *Qualitative assessment of text difficulty: A practical guide for teachers and writers.* Cambridge, MA: Brookline.

Chapman, J. W., Tunmer, W. E., Prochnow, J. E. (2000). Early reading-related skills and performance, reading self-concept, and the development of academic self-concept: A longitudinal study. *Journal of Educational Psychology, 92,* 703–708.

Chard, D. J., & Osborn, J. (1999). Phonics and reading recognition instruction in early reading programs: Guidelines for accessibility. *Learning Disabilities Research and Practice, 14,* 107–118.

Christie, J. F. (1990). Dramatic play: A context for meaningful engagement. *The Reading Teacher, 43,* 542–545.

Clarke, L .W., & Holwadel, J. (2007). "Help! What is wrong with these literature circles and how can we fix them?" *The Reading Teacher, 61,* 20–29.

Clay, M. M. (1985). *The early detection of reading difficulties* (3rd ed.). Portsmouth, NH: Heinemann.

Clay, M. M. (2000). *Running records for classroom teachers.* Portsmouth, NH: Heinemann.

Cohen, L. G., & Spenciner, L. J. (2007). *Assessment of children and youth with special needs* (3rd ed.). Boston: Allyn and Bacon.

Collins, L., & Matthey, S. (2001). Helping parents to read with their children: Evaluation of an individual and group reading motivation programme. *Journal of Research in Reading, 24,* 65–81.

Collins, M. D., & Cheek, E. H., Jr. (1999). *Assessing and guiding reading instruction.* Boston: McGraw-Hill.

Connor, C.D., Son, S., & Hindman, A. H. (2005). Teacher qualifications, classroom practices, family characteristics, and preschool experience: Complex effects on first graders' vocabulary and early reading outcomes. *Journal of School Psychology, 43,* 343–375.

Cooper, J. D., & Kiger, N. D. (2009). *Literacy: Helping children construct meaning* (7th ed.). Boston: Houghton Mifflin.

Cooper, J. O., Heron, T. E., & Heward, W. L. (2007). *Applied behavior analysis* (2nd ed.). Upper Saddle River, NJ: Merrill/Prentice Hall.

Coyne, M. D., Kame'enui, E. J., & Carnine, D. W. (2007). *Effective teaching strategies that accommodate diverse learners* (3rd ed.). Upper Saddle River, NJ: Merrill/Prentice Hall.

Crawford, P. A., & Zygouris-Coe, V. (2006). All in the family: Connecting home and school with family literacy. *Early Childhood Education Journal, 33,* 261–267.

Crawley, S. J., & Merritt, K. (2000). *Remediating reading difficulties* (2nd ed.). Boston: McGraw-Hill.

Cudd, E. T., & Roberts, L. L. (1987). Using story frames to develop reading comprehension in a 1st grade classroom. *The Reading Teacher, 41,* 74–79.

Cummins, J. (2001). Assessment and intervention with culturally and linguistically diverse learners. In S. R. Hurley & J. V. Tinajero (Eds.), *Literacy assessment of second language learners* (pp. 115–129). Boston: Allyn and Bacon.

Cunningham, J. W., Spadorcia, S. A., Erickson, K. A., Koppenhaver, D. A., Sturn, J. M., & Yoder, D. E. (2005). Investigating the instructional supportiveness of leveled texts. *Reading Research Quarterly, 40,* 410–427.

Cunningham, P. M. (2003). What research says about teaching phonics. In L. M. Morrow, L. B. Gambrell, & M. Pressley (Eds.), *Best practices in literacy instruction* (2nd ed., pp. 65–85). New York: Guilford.

Cunningham, P. M. (2009). *Phonics they use: Words for reading and writing* (5th ed.). Boston: Allyn and Bacon/Merrill.

Cunningham, P. M., & Allington, R. L. (2007). *Classrooms that work: They can all read and write* (4th ed.). Boston: Allyn and Bacon.

Cunningham, P. M., & Cunningham, J. W. (1992). Making words: Enhancing the invented spelling-decoding connection. *The Reading Teacher, 46,* 106–115.

Cunningham, P. M., Hall, D. P., & Sigmon, C. M. (1999). *The teacher's guide to the Four Blocks: A multimethod, multilevel framework for grades 1–3.* Greensboro, NC: Carson-Dellosa.

Daniels, H. (2002). *Literature circles: Voice and choice in book clubs and reading groups* (2nd ed.). Portland, ME: Stenhouse.

Davey, B. (1983). Think aloud—modeling the cognitive processes of reading comprehension. *Journal of Reading, 27,* 44–47.

Davis, Z. T. (1994). Effects of prereading story-mapping on elementary readers' comprehension. *Journal of Educational Research, 87,* 353–360.

Davis, Z. T., & McPherson, M. D. (1989). Story map instruction: A road map for reading comprehension. *The Reading Teacher, 43,* 232–240.

Dearing, E., Kreider, H., & Simpkins, S. (2006). Family involvement in school and low-income children's literacy: Longitudinal associations between and within families. *Journal of Educational Psychology, 98,* 653–664.

DiBenedetto, B. (1996). Integrating approaches to the remediation of reading disability. In L.R. Putnam (Ed.), *How to become a better reading teacher: Strategies for assessment and intervention* (pp. 199–209). Upper Saddle River, NJ: Merrill/Prentice Hall.

Dickson, S. V., Collins, V. L., Simmons, D. C., & Kame'enui, E. J. (1998). Metacognitive strategies: Instructional and curricular basics and implications. In D. C. Simmons & E. J. Kame'enui (Eds.), *What reading research tells us about children with diverse learning needs: Bases and basics* (pp. 361–380). Mahway, NJ: Lawrence Erlbaum.

Dowhower, S. L. (1989). Repeated reading: Research into practice. *The Reading Teacher, 42,* 502–507.

Dreyer, L. G. (1984). Readability and responsibility. *Journal of Reading, 27,* 334–338.

Duffelmeyer, F. A. (1994). Effective anticipation guide statements for learning from expository prose. *Journal of Reading, 37,* 452–457.

Duffelmeyer, F. A., & Banwart, B. H. (1993). Word maps for adjectives and verbs. *The Reading Teacher, 46,* 351–352.

Duffy-Hester, A. M. (1999). Teaching struggling readers in elementary school classrooms: A review of classroom reading programs and principles for instruction. *The Reading Teacher, 52,* 480–495.

Dunst, C. J., Trivette, C. M., & Deal, A. G. (1988). *Enabling and empowering families: Principles and guidelines for practice.* Cambridge, MA: Brookline.

Durkin, D. (1976). *Strategies for identifying words.* Boston: Allyn and Bacon.

Dyer, R. V. (2001). *Successful strategies in family literacy.* Augusta, ME: Maine Family Literacy Initiative, Maine Department of Education.

Dykman, R. A., & Ackerman, P. T. (1991). Attention deficit disorder and specific reading disability: Separate but often overlapping disorders. *Journal of Learning Disabilities, 24,* 96–103.

Dymock, S. (2007). Comprehension strategy instruction: Teaching narrative text structure awareness. *The Reading Teacher, 61,* 161–167.

Earle, R. A. (1969). Use of the structure overview in mathematics classes. In H. I. Herber & P. L. Sanders (Eds.), *Research in reading in the content areas: First year report* (pp. 49–58). Syracuse, NY: Syracuse University, Reading and Language Arts Center.

Earle, R. A., & Barron, R. F. (1973). An approach for teaching vocabulary in content subject. In H. I. Herber & P. L. Sanders (Eds.), *Research in reading in the content areas: Second year report* (pp. 84–100). Syracuse, NY: Syracuse University, Reading and Language Arts Center.

Echevarria, J. (1995). Interactive reading instruction: A comparison of proximal and distal effects of instructional conversations. *Exceptional Children, 61,* 536–552.

Ehri, L. C. (1991). Development of the ability to read words. In R. Barr, M. L. Kamil, P. B. Mosenthal, & P. D. Pearson (Eds.), *Handbook of reading research* (vol. 2, pp. 383–417). New York: Longman.

Ehri, L. C. (1992). Reconceptualizing the development of sight word reading and its relationship to recoding. In P. Gough, L. Ehri, & R. Treiman (Eds.), *Reading acquisition* (pp. 107–143). Hillsdale, NJ: Lawrence Erlbaum.

Ehri, L. C., Nunes, S. R., Willows, D. M., Schuster, B. V., Yaghoub-Zadeh, Z., & Shanahan, T. (2001). Phonemic awareness instruction helps children learn to read: Evidence from the National Reading panel's meta-analysis. *Reading Research Quarterly, 36,* 250–287.

Elkonin, D. B. (1963). The psychology of mastering the elements of reading. In B. Simon & J. Simon (Eds.), *Educational psychology in the U.S.S.R.* (pp. 165–179). New York: Routledge.

Elkonin, D. B. (1973). Reading in the USSR. In J. Downing (Ed.), *Comparative reading* (pp. 551–579). New York: Macmillan.

Emery, D. W. (1996). Helping readers comprehend stories from the characters' perspectives. *The Reading Teacher, 49,* 534–541.

Englert, C. S., Raphael, T. E., Anderson, L. M., Anthony, H. M., & Stevens, D. D. (1991). Making strategies and self-talk visible: Writing instruction in regular and special education classrooms. *American Educational Research Journal, 28,* 337–372.

Farris, P. J., Nelson, P. A., & L'Allier, S. (2007). Using literature circles with English language learners at middle level. *Middle School Journal, 38*(4), 38–42.

Fawson, P. C., & Reutzel, D. R. (2000). But I only have a basal: Implementing guided reading in the early grades. *The Reading Teacher, 54,* 84–97.

Feazell, V. S. (2004). Reading Acceleration Program: A schoolwide intervention. *The Reading Teacher, 58,* 66–72.

Finn, P. J. (2009). *Literacy with an attitude: Educating working-class children in their own self-interest* (2nd ed.). Albany, NY: State University of New York.

Fisher, P., & Blachowicz, C. (2007). Teaching how to think about words. *Voices from the Middle, 15*(1), 6–12.

Flood, J., Lapp, D., & Fisher, D. (2002). Parsing, questioning, and rephrasing (PQR): Building syntactic knowledge to improve reading comprehension. In C. C. Block, L. B. Gambrell, & M. Pressley (Eds.), *Improving comprehension instruction: Rethinking research, theory, and classroom practice* (pp. 181–198). San Francisco: Jossey-Bass.

Flynn, R. M. (2004/2005). Curriculum-based Readers Theatre: Setting the stage for reading and retention. *The Reading Teacher, 58,* 360–365.

Foorman, B. R., & Torgesen, J. (2003). Critical elements of classroom and small-group instruction promote reading success in all children. *Learning Disabilities Research and Practice, 16,* 203–212.

Fosnot, C. T. (2005). *Constructivism: Theory, perspectives, and practice* (2nd ed.). New York: Teachers College.

Fountas, I. C., & Pinnell, G. S. (1996). *Guided Reading: Good first teaching for all children.* Portsmouth, NH: Heinemann.

Fountas, I. C., & Pinnell, G. S. (2005). *Leveled books, K–8: Matching texts to readers for effective teaching.* Portsmouth, NH: Heinemann.

Fountas, I. C., & Pinnell, G. S. (2008). *Fountas and Pinnell leveled books website.* Retrieved July 11, 2008 from www.fountasandpinnellleveledbooks.com.

Fox, B. J. (2008). *Word identification strategies: Building phonics into a classroom reading program* (4th ed.). Englewood Cliffs, NJ: Merrill/Prentice Hall.

French, M. M. (1988). Story retelling for assessment and instruction. *Perspectives for Teachers of the Hearing Impaired, 7*(2), 20–22.

Fry, E. G. (1989). Reading formulas—maligned but valid. *Journal of Reading, 32,* 292–297.

Fuchs, L. S., Fuchs, D., & Speece, D. L. (2002). Treatment validity as a unifying construct for identifying learning disabilities. *Learning Disability Quarterly, 25,* 33–45.

Gallaudet Research Institute. (2003). *Literacy.* Retrieved July 9, 2008, from http://gri.gallaudet.edu/Literacy/index.html.

Gambrell, L. B. (1980). Think-time: Implications for reading instruction. *The Reading Teacher, 34,* 143–146.

Gambrell, L. B. (1983). The occurrence of think-time during reading comprehension instruction. *The Journal of Educational Research, 77,* 77–80.

Gambrell, L. B., & Jawitz, P. B. (1993). Mental imagery, text illustrations, and children's story comprehension and recall. *Reading Research Quarterly, 28,* 264–276.

Gambrell, L. B., Pfeiffer, W. R., & Wilson, R. M. (1985). The effects of retelling upon reading comprehension and recall of text information. *The Journal of Educational Research, 78,* 216–220.

Gardill, M. C., & Jitendra, A. K. (1999). Advance story-map instruction: Effects on the reading comprehension of students with learning disabilities. *The Journal of Special Education, 33,* 2–17.

Gaskins, I. W. (2000). *Information about word identification/spelling programs published by Benchmark School.* Media, PA: Benchmark School.

Gaskins, I. W., Ehri, L. C., Cress, C., O'Hara, C., & Donnelly, K. (1996–1997). Procedures for word learning: Making discoveries about words. *The Reading Teacher, 50,* 312–327.

Gillet, J. W., & Gentry, J. R. (1983). Bridges between Nonstandard and Standard English with extensions of dictated stories. *The Reading Teacher, 36,* 360–364.

Gipe, J. P. (2006). *Multiple paths to literacy: Assessment and differentiated instruction for diverse learners, K–12* (6th ed). Upper Saddle River, NJ: Merrill/Prentice Hall.

Goatley, V. J., Brock, C. H., & Raphael, T. E. (1995). Diverse learners participating in regular education "Book Clubs." *Reading Research Quarterly, 30,* 352–380.

Goldenberg, C. (1991). Learning to read in New Zealand: The balance of skills and meaning. *Language Arts, 68,* 555–562.

Goldenberg, C. (1993). Instructional conversations: Promoting comprehension through discussion. *The Reading Teacher, 46,* 316–326.

Gollnick, D. M., & Chinn, P. C. (2009). *Multicultural education in a pluralistic society* (8th ed.). Columbus, OH: Allyn and Bacon/Merrill.

Goodman, Y. M., Watson, D. J., & Burke, C. L. (2006). *Reading miscue inventory: From evaluation to instruction.* Katonah, NY: Richard C. Owen.

Graves, M. F. (1986). Vocabulary learning and instruction. In E. Z. Rothkopf (Ed.), *Review of research in education* (pp. 49–89). Washington, DC: American Educational Research Association.

Graves, M. F., & Braaten, S. (1996). Scaffolded Reading Experiences: Bridges to success. *Preventing School Failure, 40,* 169–173.

Graves, M. F., Cooke, C. L., & Laberge, M. J. (1983). Effects of previewing difficult short stories on low ability junior high school students' comprehension, recall, and attitudes. *Reading Research Quarterly, 17,* 262–276.

Graves, M., & Graves, B. (2007). *Scaffolded Reading Experiences: Designs for student success* (3rd ed.). Norwood, MA: Christopher-Gordon.

Gravois, T. A., & Gickling, E. E. (2002). Best practices in curriculum-based assessment. In A. Thomas & J. Grimes (Eds.), *Best practices in school psychology IV* (pp. 885–898). Bethesda, MD: National Association of School Psychologists.

Griffey, Q. Jr., Zigmond, N., & Leinhardt, G. (1988). The effects of self-questioning and story structure on the reading comprehension of poor readers. *Learning Disabilities Quarterly, 4*(1), 45–51.

Gunning, T. G. (2003). The role of readability in today's classroom. *Topics in Language Disorders, 23,* 175–189.

Gunning, T. G. (2006). *Assessing and correcting reading and writing difficulties* (3rd ed.). Boston: Allyn and Bacon.

Guthrie, J. T., & McCann, A. D. (1997). Characteristics of classrooms that promote motivations and strategies for learning. In J. T. Guthrie & A. Wigfield (Eds.), *Reading engagement: Motivating readers through integrated instruction* (pp. 128–148). Newark, DE: International Reading Association.

Guthrie, J. T., McRae, A., & Klauda, S. L. (2007). Contributions of Concept-Oriented Reading Instruction to knowledge about interventions for motivation in reading. *Educational Psychologist, 42,* 237–250.

Guthrie, J. T., & Wigfield, A. (2000). Engagement and motivation in reading. In M. L. Kamil, R. B. Mosenthal, P. D. Pearson, & R. Barr (Eds.), *Handbook of reading research, volume III* (pp. 403–422). Mahwah, NJ: Erlbaum.

Guthrie, J. T., Wigfield, A., Metsala, J. L., & Cox, K. E. (1999). Motivational and cognitive predictors of text comprehension and reading amount. *Scientific Studies of Reading, 3,* 231–256.

Guthrie, J. T., Wigfield, A., & VonSecker, C. (2000). Effects of integrated instruction on motivation and strategy use in reading. *Journal of Educational Psychology, 92,* 331–341.

Hancock, M. R. (1993a). Character journals: Initiating involvement and identification through literature. *Journal of Reading, 37,* 42–50.

Hancock, M. R. (1993b). Exploring and extending personal response through literature journals. *The Reading Teacher, 46,* 466–474.

Hansen, J. (1981). The effects of inference training and practice on young children's reading comprehension. *Reading Research Quarterly, 16,* 391–417.

Hansen, J. (2001). *When writers read* (2nd ed.). Portsmouth, NH: Heinemann.

Hansen, J., & Pearson, P. D. (1983). An instructional study: Improving the inferential comprehension of good and poor fourth-grade readers. *Journal of Educational Psychology, 75,* 821–829.

Hargis, C. H. (2004). *Curriculum based assessment* (3rd ed.). Springfield, IL: Thomas.

Harmon, J. M. (2002). Teaching independent word learning strategies to struggling readers. *Journal of Adolescent and Adult Literacy, 45,* 606–615.

Harris, T. L., & Hodges, R. E. (Eds.). (1995). *The literacy dictionary.* Newark, DE: International Reading Association.

Harste, J. C., Short, K. G., & Burke, C. (1988). *Creating classrooms for authors: The reading-writing connection.* Portsmouth, NH: Heinemann.

Hasbrouk, J., & Tindal, G. (2006). Oral reading fluency norms: A valuable assessment tool for reading teachers. *The Reading Teacher, 59,* 636–644.

Hashey, J. M., & Connors, D. J. (2003). Learn from our journey: Reciprocal teaching action research. *The Reading Teacher, 57,* 224–232.

Heckelman, R. G. (1969). A neurological impress method of reading instruction. *Academic Therapy, 4,* 277–282.

Hedrick, W. B., & Pearish, A. B. (1999). Good reading instruction is more important than who provides the instruction or where it takes place. *The Reading Teacher, 52,* 716–726.

Heller, M. F. (1988). Comprehending and composing through language experience. *The Reading Teacher, 42,* 130–135.

Hendricks, C., & Rinsky, L. A. (2007). *Teaching word recognition skills* (7th ed.). Upper Saddle River, NJ: Merrill/Prentice Hall.

Heward, W. L. (2009). *Exceptional children: An introduction to special education* (9th ed.). Upper Saddle River, NJ: Allyn and Bacon/Merrill.

Hill, J. L. (1999). *Meeting the needs of children with special physical and health care needs.* Upper Saddle River, NJ: Merrill/Prentice Hall.

Hoffman, J. V. (1987). Rethinking the role of oral reading in basal instruction. *The Elementary School Journal, 87,* 367–373.

Hollingsworth, P. M. (1978). An experimental approach to the impress method of teaching reading. *The Reading Teacher, 31,* 624–626.

Idol, L. (1987). Group story mapping: A comprehension strategy for both skilled and unskilled readers. *Journal of Learning Disabilities, 20,* 196–205.

Irwin, J. W., & Davis, C. A. (1980). Assessing readability: The checklist approach. *Journal of Reading, 24,* 124–130.

Ivey, G., & Broaddus, K. (2001). "Just plain reading": A survey of what makes students want to read in middle school classrooms. *Reading Research Quarterly, 36,* 350–377.

Jansen, S. J., & Duffelmeyer, F. A. (1996). Enhancing possible sentences through cooperative learning. *Journal of Adolescent and Adult Literacy, 39,* 658–659.

Jenkins, J. R., Matlock, B., & Slocum, T. A. (1989). Two approaches to vocabulary instruction: The teaching of individual word meanings and practice in deriving word meaning from context. *Reading Research Quarterly, 24,* 215–235.

Jenkins, J. R., Stein, M. L., & Wysocki, K. (1984). Learning vocabulary through reading. *American Educational Research Association, 21,* 767–787.

Jeynes, W. H. (2005). A meta-analysis of the relation of parental involvement to urban elementary school student academic achievement. *Urban Education, 40,* 237–269.

Johnson, D. D., & Pearson, P. D. (1984). *Teaching reading vocabulary* (2nd ed.). New York: Holt, Rinehart and Winston.

Johnson, G. S., & Bliesmer, E. P. (1983). Effects of narrative schema training and practice in generating questions on reading comprehension of seventh grade students. In G. H. McNinch (Ed.), *Reading research to reading practice* (pp. 91–94). Athens, GA: The American Reading Forum.

Johnson, K. L. (1987). Improving reading comprehension through prereading and post-reading exercises. *Reading Improvement, 24,* 81–83.

Juel, C. (1991). Beginning reading. In R. Barr, M. L. Kamil, P. B. Mosenthal, & P. D. Pearson (Eds.), *Handbook of reading research* (vol. 2, pp. 759–788). New York: Longman.

Kapinus, B. A., Gambrell, L. B., & Koskinen, P. S. (1987). Effects of practice in retelling upon the reading comprehension of proficient and less proficient readers. In J. E. Readence & R. S. Baldwin (Eds.), *Research in literacy: Merging perspectives* (pp. 135–141). Rochester, NY: The National Reading Conference.

Karnowski, L. (1989). Using LEA with process writing. *The Reading Teacher, 42,* 462–465.

Kavale, K. A., & Forness, S. R. (2000). History, rhetoric and reality: Analysis of the inclusion debate. *Remedial and Special Education, 21,* 279–296.

Keehn, S. (2003). The effect of instruction and practice through Readers Theatre on young readers' oral reading fluency. *Reading Research and Instruction, 42*(4), 40–61.

Keeler, M. A. (1993). Story map game board. *The Reading Teacher, 46,* 626–628.

Kelly-Vance, L., & Schreck, D. (2002). The impact of a collaborative family/school reading programme on student reading rate. *Journal of Research in Reading, 25,* 43–53.

Kibby, M. W. (1995a). *Practical steps for informing literacy instruction: A diagnostic decision-making model.* Newark, DE: International Reading Association.

Kibby, M. W. (1995b). The organization and teaching of things and the words that signify them. *Journal of Adolescent and Adult Literacy, 39,* 208–223.

Kingsley, M. (1997). The effects of a visual loss. In H. Mason & S. McCall (Eds.), *Visual impairment: Access to education for children and young people* (pp. 23–29). London: Fulton.

Kinniburgh, L., & Shaw, E., Jr. (2007). Building reading fluency in elementary science through Readers' Theatre. *Science Activities, 44*(1), 16–22.

Klingner, J. K., & Vaughn, S. (1999). Promoting reading comprehension, content learning, and English acquisition through Collaborative Strategic Reading (CSR). *The Reading Teacher, 52,* 738–747.

Klingner, J. K., Vaughn, S., Arguelles, M. E., Hughes, M. T., & Leftwich, S. A. (2004). Collaborative Strategic Reading: "Real world" lessons from classroom teachers. *Remedial and Special Education, 25,* 291–302.

Klingner, J. K., Vaughn, S., Dimino, J., Schumm, J. S., & Bryant, D. P. (2001). *From clunk to click: Collaborative Strategic Reading.* Longmont, CO: Sopris West.

Koskinen, P. S., Gambrell, L. B., Kapinus, B. A., & Heathington, B. S. (1988). Retelling: A strategy for enhancing students' reading comprehension. *The Reading Teacher, 41,* 892–896.

Koskinen, P. S., & O'Flahavan, J. F. (1995). Teacher role options in peer discussions about literature. *The Reading Teacher, 48,* 354–356.

Kotula, A. W. (2003). Matching readers to instructional materials: The use of classic readability measures for students with language learning disabilities and dyslexia. *Topics in Language Disorders, 23,* 190–203.

Langer, J. A. (1981). From theory to practice: A prereading plan. *Journal of Reading, 25,* 152–157.

Leal, D. J. (1993). The power of literacy peer-group discussions: How children collaboratively negotiate meaning. *The Reading Teacher, 47,* 114–120.

Lee, N. G., & Neal, J. C. (1992/1993). Reading Rescue: Intervention for a student "at promise." *The Reading Teacher, 36,* 276–283.

Lenz, B. K., Alley, G. R., & Schumaker, J. B. (1987). Activating the inactive learner: Advance organizers in the secondary content classroom. *Learning Disability Quarterly, 10,* 53–67.

Leu, D. J., Jr., & Kinzer, C. K. (2003). *Effective literacy instruction, K–8* (4th ed.). Upper Saddle River, NJ: Merrill/Prentice Hall.

Literacy Collaborative at The Ohio State University. (2008). *Literacy collaborative framework.* Retrieved July 11, 2008 from www.lcosu.org/framework.htm.

Long, S. A., Winograd, P. N., & Bridge, C. A. (1989). The effects of reader and text characteristics on imagery reported during and after reading. *Reading Research Quarterly, 24,* 353–372.

Lovett, M. W., Steinbach, K. A., & Frijters, J. C. (2000). Remediating the core deficits of developmental reading disability: A double-deficit perspective. *Journal of Learning Disabilities, 33,* 334–358.

Lutz, S. L., Guthrie, J. T., & Davis, M. H. (2006). Scaffolding for engagement in elementary reading instruction. *The Journal of Educational Research, 100,* 3–20.

Madden, N. A., Slavin, R. E., Wasik, B. A., & Dolan, L. J. (1997). Reading, writing, and language arts in Success for All. In S. A. Stahl & D. A. Hayes (Eds.), *Instructional models in reading* (pp. 109–130). Mahwah, NJ: Erlbaum.

Manzo, A. V. (1969). The ReQuest procedure. *Journal of Reading, 13,* 123–126, 163.

Manzo, A. V., & Manzo, U. C. (2008). *Content area literacy: Interactive teaching for active learning* (5th ed.). Hoboken, NJ: John Wiley & Sons.

Marinak, B. A., & Gambrell, L. B. (2008). Intrinsic motivation and rewards: What sustains young children's engagement with text? *Literacy Research and Instruction, 47,* 9–26.

Marzano, R. J., & Kendall, J. S. (2007). *The new taxonomy of educational objectives* (2nd ed.). Thousand Oaks, CA: Sage.

Mason, L. H., Meadan, H., Hedin, L., & Corso, L. (2006). Self-regulated strategy development instruction for expository text comprehension. *Teaching Exceptional Children, 38*(4), 47–52.

Mason, L. H., Snyder, K. H., Sukhram, D. P., & Kedem, Y. (2006). TWA + PLANS strategies for expository reading and writing: Effects for nine fourth-grade students. *Exceptional Children, 73,* 69–89.

McCauley, J. K., & McCauley, D. S. (1992). Using choral reading to promote language learning for ESL students. *The Reading Teacher, 45,* 526–533.

McCormick, S. (2007). *Instructing students who have literacy problems* (5th ed.). Upper Saddle River, NJ: Merrill/Prentice Hall.

McGee, L. M. (1982). Awareness of text structure: Effects on children's recall of expository text. *Reading Research Quarterly, 17,* 581–590.

McKenna, M. C. (2002). *Help for struggling readers: Strategies for grades 3–8.* New York: Guilford.

McKenna, M. C., Ellsworth, R. A., & Kear, D. J. (1995). Children's attitudes toward reading: A national survey. *Reading Research Quarterly, 30,* 934–956.

McKeown, M. G. (1993). Creating effective definitions for young word learners. *Reading Research Quarterly, 28,* 16–31.

McKeown, M. G., & Beck, I. L. (2004). Transforming knowledge into professional development resources: Six teachers implement a model of teaching for understanding text. *The Elementary School Journal, 104,* 391–408.

McKool, S. S. (2007). Factors that influence the decision to read: An investigation of fifth grade students' out-of-school reading habits. *Reading Improvement, 44,* 111–131.

McMahon, S. I., & Raphael, T. E. (1997). *The Book Club connection: Literacy learning and classroom talk.* New York: Teachers College.

McNeil, J. D. (1992). *Reading comprehension: New directions for classroom practice* (3rd ed.). New York: Harper-Collins.

McTavish, M. (2007). Constructing the big picture: A working class family supports their daughter's pathways to literacy. *The Reading Teacher, 60,* 476–485.

Meece, J. L., & Miller, S. D. (1999). Changes in elementary school children's achievement goals for reading and writing: Results of a longitudinal and an intervention study. *Scientific Studies of Reading, 3,* 207–229.

Miller, D. E. (1993). The Literature Project: Using literature to improve the self-concept of at-risk adolescent females. *Journal of Reading, 36,* 442–448.

Miller, S. D., & Meece, J. L. (1999). Third graders' motivational preferences for reading and writing tasks. *The Elementary School Journal, 100,* 19–35.

Mohr, K. A. J., & Mohr, E. S. (2007). Extending English-language learners' classroom interactions using the Response Protocol. *The Reading Teacher, 60,* 440–450.

Moore, D. W., & Moore, S. A. (1986). Possible sentences. In E. K. Dishner, T. W. Bean, J. E. Readence, & D. W. Moore (Eds.), *Reading in the content areas: Improving classroom instruction* (2nd ed., pp. 174–179). Dubuque, IA: Kendall/Hunt.

Moore, P. (1987). On the incidental learning of vocabulary. *Australian Journal of Reading, 10,* 12–19.

Morningstar, J. W. (1999). Home response journals: Parents as informed contributors in the understanding of their child's literacy development. *The Reading Teacher, 52,* 690–697.

Morris, D. (1995). *First Steps: An early reading intervention program.* Boone, NC: Appalachian State University Reading Clinic. (ERIC Document Reproduction Service No. ED 388 956).

Morris, D., Tyner, B., & Perney, J. (2000). Early Steps: Replicating the effects of a first-grade reading intervention program. *Journal of Educational Psychology, 92,* 681–693.

Morrow, L. M. (1985). Retelling stories: A strategy for improving young children's comprehension, concept of story structure, and oral language complexity. *The Elementary School Journal, 85,* 647–661.

Nagy, W. E. (1988). *Teaching vocabulary to improve reading comprehension.* Newark, DE/Urbana, IL: International Reading Association/National Council of Teachers of English.

Nagy, W. E., Diakidoy, I. N., & Anderson, R. C. (1993). The acquisition of morphology: Learning the contribution of suffixes to the meanings of derivatives. *Journal of Reading Behavior, 25,* 155–170.

Nagy, W. E., Herman, P. A., & Anderson, R. C. (1985). Learning words from context. *Reading Research Quarterly, 20,* 233–253.

National Joint Committee on Learning Disabilities. (1998). *Operationalizing the NJCLD definition of learning disabilities for ongoing assessment in schools.* Retrieved July 9, 2008 from www.ldonline.org/article/12205.

National Reading Panel. (2000). *Report of the National Reading Panel. Teaching children to read: An evidence-based assessment of the scientific research literature on reading and its implications for reading instruction.* Washington, DC: U.S. Department of Health and Human Services.

Nippold, M. A. (2007). *Later language development: School-age children, adolescents, and young adults.* Austin, TX: Pro-Ed.

Noyce, R. M., & Christie, J. F. (1989). *Integrating reading and writing instruction in grades K–8.* Boston: Allyn and Bacon.

Ogle, D. M. (1986). K-W-L: A teaching model that develops active reading of expository text. *The Reading Teacher, 39,* 564–570.

Ohlhausen, M. M., & Roller, C. M. (1988). The operation of text structure and content schemata in isolation and in interaction. *Reading Research Quarterly, 23,* 70–88.

Oldrieve, R. (1997). Success with reading and spelling: Students internalize words through structured lessons. *Teaching Exceptional Children, 29*(4), 57–61.

O'Masta, G. A., & Wolf, J. M. (1991). Encouraging independent reading through the Reading Millionaires project. *The Reading Teacher, 44,* 656–662.

Orlich, D. C., Harder, R. J., Callahan, R. C., Trevison, M. S., & Brown, A. H. (2007). *Teaching strategies: A guide to effective instruction* (8th ed.). Boston: Houghton Mifflin.

O'Shea, L. J., & O'Shea, D. J. (1994). What research in special education says to reading teachers. In K. D. Wood & B. Algozzine (Eds.), *Teaching reading to high-risk learners: A unified perspective* (pp. 49–81). Boston: Allyn and Bacon.

Padak, N. D., & Rasinski, R. V. (2008). *Evidence-based instruction in reading: A professional development guide to fluency.* Columbus, OH: Allyn and Bacon/Merrill.

Palincsar, A. S., & Brown, A. L. (1986). Interactive teaching to promote independent learning from text. *The Reading Teacher, 39,* 771–777.

Palincsar, A. S., & Brown, A. L. (1988). Teaching and practicing thinking skills to promote comprehension in the context of group problem solving. *Remedial and Special Education, 9,* 53–59.

Pappas, C. C., & Brown, E. (1987). Young children learning story discourse: Three case studies. *The Elementary School Journal, 87,* 455–466.

Paratore, J. R. (2002). Home and school together: Helping beginning readers succeed. In A. E. Farstrup & S. J. Samuels (Eds.), *What research has to say about reading instruction* (3rd ed., pp. 48–68). Newark, DE: International Reading Association.

Pearson, P. D., & Johnson, D. D. (1978). *Teaching reading comprehension.* New York: Holt, Rinehart and Winston.

Pellegrini, A. D., & Galda, L. (1982). The effects of thematic-fantasy play training on the development of children's story comprehension. *American Educational Research Journal, 19*, 443–452.

Pittelman, S. D., Heimlich, J. E., Berglund, R. L., & French, M. P. (1991). *Semantic Feature Analysis.* Newark, DE: International Reading Association.

Pomerantz, E. M., Moorman, E. A., & Litwack, S. D. (2007). The how, whom, and why of parents' involvement in children's academic lives: More is not always better. *Review of Educational Research, 77*, 373–410.

Pressley, M. (2006). *Reading instruction that works: The case for balanced teaching* (3rd ed.). New York: Guilford.

Pressley, M., Roehrig, A., Bogner, K., Raphael, L. M., & Dolezal, S. (2002). Balanced literacy instruction. *Focus on Exceptional Children, 34*(5), 1–14.

Pressley, M., & Woloshyn, V. (1995). *Cognitive strategy instruction that really improves children's academic performance.* Cambridge, MA: Brookline.

Purcell-Gates, V., L'Allier, S., & Smith, D. (1995). Literacy at the Harts' and the Larsons': Diversity among poor, innercity families. *The Reading Teacher, 48*, 572–578.

Rahman, T., & Bisanz, G. L. (1986). Reading ability and use of a story schema in recalling and reconstructing information. *Journal of Educational Psychology, 78*, 323–333.

Raphael, T. E. (1984). Teaching learners about sources of information for answering comprehension questions. *Journal of Reading, 27*, 303–311.

Raphael, T. E. (1986). Teaching question-answer relationships, revisited. *The Reading Teacher, 39*, 516–522.

Raphael, T. E., & Au, K. H. (2005). QAR: Enhancing comprehension and test taking across grades and content areas. *The Reading Teacher, 59*, 206–221.

Raphael, T. E., & McMahon, S. I. (1994). Book Club: An alternative framework for reading instruction. *The Reading Teacher, 48*, 102–116.

Raphael, T. E., Pardo, L. S., & Highfield, K. (2002). *Book Club: A literature based curriculum.* Newark, DE: International Reading Association.

Raphael, T. E., & Pearson, P. D. (1985). Increasing students' awareness of sources of information for answering questions. *American Educational Research Association, 22*, 217–235.

Rasinski, T. (1999a). Making and writing words. *Reading Online.* Retrieved July 30, 2008 from www.readingonline.org/articles/art_index.asp?HREF=words/index.html.

Rasinski, T. (1999b). Making and writing words using letter patterns. *Reading Online.* Retrieved July 30, 2008, from www.readingonline.org/articles/art_index.asp?HREF=rasinski/index.html.

Rasinski, T., & Padak, N. (2004). *Effective reading strategies: Teaching children who find reading difficult* (3rd ed.). Upper Saddle River, NJ: Merrill/Prentice Hall.

Recht, D. R., & Leslie, L. (1988). Effect of prior knowledge on good and poor readers' memory of text. *Journal of Educational Psychology, 80*, 16–20.

Reed, S. K. (2007). *Cognition: Theory and applications* (7th ed.). Belmont, CA: Wadsworth.

Reutzel, D. R. (1985a). Reconciling schema theory and the basal reading lesson. *The Reading Teacher, 39*, 194–197.

Reutzel, D. R. (1985b). Story maps improve comprehension. *The Reading Teacher, 38*, 400–404.

Reutzel, D. R., & Cooter, R. B. (2007). *Strategies for reading assessment and instruction: Helping every child succeed* (3rd ed.). Upper Saddle River, NJ: Merrill/Prentice Hall.

Reutzel, D. R., & Cooter, R. B., Jr. (2009). *The essentials of teaching children to read: The teacher makes the difference* (2nd ed.). Boston: Allyn and Bacon.

Rhodes, L. K., & Dudley-Marling, C. (1996). *Readers and writers with a difference: A holistic approach to teaching struggling readers and writers.* Portsmouth, NH: Heinemann.

Riccio, C. A., & Hynd, G. W. (1996). Neuroanatomical and neurophysiological aspects of dyslexia. *Topics in Language Disorders, 16*, 1–13.

Richards, J. C., & Gipe, J. P. (1993). Getting to know story characters: A strategy for young and at-risk readers. *The Reading Teacher, 47*, 78–79.

Richardson, E., & Bradley, C. (1975). The ISM: A teacher-oriented method of reading instruction for the child-oriented teacher. *Journal of Learning Disabilities, 7*, 341–352.

Richardson, M. V., Miller, M. B., Richardson, J. A., & Sacks, M. K. (2008). Literacy bags to encourage family involvement. *Reading Improvement, 45*, 3–9.

Richek, M. A., Caldwell, J. S., Jennings, J. H., & Lerner, J. W. (2002). *Reading problems: Assessment and teaching strategies* (4th ed.). Boston: Allyn and Bacon.

Rinehart, S. D., Stahl, S. A., & Erickson, L. G. (1986). Some effects of summarization training on reading and studying. *Reading Research Quarterly, 21*, 422–438.

Risko, V. J., & Alvarez, M. C. (1983). Thematic organizers: Application to remedial reading. In G. H. McNinch (Eds.), *Reading research to reading practice* (pp. 85–87). Athens, GA: The American Reading Forum.

Rogevich, M. E., & Perin, D. (2008). Effects on science summarization of a reading comprehension intervention for adolescents with behavior and attention disorders. *Exceptional Children, 74*, 135–154.

Roller, C. M. (1996). *Variability not disability: Struggling readers in a workshop classroom.* Newark, DE: International Reading Association.

Romeo, L. (2002). At-risk students: Learning to break through comprehension barriers. In C. C. Block, L. B. Gambrell, & M. Pressley (Eds.), *Improving comprehension instruction: Rethinking research, theory, and classroom practice* (pp. 354–369). San Francisco: Jossey-Bass.

Rosenshine, B., & Meister, C. (1997). Cognitive strategy instruction in reading. In S. Stahl & D. Hayes (Eds.), *Instructional models in reading* (pp. 85–107). Mahwah, NJ: Erlbaum.

Rosenshine, B., Meister, C., & Chapman, S. (1996). Teaching students to generate questions: A review of the intervention studies. *Review of Educational Research, 66,* 181–221.

Rowe, M. B. (1974). Wait-time and rewards as instructional variables, their influence on language, logic, and fate control: Part one—wait-time. *Journal of Research in Science Teaching, 11,* 81–94.

Rowe, M. B. (1986). Wait time: Slowing down may be a way of speeding up. *Journal of Teacher Education, 37*(1), 43–50.

Rupley, W. H., Logan, J. W., & Nichols, W. D. (1999). Vocabulary instruction in a balanced reading program. *The Reading Teacher, 52,* 336–346.

Rush, R. T. (1985). Assessing readability: Formulas and alternatives. *The Reading Teacher, 39,* 274–283.

Sadoski, M. (1985). The natural use of imagery in story comprehension and recall: Replication and extension. *Reading Research Quarterly, 20,* 658–667.

Sadoski, M., & Paivio, A. (2001). *Imagery and text: A dual coding theory of reading and writing.* Mahwah, NJ: Lawrence Erlbaum.

Salvia, J., Ysseldyke, J. E., & Bolt, S. (2007). *Assessment in special and inclusive education* (10th ed.). Boston: Houghton Mifflin.

Samuels, S. J. (2002a). Automaticity and reading fluency. In B. J. Guzzetti (Eds.), *Literacy in America: An encyclopedia of history, theory, and practice* (pp. 40–42). Santa Barbara, CA: ABC-CLIO.

Samuels, S. J. (2002b). Reading fluency: Its development and assessment. In A. E. Farstrup & S. J. Samuels (Eds.), *What research has to say about reading instruction* (pp. 166–183). Newark, DE: International Reading Association.

Santa, C. M., & Hoien, T. (1999). An assessment of Early Steps: A program for early intervention of reading problems. *Reading Research Quarterly, 34,* 54–73.

Saunders, W. M., & Goldenberg, C. N. (1999). Effects of instructional conversations and literature logs on limited- and fluent-English-proficient students' story comprehension and thematic understanding. *The Elementary School Journal, 99,* 277–301.

Schatz, E. K., & Baldwin, R. S. (1986). Context clues are unreliable predictors of word meanings. *Reading Research Quarterly, 21,* 439–453.

Schirmer, B. R. (1995). Mental imagery and the reading comprehension of deaf children. *Reading Research and Instruction, 34,* 177–188.

Schirmer, B. R. (2000). *Language and literacy development in children who are deaf* (2nd ed.). Boston: Allyn and Bacon.

Schirmer, B. R., & Bond, W. L. (1990). Enhancing the hearing impaired child's knowledge of story structure to improve comprehension of narrative text. *Reading Improvement, 27,* 242–254.

Schirmer, B. R., & Schaffer, L. (2008, May). *Guided Reading Approach: Application to deaf students.* Paper presented at the Annual Convention of the International Reading Association, Atlanta, Georgia.

Schirmer, B. R., & Woolsey, M. L. (1997). Effect of teacher questions on the reading comprehension of deaf children. *Journal of Deaf Studies and Deaf Education, 2,* 47–56.

Schmitt, M. C., & O'Brien, D. G. (1986). Story grammars: Some cautions about the translation of research into practice. *Reading Research and Instruction, 26,* 1–8.

Schwartz, R. M., & Raphael, T. E. (1985). Concept of definition: A key to improving students' vocabulary. *The Reading Teacher, 39,* 198–205.

Searfoss, L. W. (1975). Radio reading. *The Reading Teacher, 29,* 295–296.

Serafini, F. (2001). *Reading Workshop: Creating space for readers.* Portsmouth, NH: Heinemann.

Share, D. (1999). Phonological recoding and orthographic learning: A direct test of the self-teaching hypothesis. *Journal of Experimental Child Psychology, 72,* 95–129.

Shaywitz, B. A., Fletcher, J. M., & Shaywitz, S. E. (1995). Defining and classifying learning disabilities and attention-deficit/hyperactivity disorder. *Journal of Child Neurology, 10*(Supplement 1), S50–S57.

Shaywitz, B. A., Pugh, K. R., Jenner, A. R., Fulbright, R. K., Fletcher, J. M., Gore, J. C., & Shaywitz, S. E. (2000). The cognitive basis of dyslexia. In M. L. Kamil, P. B. Mosenthal, P. D. Pearson, & R. Barr (Eds.), *Handbook of reading research, Volume III* (pp. 229–249). Mahwah, NJ: Erlbaum.

Slavin, R. E., & Madden, N. A. (2000). *One million children: Success for All.* Thousand Oaks, CA: Corwin.

Slavin, R. E., Madden, N. A., Farnish, A. M., & Stevens, R. J. (1995). *Cooperative Integrated Reading and Composition (CIRC): A brief overview.* Baltimore, MD: Center for Organization of Schools, Johns Hopkins University. (ERIC Document Reproduction Service No. ED 378 569).

Smith, S. B., Simmons, D. C., Gleason, M. M., Kame'enui, E. J., Baker, S. K., Sprick, M., Gunn, B., Thomas, C. L., Chard, D. J., Plasencia-Peinado, J., & Peinado, R. (2001). An analysis of phonological awareness instruction in four kindergarten basal reading programs. *Reading and Writing Quarterly, 17,* 25–52.

Smith, S. B., Simmons, D. C., & Kame'enui, E. J. (1998). Phonological awareness: Instructional and curricular basics and implications. In D. C. Simmons & E. J. Kame'enui (Eds.), *What reading research tells us about children with diverse learning needs: Bases and basics* (pp. 129–140). Mahwah, NJ: Lawrence Erlbaum.

Snow, C. E., Burns, M. S., & Griffin, P. (Eds.). (1998). *Preventing reading difficulties in young children*. Washington, DC: National Academy.

Snyder, L. S., & Godley, D. (1992). Assessment of word-finding disorders in children and adolescents. *Topics in Language Disorders, 13*, 15–32.

Sparks-Langer, G. M., Starko, A. J., Pasch, M., Burke, W., Moody, C. D., & Gardner, T. G. (2004). *Teaching as decision making: Successful practices for the secondary teacher* (2nd ed.). Upper Saddle River, NJ: Merrill/Prentice Hall.

Spinelli, C. G. (2006). *Classroom assessment for students in special and general education* (2nd ed.). Upper Saddle River, NJ: Merill/Prentice Hall.

Stahl, S. A. (1999). *Vocabulary development* (Vol. 2). Cambridge, MA: Brookline.

Stahl, S. A., & Fairbanks, M. M. (1986). The effects of vocabulary instruction: A model-based meta-analysis. *Review of Educational Research, 56*, 72–110.

Stahl, S. A., & Kapinus, B. A. (1991). Possible Sentences: Predicting word meanings to teach content area vocabulary. *The Reading Teacher, 45*, 36–43.

Staires, J. (2007). Word Wall connections. *Science scope, 30*(5), 64–65.

Stanovich, K. E. (2000). *Progress in understanding reading: Scientific foundations and new frontiers*. New York: Guilford.

Starko, A. J., Sparks-Langer, G. M., Pasch, M., Franks, L., Gardner, T. G., Moody, C. D. (2002). *Teaching as decision making: Successful practices for elementary teachers* (3rd ed.). Upper Saddle River, NJ: Merrill/Prentice Hall.

Stauffer, R. G. (1969). *Teaching reading as a thinking process*. New York: Harper and Row.

Stauffer, R. G. (1970). *The Language Experience Approach to the teaching of reading*. New York: Harper and Row.

St. Pierre, R. G., Ricciuti, A. E., & Riihdzius, T. A. (2005). Effects of a family literacy program on low-literate children and their parents: Findings from an evaluation of the Even Start Family Literacy Program. *Developmental Psychology, 41*, 953–970.

Strickland, D. S., Dillon, R. M., Funkhouser, L., Glick, M., & Rogers, C. (1989). Classroom dialogue during literature response groups. *Language Arts, 66*, 192–200.

Strickland, D. S., Ganske, K., & Monroe, J. K. (2002). *Supporting struggling readers and writers: Strategies for classroom intervention 3–6*. Portland, ME: Stenhouse.

Swan, E. A. (2003). *Concept-Oriented Reading Instruction: Engaging classrooms, lifelong learners*. New York: Guilford.

Tatham, S. M. (1978). Comprehension taxonomies: Their uses and abuses. *The Reading Teacher, 32*, 190–194.

Taylor, B. M., Pearson, P. D., Clark, K., & Walpole, S. (2000). Effective schools and accomplished teachers: Lessons about primary-grade reading instruction in low-income schools. *The Elementary School Journal, 101*, 121–165.

Taylor, R. L. (2006). *Assessment of exceptional students* (7th ed.). Boston: Allyn and Bacon.

Therrien, W. J. (2004). Fluency and comprehension gains as a result of repeated reading: A meta-analysis. *Remedial and Special Education, 25*, 252–261.

Therrien, W. J., Gormley, S., & Kubina, R. M. (2006). Boosting fluency and comprehension to improve reading achievement. *Teaching Exceptional Children, 38*(3), 22–26.

Therrien, W. J., Wickstrom, K., & Jones, K. (2006). Effect of a combined repeated reading and question generation intervention on reading achievement. *Learning Disabilities Research and Practice, 21*, 89–97.

Tierney, R. J., & Cunningham, J. W. (1984). Research on teaching reading comprehension. In P. D. Pearson (Ed.), *Handbook of reading research* (pp. 609–655). New York: Longman.

Tobin, K. (1986). Effects of teacher wait time on discourse characteristics in mathematics and language arts classes. *American Educational Research Association, 23*, 191–200.

Tobin, K. (1987). The role of wait time in higher cognitive learning. *Review of Educational Research, 57*, 69–95.

Tompkins, G. E. (2006). *Literacy for the 21st century: A balanced approach* (4th ed.). Upper Saddle River, NJ: Merrill/Prentice Hall.

Topping, K. (1989). Peer tutoring and paired reading: Combining two powerful techniques. *The Reading Teacher, 42*, 488–494.

Torgesen, J. K. (1996). *Phonological awareness: A critical factor in dyslexia*. Baltimore: Orton Dyslexia Society.

Torgesen, J. K., Alexander, A. W., Wagner, R. K., Rashotte, C. A., Voeller, K. K. S., & Conway, T. (2001). Intensive remedial instruction for children with severe reading disabilities: Immediate and long-term outcomes from two instructional approaches. *Journal of Learning Disabilities, 34*, 33–58, 78.

Torgesen, J. K., & Wagner, R. K. (1998). Alternative diagnostic approaches for specific developmental reading disabilities. *Learning Disabilities Research and Practice, 13*, 220–232.

Turnbull, A., & Turnbull, R., Erwin, E., & Soodak, L. (2005). *Families, professionals, and exceptionality: Positive outcomes through partnership and trust* (5th ed.). Upper Saddle River, NJ: Merrill/Prentice Hall.

Unrau, N., & Schlackman, J. (2006). Motivation and its relationship with reading achievement in an urban middle school. *The Journal of Educational Research, 100*, 81–101.

Vacca, J. L., Vacca, R. T., Gove, M. K., Burkey, L. C., Lenhart, L. A., & McKeon, C. A. (2009). *Reading and learning to read* (7th ed.). Boston: Allyn and Bacon.

Vaughn, S., Linan-Thompson, S., & Hickman, P. (2003). Response to instruction as a means of identifying students with reading/learning disabilities. *Exceptional Children, 69*, 391–409.

Vygotsky, L. S. (1978). *Mind in society: The development of higher psychological processes.* Cambridge, MA: Harvard University.

Wagstaff, J. M. (1999). *Teaching reading and writing with Word Walls.* New York: Scholastic.

Walpole, S., & McKenna, M. C. (2006). The role of informal reading inventories in assessing word recognition. *The Reading Teacher, 59,* 592–594.

Wang, X. C., & Aldridge, J. (Eds.). (2007). Re-examining diversity issues in childhood education. *Childhood Education, 83,* 261–308.

Wells, G. (1986). *The meaning makers: Children learning language and using language to learn.* Portsmouth, NH: Heinemann.

Welsch, R. G. (2007). Using experimental analysis to determine interventions for reading fluency and recalls of students with learning disabilities. *Learning Disability Quarterly, 20,* 115–129.

Whitaker, S. (2008). Finding the joy of language in authentic wordplay. *English Journal, 97*(4), 45–48.

Wigfield, A., Eccles, J. S., Yoon, K. S., Harold, R. D., Arbreton, A. J. A., Freedman-Doan, C., & Blumenfeld, P. C. (1997). Change in children's competence beliefs and subjective task values across the elementary school years: A 3-year study. *Journal of Educational Psychology, 89,* 451–469.

Wigfield, A., Guthrie, J. T., Perencivich, K. C., Taboada, A., Klauda, S. L., McRae, A., & Barbosa, P. (2008). Role of reading engagement in mediating effects of reading comprehension instruction on reading outcomes. *Psychology in the Schools, 45,* 432–445.

Wiig, E. H. (1994). The role of language in learning disabilities. In A. J. Capute, P. J. Accardo, & B. K. Shapiro (Eds.), *Learning disabilities spectrum: AD, ADHD, and LD* (pp. 111–131). Baltimore: York.

Wilen, W. W. (1990). Forms and phases of discussion. In W. W. Wilen (Ed.), *Teaching and learning through discussion* (pp. 3–24). Springfield, IL: Charles C. Thomas.

Winton, P. (1986). Effective strategies for involving families in intervention efforts. *Focus on Exceptional Children, 19*(2), 1–10, 12.

Wixson, K. K. (1986). Vocabulary instruction and children's comprehension of basal stories. *Reading Research Quarterly, 21,* 317–329.

Wolf, M. A. (1991). Naming speed and reading: The contribution of the cognitive neurosciences. *Reading Research Quarterly, 26,* 123–141.

Wolf, S. A. (1994). Learning to act/acting to learn: Children as actors, critics, and characters in classroom theatre. *Research in the Teaching of English, 28,* 7–44.

Wollman-Bonilla, J. E. (1994). Why don't they "just speak"? Attempting literature discussion with more and less able readers. *Research in the Teaching of English, 28,* 231–258.

Wong, B. Y. L. (1985). Self-questioning instructional research: A review. *Review of Educational Research, 55,* 227–268.

Wood, E., Pressley, M., & Winne, P. H. (1990). Elaborative interrogation effects on children's learning of factual content. *Journal of Educational Psychology, 82,* 741–748.

Wood, E., Winne, P. H., & Carney, P. A. (1995). Evaluating the effects of training high school students to use summarization when training includes analogically similar information. *Journal of Reading Behavior, 27,* 605–626.

Worthy, J. (1996). A matter of interest: Literature that hooks reluctant readers and keeps them reading. *The Reading Teacher, 50,* 204–212.

Worthy, J. (2002). What makes intermediate-grade students want to read? *The Reading Teacher, 55,* 568–569.

Worthy, J., Moorman, M., & Turner, M. (1999). What Johnny likes to read is hard to find in school. *Reading Research Quarterly, 34,* 12–27.

Worthy, J., Patterson, E., & Salas, R. (2002). "More than just reading": The human factor in reaching resistant readers. *Reading Research and Instruction, 41,* 177–201.

Worthy, J., & Prater, K. (2002). "I thought about it all night": Readers Theatre for reading fluency and motivation. *The Reading Teacher, 56,* 294–297.

Wright, G., Sherman, R., & Jones, T. B. (2004). Are silent reading behaviors of first graders really silent? *The Reading Teacher, 57,* 546–553.

Yopp, H. K., & Yopp, R. H. (2003). Ten important words identifying the big ideas in informational text. *Journal of Content Area Reading, 2,* 7–13.

Yopp, R. H., & Yopp, H. K. (2007). Ten important words plus: A strategy for building word knowledge. *The Reading Teacher, 61,* 157–160.

Zakaluk, B. L., & Samuels, S. J. (Eds.). (1988). *Readability: Its past, present, and future.* Newark, DE: International Reading Association.

Zygouris-Coe, V. (2007). Family literacy: The missing link in school-wide literacy efforts. *Reading Horizons, 48*(1), 57–70.

Index